Blueberries, Cranberries and Other Vacciniums

Royal Horticultural Society Plant Collector Guide

Blueberries, Cranberries and Other Vacciniums

Jennifer Trehane

Timber Press

Portland • Cambridge

ROYAL HORTICULTURAL SOCIETY

To my late father, David, who not only inspired my interest
in blueberries but also opened my eyes to the fascinating world
of plants in general.

Published in association with the Royal Horticultural Society in 2004 by

Timber Press, Inc.
The Haseltine Building
133 S.W. Second Avenue, Suite 450
Portland, Oregon 97204-3527, U.S.A.

Timber Press
2 Station Road
Swavesey
Cambridge CB4 5QJ, U.K.

Design by Dick Malt
Printed through Colorcraft Ltd., Hong Kong

Library of Congress Cataloging-in-Publication Data
Trehane, Jennifer.
    Blueberries, cranberries, and other vacciniums / Jennifer Trehane.
        p. cm.
    Includes bibliographical references and index.
    ISBN 0-88192-615-9
    1.Blueberries. 2. Cranberries. 3. Vaccinium. I.Title.

SB386.B7T74 2004
634′.737–dc22   2003053376

A catalog record for this book is also available from the British Library.

Contents

Foreword

I first encountered vacciniums on a walk in the Scottish highlands. As a child I was aware of plants but wasn't alert to their significance. Still, the succulent blaeberries and cranberries diverted my attention from the clouds of midges hovering overhead, and the berries left an impression, initially, when I found it difficult to remove their richly colored juice from my fingers!

Years later I again encountered vacciniums in the wild, in the Cascade mountain ranges of western North America, but this time I was fully aware of what they were. Huckleberries are found around Mt. Adams in Washington State, where they were refreshing on the hill but delicious when made into jam. This economic value is not the preserve of the wild; highbush blueberries have become fashionable and are now a regular feature on supermarket shelves.

Many species, both temperate and hardy, are also invaluable flowering, foliage or fruiting plants in the ornamental garden, as I learned while working at the Royal Botanic Garden Edinburgh. *Vaccinium glaucoalbum*, which Roy Lancaster collected in Nepal, is making its way into garden plantings; *V. acrobracteatum* is grown for its stunning bright red new growth; and the hardy exotic *V. cylindraceum*, native to the Azores, is a revelation, with its yellowish green flowers followed by showy bunches of blue-black fruit in winter.

So this genus of many talents has been profiled in depth by Jennifer Trehane. Known for her authoritative knowledge of camellias, Jennifer has turned her energies to producing this most comprehensive of volumes. As the text makes clear, she left no stone unturned in her search for information, all of it enthusiastically presented. The result is not only for the keen gardener; this book will surely engage the scientist and commercial grower—those who have an interest far beyond the garden fence—for many years.

Jim Gardiner *RHS Garden Wisley*

Preface

Blueberry pie, blueberry yoghurt, cranberry juice, cranberry sauce—well-known products available almost all over the world and very much associated with North America, though there is much more to the story than that. Blueberries and cranberries are part of the genus *Vaccinium*, which includes around 460 species that are distributed worldwide from the coldest regions near the Arctic Circle through temperate regions and into the tropics and neotropical regions. Several species that grow on islands such as Madagascar and the Azores appear to be entirely native, though their arrival on those islands is an interesting puzzle to botanists.

Much confusion surrounds the nomenclature of *Vaccinium*. On an everyday level, this confusion is often the result of the many "common" names given to some of the more widely distributed and much used species. I have lost count of the number of people who see our highbush blueberry fruit for sale and remember with nostalgia picking whortleberries—or bilberries or blaeberries or hurts—on the moors near their childhood homes. Then they want to know if those wild fruits and our cultivated ones are the same. The quick, typical answer is, "They are related, like cousins, but they are not the same." The next question is usually, "What's the difference, apart from yours being much bigger?" Many want to know more about the different species of *Vaccinium*, how they can be used in the garden and the history of human use.

The wonderful work of Swedish botanist Carl Linnaeus in classifying plants by assigning them Latin names makes it possible, in theory at least, for people all over the world to identify and describe a particular plant in a universal language. Botanists have their disagreements, however, usually about some seemingly minor morphological detail. In addition, different collectors have collected and named species in the wild quite independently of each other. Some have been more meticulous than others in their written descriptions, in the way they have preserved their specimens in the herbaria round the world and in their publicized findings. A lack of coordination in the past has resulted in the nomenclature scene being highly confused and the botanical classification of the genus being muddy, to say the least; hundreds of synonyms are now listed. The general consensus is that, as of the late twentieth century, the genus is at least defined, although a few species should be demoted to "subspecies" or "variety" because many plants given specific (species) status have only slight variations, the majority of which are due to adaptations to differing climate or other habitat situations. In this book I adopt the most recent botanical names, and they will, I hope, remain unaltered for at least a few years, but there are no guarantees. The book is, however, not a botanical book but more a general interest horticultural one.

It is not surprising that the value of the fruit of blueberries, cranberries and lingonberries has long been appreciated, both for flavor and for health-giving properties, both of which have attracted considerable attention since approximately 1998. Some research results, particularly into the health benefits of blueberries, are included in this book.

It is only in the late 1990s that the ornamental value of so many *Vaccinium* species has been truly appreciated, and there is a wealth of species that has not yet reached our gardens in any significant numbers but that will, given time to propagate and adequate promotion, be doing so. Many have attractive, brightly colored young growth, pretty, sometimes scented flowers, edible fruit that is visually attractive and often tasty and either glossy evergreen leaves or, if deciduous, bright fall color. Some grow into big bold shrubs or have light dainty growth, while others stay small and compact, making them ideal for small gardens and containers. Some require a degree of shade while others thrive in exposed situations in full sun; some have their roots in or near water while others prefer arid conditions. There are also some species with epiphytic tendencies that do well in the humus-lined crooks of living trees or that colonize dead tree stumps or horizontal tree trunks. We have the whole range of possibilities in this genus: what more could any gardener want?

The book begins by tracing the story of the most widely grown species of *Vaccinium*, the blueberries and cranberries; they have a fascinating history going back thousands of years. The book deals with their propagation, cultivation, harvest and uses, including their health benefits, and varieties are also fully described. Pests and diseases, some of which are quite fascinating in their own right, are discussed, although most cause problems only in areas where there are concentrations of crops or extensive wild populations. United States and United Kingdom (RHS) hardiness zone classifications have been omitted as many of the so-called tender species thrive in microclimates in areas where, according to the zone classifications, they should fail. Our changing world climates are making a mockery of these ratings, so I offer only general guidelines.

Other, relatively unfamiliar, fruiting vacciniums are dealt with in the section on garden cultivation, as are some cold-hardy and neo- or subtropical species and "forms," as well as cultivars (cultivated varieties) that have merit solely as ornamental garden plants or as a valuable source of food for birds and mammals in "wildlife" gardens. Some are readily available from nurseries, and others are not but should be! Site selection, climate, soils and cultivation techniques are all included, which will, I hope, give general guidance to gardeners in differing conditions around the world. The intention is to provide a general interest book that may also be used as a basic manual for the cultivation of currently available vacciniums, plus those that are still difficult to acquire but that are likely to be introduced in the future.

This book is an effort to clarify the *Vaccinium* story for any reader, whether an enthusiastic gardener or someone who is simply curious about blueberries and cranberries and would like to widen the picture and maybe even learn a little about some of the other lesser known vacciniums. I also hope that it will inform and inspire those who have either never grown *Vaccinium* plants before or have put just a tentative toe in the water and would now like to go in a little deeper. The book contains sufficient information to get a reader started on growing blueberries, cranberries and even lingonberries on a small-scale commercial basis, but it is not intended as a complete manual for large-scale commercial growing.

Acknowledgments

I should like to give very grateful thanks to Barry Starling, whose guidance, help and encouragement with information on ornamental vacciniums have been so freely given. Without his extensive knowledge of a very wide range of *Vaccinium* species and the loan of some of his books and journals, as well as many of his transparencies, this section of the book would have been extremely thin. Barry even gave me a collection of nearly 30 species to grow, propagate from and observe for myself. The rapidly increasing species section of our commercial nursery is due entirely to his inspiration.

Michael Michaud has been generous with the long-term loan of books, particularly S. P. Vander Kloet's excellent *The Genus Vaccinium in North America*, which is out of print and very difficult to obtain.

I am also grateful to Joan Lorraine for giving up a whole day's gardening to show me her national collection of *Vaccinium* in her woodland garden in North Devon and for allowing me to take notes from some of her books.

Help from overseas has been equally generously given over the years. A visit to New Jersey was greatly enhanced by Gary Pavlis and Mark Ehlenfeldt of the United States Department of Agriculture (USDA) who took my son (who is my business partner) and me to see many places of both blueberry and cranberry interest. The Allen family were unstinting with their knowledge and practical experience of lowbush blueberry growing in Maine, as was the marketing director of the Wild Blueberry Growers Association (WBANA) based in Bar Harbor. On the West Coast I was grateful for the time I spent with Dick Mombell at Fall Creek Wholesale Nursery in Oregon, learning about and photographing some of the huge number of *Vaccinium* cultivars in production or on trial there.

In Europe, Sonja and Wilhelm Dierking kindly allowed me to have the freedom of their extensive and very well run plant nursery, including their protected and open-grown blueberry crops, cranberry beds and their trial grounds. They also took me into the forest to see three species, *Vaccinium myrtillus, V. uliginosum* and *V. vitis-idaea*, growing wild in a very interesting location.

In Australia the staff at the very commercial Blueberry Farms of Australia in New South Wales were extremely helpful, and I even had a chance to catch up with renowned blueberry breeder Ridley Bell, who had visited our blueberry plantations in the 1980s.

Narandra Patel and Syd Solomona of HortResearch in New Zealand have been a wonderful inspiration, and Syd has passed on a great many documents and papers of value, as well as first-hand information about cultivation in New Zealand, on his visits to us.

Thanks also to Roger Holman for taking the photograph of me that appears on the dust jacket.

Lastly, but by no means least, I should like to thank my son, David, who has helped with the computer side of things and who has also been remarkably tolerant of my absences from our own business, the Dorset Blueberry Company.

Part I

The Genus *Vaccinium*

A Little History

The name "*Vaccinium*" seems a good point to start with. It is Latin but its origins probably go much further back to thraco pelagian, a prehistoric European language (Stearn 1995). The other theory is that the name comes from the Latin "vacca," meaning cow. The "cowberry," *V. vitis-idaea*, is plentiful in the wild in Sweden, where Linnaeus was born. Could it possibly be that the name *Vaccinium* came from such a source? This is pure speculation, and we will probably never know the answer.

Blueberries and cranberries in many shapes and sizes have been gathered from the wild and appreciated as a source of food by humans for thousands of years. The earliest evidence comes from a Bronze Age tomb found in Jutland, Denmark, where sediment from an excavated clay jug was analyzed and found to be the remains of a drink containing wheat, cranberries, bog myrtle and honey. A 200-year-old sealskin pouch with wild blueberries well preserved in ice by Inuit in northern Canada has also been found.

Birds such as the various species of grouse, partridge, quail, American robins, European blackbirds and thrushes appreciate blueberries and cranberries too, as do many mammals. On the North American continent the berries form an important part of the diet of bears and chipmunk, while deer, elk, rabbit and hare graze on the leaves and young stems of plants. In Europe game birds thrive on the berries of wild blueberries, as do badgers.

It is to the United States and Canada that most people turn for the biggest range of edible and economically important *Vaccinium* species although some, especially *V. myrtillus*, *V. oxycoccus* and *V. vitis-idaea*, are found in sufficient quantities in many European countries to be of commercial value. Wild berries are still harvested in commercial quantities and exported from Poland, Lithuania and other neighboring countries.

Wild vaccinium berries figure in the folklore of countries from China to the Northern Hemisphere countries already mentioned. Their use for both food and medicinal purposes has long been appreciated and has become part of the symbolism or even ritual in some native tribes, especially those in China and on the North American continent where the population has depended on local resources. Blueberries have a five-pointed, star-shaped calyx that remains on the fruit. One of the Native American folktales tells of times of starvation when "the Great Spirit sent the star berries down from the night of heaven to feed the children."

The Inuit harvested the ¼ in. (5 mm) berries of *Vaccinium uliginosum* during the late summer and stored them in sealskin pouches in pockets of frozen tundra to give some added interest to the tedious diet of seal and fish during the long winter months. (Seal oil was also used as a preservative especially where ice was not available.) Cranberries, *V. oxycoccus*, were also harvested. Their tart flavor must have been a welcome counterbalance to the fatty food, while the mixture of salmon spawn, blueberries and seal fat was likely quite a gourmet dish for the coastal Inuit of Labrador.

The mountain bilberry or mountain huckleberry, *Vaccinium membranaceum*, has its devotees, especially in the Rocky Mountains, following in the tradition of the Native American tribes who have for centuries harvested the fruit for their own use as raw fruit or as dried fruit after having dried them in the sun or over a fire, then storing them for winter use. The Ojibwa used both the velvet-leafed blueberry, *V. myrtilloides*, and the small cranberry, *V. oxycoccus*, for this winter purpose, sometimes constructing platforms of rush mats to spread the fruit out in the sun out of reach of predators. *Vaccinium myrtilloides* is plentiful and produces prolific fruit crops in many mountainous western areas, and as the fruit ripens early on the lower slopes, it was harvested here first, usually in July, with family groups gradually moving their camps up the slopes until picking finished in September. They found a ready market when European settlers arrived.

The shiny red berries of *Vaccinium parvifolium* were used extensively by coastal tribes in the plant's native Pacific Northwest region as a means of luring fish in streams by deceiving them into thinking they were salmon eggs. The berries of this species were also spread out on the very large leaves (commonly referred to as "Indian wax paper") of skunk cabbage, *Lysichiton americanum*, to dry in the sun in readiness for winter storage.

Vaccinium vitis-idaea grows over a wide area from the colder parts of the United States, Canada, Greenland and Scandinavia to northern Europe and Asia and is known as the mountain cranberry, cowberry or lingonberry. It produces red berries that have traditionally been used to make a tart jelly with a high vitamin C content. It is excellent for relieving symptoms of sore throats and colds as well as being delicious with meats. Lingonberries are undergoing a revival and are being increasingly grown commercially in Europe. Lingonberry compote and lingonberry relish are regarded as gourmet foods by the cognoscenti.

In Newfoundland, where *Vaccinium vitis-idaea* subsp. *minus* ('Minus') is particularly valued by descendants of the European settlers, it is called the partridgeberry. Many families took over patches of partridgeberries as their own, and descendants of the same families jealously guard those patches to this day. Native Americans who also pick and sell the berries have preserved other areas. They are even protected by law. Interestingly, the Newfoundlanders still say "to go a-hurting," a term used by country folk in the English counties of Somerset and Devon who call the local bilberries "whorts" or, in the local west country dialect, "hurts."

The early settlers, who arrived on the eastern seaboard of North America after what were long and often hazardous voyages from Europe across the Atlantic in sailing ships from early in the sixteenth century, certainly benefited from both blueberries and cranberries. Many would have been familiar with the similar wild bilberries found on the moors near their former homes in Britain. The *Mayflower* brought the Pilgrims or Separatists to Cape Cod, Massachusetts, arriving on 20 December 1620, after a voyage that had started on 6 September in Plymouth, England. Most of the passengers were idealists, obviously with very strong willpower and survival instincts, but they were not naturally practical. They were not artisans and "peasants," so it does not take much to imagine how relieved they were to be welcomed and guided by friendly, generous Indians who showed them where to hunt and fish and who shared their corn with them. Winter was beginning to bite but this was Cape Cod, one of the areas where wild American cranberries, *Vaccinium macrocarpon*, grow well. The cranberries are at their best in this area at this time of year; in fact many regard them to be of superior value after there have been a few light frosts.

The less fortunate arrivals may have found the bearberry, *Vaccinium erythrocarpum*, growing on the more upland, sandy areas of the Cape. It is an inferior blueberry that grows on tall bushes and has an acidic tastelessness.

However, any berry as rich in vitamin C as these would have been was both welcome and health giving, especially with the long winter to face in a strange new country.

Many Native Americans and First Peoples of Canada had long since combined dried, pounded meat with melted fat and any available dried berries that were added for flavor. These were often wild blueberries, cranberries or whatever other vacciniums were available. This mixture was called "pemmican," a word that is derived from the Cree "pimecan" with "pime" meaning fat. It was also a staple diet for the early settlers and could be easily transported as they traveled inland to find new lands to settle and farm. They also followed the Indian's example and added fresh or, if in winter, dried berries to the stews they made from the wild game they caught. The settlers, in turn, brought with them from their home countries in Europe recipes that used the wild berries. Thus, jams, jellies, cakes, cookies and so on were all adapted to incorporate wild blueberries and cranberries.

It is said that blaeberry jam was first introduced to the court of King James V of Scotland in 1513 by the cooks who accompanied his French bride to Scotland. They would probably have been familiar with the wild berries, which they will have known as "myrtilles."

The combination of well-established Native American uses with European influences has produced a long list of products in which ingredients from the surrounding countryside or family plots have been combined with wild blueberries and cranberries for immediate consumption or storage. Berries boiled and combined with moose fat and deer tallow are a food of the Chippewa, while the Iroquois mash the berries and make them into little cakes before drying and storing them. The Nitinaht mash the raw fruit and put the resultant pulp into rectangular wooden frames to dry for winter use. The Coeur d'Alene tribe use boiled dried berries with roots to make a warming winter soup. In areas where maple syrup is extracted, it is used to sweeten berries, and birch-bark baskets have provided containers for underground winter storage of berries that have been mixed with grease. Corn, grown for centuries by Indians and cultivated as a staple by farmers to this day, is used to make a huge range of cakes, breads and puddings, to name a few, with blueberries and cranberries being added for their distinctive flavors.

In Europe the most commonly found European species is *Vaccinium myrtillus*, which has berries of only $1/4$ to $1/3$ in. (5 to 8 mm) in diameter and a low-growing habit that makes picking laborious. The fruit has, however, been picked for centuries and is still harvested by enthusiasts who have sufficient time. It is also picked as a commercial crop in countries where labor is cheap. Vast colonies of *V. myrtillus* grow on the upland moors of northern England and Scotland and along roadsides. (Plate 1) Sheep often graze these colonies to a few centimeters but they still manage to survive in places. *Vaccinium myrtillus* is also found on many moors in southern England or in scrub woodland situations, with plants achieving $3^1/_3$ ft. (1 m) in height in shady sites in the New Forest in Hampshire but yielding very few berries. They are often associated with crowberries (*Empetrum nigrum*), which have shiny black berries of similar size and are, fortunately, also edible, if rather bland.

In the British Isles, *Vaccinium myrtillus* has a large number of common names depending on the region:

blaeberry	Cumbria, Lancashire, Northumberland, Shropshire, Yorkshire; Scotland
blueberry	Cumbria, Yorkshire
brylocks	Scotland
hartberry	Dorset, Somerset
hurtleberry	Devon, Somerset
hurts	Cornwall, Devon, Gloucestershire, Hampshire, Surrey, Sussex; Pembrokeshire in Wales
whortleberry	Somerset, Wiltshire
whorts	Cornwall, Devon, Gloucestershire, Hampshire, Surrey, Sussex
wimberry	Cheshire, Derbyshire, Gloucestershire, Herefordshire, Shropshire

Whatever these berries are called, many older folks have happy childhood memories of "picnics out on the moors, with our cans and baskets, picking berries to take home for mother to make into pies." Many of the cities in the north of England, which were hubs of the industrial life of the country in the nineteenth and most of the twentieth century, are surrounded by moorland, where large colonies of bilberries grow. Each city had an annual "wakes week" in July or August when the mills closed to allow the workers a holiday and to carry out maintenance of the machinery. Families used to get together to go to the seaside or out to the moors to pick bilberries. Some of the more commercially minded sold surplus fruit to stall-holders in the local markets or to the local greengrocer. The fruit added a healthy touch to the usual stodgy diet of pies and bread, the occasional fish or meat offal, and maybe a cabbage to add variety. The Victorian invention of the Kilner jar (a glass jar that was filled with fruit and then heated to boiling point) for winter preservation helped to prolong the pleasure during the winter. After it reached boiling point, it was hermetically sealed with a rubber ring between the jar and its glass lid.

The Swedes recognize *Vaccinium myrtillus* as blabar, people from northern Germany call it bickberren and those from southern Germany call it blauberren. All three names mean blueberry. In France the fruit are called myrtilles. Often the berries are stewed and served with milk, but there are countless more recipes that have been handed down from generation to generation.

In China, Zixishan (Zixi Mountain) in Yunnan Province is a holy mountain, one of the most important Buddhist sites, with present-day temples and over 80 sites of older buildings. It is also a cultural and religious center for the Yi people. Among the benefits of being a holy mountain is that the flora has not been ravaged for firewood, and Zixishan has a vast variety of plants. It is a virtual paradise for the botanist or horticulturist. Five species of *Vaccinium* have been recorded (1992–1993) by Chinese botanists on the mountain: *V. brachybotrys*, *V. dunalianum* var. *urophyllum* Rehder and Wilson, *V. fragile* Franchet, *V. iteophyllum* Hance and *V. pubicalyx* Franchet. Berries were valued by the Yi for food, and leaves and young stems are used for medicinal purposes.

Vacciniums for Medicine

Many species of *Vaccinium* have a long history of being used for medicinal purposes. Headaches, fever, eye problems, diarrhea and other problems have all apparently been eased or cured by various vacciniums. All parts of the plant have been used, with the fruit being favored in Europe, and the leaves, stems and bark being more widely used by Native Americans.

As far back as the twelfth century, Saint Hildegard of Bingen, the first woman to write a herbal, noted that bilberry fruits were good for inducing menstruation. The sixteenth-century German herbalist Hieronymus Bock wrote that the berries were useful for the treatment of bladder stones and lung and liver disorders. Berries were used fresh or dried for winter use and then soaked in water to make infusions or syrups such as those that have been used for centuries to treat coughs.

In North America, Indian tribes have used—and indeed continue to use—various species of *Vaccinium* for medicinal purposes, using every part of the plant, from flowers and fruit to leaves, young shoots, bark and even occasionally roots. While not quite a cure-all, it is apparent that where cures involving the many problems regarding blood and its circulation are concerned, blueberry and cranberry plants have provided important infusions. Thus, decoctions of the leafy stems of velvet-leafed blueberry (*V. myrtilloides*) have been used by the Cree of Canada to bring on menstruation, as a contraceptive, after childbirth to "clean out the womb," to prevent miscarriage and to slow down excessive bleeding. Blue huckleberry (*V. membranaceum*) has provided infusions for the Flatheads tribe as a treatment for rheumatism, arthritis and heart trouble. The red fruits of *V. vitis-idaea* (lingonberry) have provided treatment, either whole or as a juice, for coughs and colds. Dried flowers placed on hot stones have been used as an inhalant "for craziness," while a decoction made from the roots has provided relief from "hog sickness."

In the eighteenth century, bilberries, probably *Vaccinium myrtillus*, became a valuable resource, especially in Germany, for herbalists and physicians who used extracts from dried berries as an infusion or tisane. The latter was used as an astringent to treat diarrhea, as a diuretic, to prevent scurvy and as a mouthwash to soothe mouth ulcers. It was also used in the treatment of gout and rheumatism, and even to relieve symptoms of typhoid fever.

During the Second World War when British and Canadian Royal Air Force pilots were on nighttime bombing or defense missions, they reported that their sight improved after eating bilberry jam over a prolonged period. This led to the first laboratory and clinical research in Britain, Italy and Sweden in the 1960s into the effects of bilberry fruit extracts on the eyes, and indeed on the wider subject of its effects on the whole vascular system. Air-traffic controllers, airline pilots and truck drivers have also reported improved night vision when regularly given extracts of bilberry fruit. Italian researchers working between 1982 and 1987 reported that 76 percent of patients in their trials experienced a marked improvement in their myopia (shortsightedness) after being given 5 ounces (150 mg) a day of a bilberry extract, plus vitamin A, for 15 days. They also reported a significant reduction or disappearance of hemorrhages in the retina of diabetics who were given a higher dose of extract for 30 days up to one year.

In another experiment done in Japan, 26 people were divided into two groups. One group received a placebo for 28 days. The other group was given 4 ounces (125 mg) of blueberry extract (which contains 1 ounce or 28 g of anthocyanins, the chemicals responsible for the blue color in blueberries) twice a day for the same period. After 28 days the groups were switched and the experiment repeated. Tests were made before and after each period to measure improvement or deterioration of eyesight. The results showed that after the extract was taken for 28 days, symptoms associated with weak eyesight improved. The greatest benefit was the relief of the symptoms of tired eyes. Eyes that were already weak or had cataracts did not receive much benefit.

Fruit with a dark skin, including blueberries, has long been a favorite ingredient in wine making in the home. Many a glass has been tossed back with the toast "to your good health," perhaps without the realization that these were not empty words. It has always been known in country folklore that red wine made from wild fruits with dark skins has preventative and healing power and is taken "for a strong heart and long life," as well as pure enjoyment.

The blueberries picked and regularly sold today are of great benefit to health and we now know a lot more about the reasons for this. Considerable study has been carried out, particularly on the effects of eating blueberries or taking extracts made from bilberries or the North American wild blueberries. Much of the research has been carried out at the United States Department of Agriculture (USDA) Human Nutrition Research Center on Aging at Tufts University in Boston. There is now much more understanding of the action on the body of the complex chemicals involved. It is a tricky subject for nonscientists to understand, especially as current terminology is confusing, even among scientists.

The red, blue or violet plant pigments in the skin of *Vaccinium* fruit are due to the presence of organic chemicals. Scientists give these chemicals a variety of names, but the term "polyphenols" covers them as a general term. They provide a range of health benefits, acting primarily as antioxidants, which mop up harmful free radicals but also act in other ways, from having some antibacterial and antiviral action, to anticarcinogenic, antiangiogenic and antiallergenic actions. Free radicals are produced by the normal process of converting oxygen into energy in the cells of the body, and the toxins associated with them are normally disposed of by a healthy body. However, when produced in excess or not removed efficiently, they can be highly destructive and destroy the outer membranes of healthy cells, causing degeneration and death of cells in tissues where they are active. This imbalance is called oxidative stress and is more common in today's polluted society than in the past. Antioxidants combine with free radicals and render them harmless.

Glutathione is an important agent in the body, active in preventative functions, helping to repair damaged DNA. In the liver it is used in great quantities to detoxify carcinogens and other toxins to which the body is constantly exposed. Its levels are boosted by polyphenols, including those provided by blueberries. In addition to polyphenols, blueberries and other berries contain ellagic acid, which is a powerful anticarcinogen. People suffering from age-related diseases tend to have low glutathione levels, and animal studies have shown that by raising those levels, the life span of the animals was increased. In addition to combating disease, chemicals present in blueberries can have the benefit of delaying other effects of aging. It is thought that they may increase the flexibility of cell membranes, which can help combat inflammatory diseases such as arthritis. Polyphenols also boost the activity of vitamin C, which in turn increases the levels of vitamin E.

It is clear that current research indicates that blueberries have both age-extending and disease-preventing functions. The greatest concentration per ounce or gram of these chemicals (known as polyphenols) is in the small-berried species and varieties. These chemicals are three or four times more potent than vitamin C and are not destroyed by cooking. The marketing arm of the WBANA, which is responsible for the marketing of the thousands of tons of lowbush blueberries, has not been slow to capitalize on this.

At least 15 different anthocyanoside compounds have been identified from bilberry extracts. In addition, up to 7 percent tannins, several alkaloids, 12 different phenolic acids and three glycosides all may play a positive role in medicine.

Experiments have been carried out on the effect of blueberry extract on brainpower. In one experiment elderly rats were fed blueberry extract for nine weeks. A control group did not receive the extract. The older rats outperformed the control group when asked to navigate mazes and balance on rotating logs. After four months they performed equally well as young rats in memory tests. So far there are no reports of elderly humans being asked to navigate mazes or balance on rotating logs, but more appropriate tests are indicating similar benefits.

Improving microcirculation appears to be among the most effective medicinal uses for bilberry or blueberry extract. Its effects on the capillaries serving the eyes and mucous membranes of the digestive and pulmonary systems are thus expected. Improved capillaries also help to improve circulation to the connective tissues, which should help arthritis sufferers. Water retention in the legs and varicose veins, general bruising and hemorrhoids are all problems that, according to the research so far, can be treated successfully with bilberry extract.

There are no reports of adverse effects due to the use of bilberry extract, nor are any expected. (Allergic reactions, in the form of rashes, vomiting and diarrhea, to fresh blueberry fruit do sometimes occur, but they are very rare.) The extract is given orally, but there are plans to make an injectable extract in the future.

Pierre Jean Cousins's book *Food Is Medicine* (2001) adds that, in addition to the above benefits, blueberries have powerful antibacterial action in the intestine, especially on coli bacteria, and they promote healing of gastric ulcers. Mild diabetes sufferers should also eat plenty of blueberries. He also recommends a blueberry decoction for diarrhea, colitis and poor night vision, as a mouthwash for sore throats and ulcers and as a face wash for eczema sufferers. He simply boils 2½ ounces (70 g) of blueberries in ¼ gallon (1 liter) of water till the volume of water is halved, then strained, cooled and bottled. He uses either cranberry or blueberry juice to prevent or treat urinary tract infections such as cystitis.

Cranberry juice is well established as being excellent for fighting urinary infections. Blueberry juice has similar qualities. This is due to tannins, which prevent bacteria from sticking to the bladder lining. (They also help fight tooth decay by the same method.) Cranberries also have similar anti-carcinogenic properties but the problem with cranberries is that most people, and many manufacturers, add sugar or another sweetener to make the rather tart fruit more palatable. This suppresses the immune system.

In practical, everyday terms, the conclusion must be that if you eat at least half a cup of blueberries per day you should benefit in terms of general health and a delay in the onset of degenerative diseases associated with aging. If you use your eyes a lot, a diet rich in blueberries should help combat tired eyes and, if you suffer from urinary infections, nonsweetened cranberry or blueberry juice acts as a useful antibacterial agent.

A Botanical Overview

The genus *Vaccinium*, which belongs to the family Ericaceae, consists of around 450 species distributed worldwide and is usually found in acidic soils that may be sandy or peaty or of other organic matter such as leaf litter, especially that from pine trees. A few subtropical and neotropical species are loosely epiphytic. They grow in humus collected in the clefts formed where branches emerge from living trees, and a number of temperate species native to forests, such as *V. parvifolium* and *V. ovatum*, quite frequently colonize rotting logs or even stumps of pine trees still standing 25 ft. (7.5 m) high or more in the Oregon and Washington coastal forests.

The Canadian botanist Vander Kloet has probably done more botanical research on *Vaccinium* than anyone and his book *The Genus* Vaccinium *in North America* (1985) is still the main reference work on the genus in Britain. He writes that 26 species occur wild in North America, six in Europe. There are a further 47 in the neotropical area including Mexico, the Caribbean and as far as south as northern Argentina in South America. In addition, five are to be found in Africa, 19 in Japan, possibly five in the Pacific area, and 70 in China and other Southeast Asian countries. The rest, about 250, are in the Malaysian region.

There has been great confusion (and discussion) over the years about the classification of this genus, not helped by the very large number of botanical synonyms accumulated over the years and, of course, by the common names given to the wild plants from which berries have been traditionally harvested. Thus, the widely distributed *Vaccinium vitis-idaea* is known as partridgeberry, foxberry, rock cranberry, mountain cranberry and upland cranberry in the United States and Canada. (This list does not include the names given to them by the various Native American tribes.) A larger leafed form of the species is known as the cowberry in Britain, lingonberry in Scandinavia and preisselbeere in Germany.

The existence of "forms" is largely the result of evolution in different geological locations, some of which may be quite local. Some botanists have allocated species names to a number of these, but the modern tendency is to reduce the number of species while recognizing the previous synonyms and forms as such. Modern taxonomists use a combination of morphological features, genetic makeup (DNA fingerprinting is useful here) and data, which gives information such as the type of habitat in which the plants thrive and, on occasion, other factors such as blooming periods.

With a genus as large and diverse as *Vaccinium* it is beyond the scope of this book to classify and describe all the taxa and cultivars, and especially to sort out the many synonyms which some species have accumulated over the years. It is a taxonomic nightmare that botanists must sort out, horticulturists leaving well enough alone. Many neotropical species and some tropical species are still not firmly placed in their correct taxonomic place. Therefore, for the purposes of this book, the botanical descriptions of what I would call the "cooler climate" vacciniums are given, as are those that are native to North America and Europe and have been the subject of study over many years, as well as those that have garden merit or are in cultivation as food crops. Some of the subtropical and neotropical species in cultivation are described under their currently classified names which seem safely established but may possibly be changed in the future as further botanical studies are carried out.

Part II

Cranberries and Lingonberries

General Classification

If you read any book on wild berries, be it a cookbook, trail guide or wild-flower companion, it will probably have a variety of "cranberries" included. The only obvious feature linking them appears to be that they all have edible red berries. The red fruits of *Viburnum edule* appear as highbush cranberry in an Alaskan cookery book, and *V. trilobum* is sometimes called the cranberry viburnum.

Botanists are united in classifying true cranberries under the family Ericaceae. Cranberries all belong to the genus *Vaccinium*, and only the creeping plants, which produce stolons or rhizomes, are regarded as true cranberries. The large shrubby vacciniums that have red berries, such as the southern mountain cranberry, are not considered true cranberries.

Apart from the relatively simple matter of sorting out what are "true" cranberries and what are impostors, there has been disagreement in the broader classification of these creeping plants. It has long been agreed that they belong to the family Ericaceae, but they used to be given generic status under the heading *Oxycoccus. Oxycoccus macrocarpon, O. palustris* and *O. microcarpus* are listed and described in W. J. Bean's 1976 edition of *Trees and Shrubs Hardy in the British Isles.* It has now been accepted that the generic name "Oxycoccus" should be dropped and that cranberries be listed under *Vaccinium*, section *Oxycoccus*, with only two specific names allocated, namely *V. macrocarpon* and *V. oxycoccus.* It is also suggested that *V. oxycoccus* migrated, over thousands of years, southward into the eastern parts of North America as glaciation spread. It eventually came into contact with the resident *V. macrocarpon*, resulting in hybrid swarms.

Chapter 1

Cranberries

Geographic Range

The large or American cranberry (*Vaccinium macrocarpon*) is the species most used in commercial production and in garden situations, where it is cultivated for its fruit. It is found growing wild in damp acidic soils mainly between latitudes 40°N and 50°N and longitudes 70°W and 80°W in the eastern coastal regions of Canada and the United States from Newfoundland to Long Island and inland from western Ontario to Minnesota. This species is also found in similar soils in the cooler, more mountainous regions of Arkansas, Illinois, North Carolina, Ohio and Virginia, although many "wild" colonies are in fact thought to be introductions. This certainly applies to those found in western Canada and the United States, Britain and other parts of Europe. Carbon dating has, however, indicated that some of the present-day, genuinely native plants in the eastern areas have grown from colonies that have origins thousands of years old.

History of Human Use and Early Cultivation

The early settlers in North America quickly discovered the benefits of cranberries from the Indians, and the first description sent to Europe is probably that of Captain John Smith in 1614. He described "red berries called Kermes," so it is possible that when the Pilgrims arrived in 1620, they already had some idea of the existence of cranberries. The first cranberries to reach Europe were those the settlers sent in 1677: ten barrels (plus Indian corn or maize and 3,000 codfish) to King Charles II, who had been displeased with them for minting their own "pine tree shillings." It was probably Mahlon Stacy, who lived near what is now Trenton, New Jersey, who first described, in a 1689 letter to his brother in Yorkshire, the use and keeping qualities of cranberries in those early days. Stacy was also the first to report the use of cranberry sauce with turkey, a Thanksgiving tradition to this day.

Little of interest is written about cranberries in the eighteenth century, except that a statute was passed in 1789 by the governing body of New Jersey forbidding the settlers to pick cranberries before 10 October. Those who were caught had to pay a fine of ten shillings, a hefty penalty for people trying to get in before their neighbors by picking berries before they were ripe.

The English landowner, plantsman, plant hunter and horticulturist Sir Joseph Banks received some cranberry plants from North America at the turn of the eighteenth century. He had previously received some fruit, which was sent across the Atlantic in barrels of water, and had found these to be "vapid and almost tasteless" as a result, he thought, of their long journey soaking in the water (Banks 1808). He decided he would try to grow his own. The species is not described. Banks's article appeared in the Transactions of the Horticultural Society (now the Royal Horticultural Society) describing his methods. He wrote, "A short account of the management of this unimproved Plant will, it is to be hoped, prove acceptable to the Members of this useful Society, and not uninteresting to the Public at large." His house, Spring Grove, in the country to the north of London was supplied with clean water from the nearby spring, and wastewater from the house was "suffered to drain through a small basin and into a large pond in the pleasure ground." Here it emerged as a fountain. Banks removed the fountain in this shallow pond and allowed the wastewater to bubble up as a spring instead and constructed a circular wooden box "22 ft. in diameter and 13 in. deep, with the sides emerging 8 in. above the water." He made sure the sides were "bored through with many holes" and filled the bottom with stones and rubble. He (or more probably a team of staff members) then took a trip—or more likely several trips—to Hounslow Heath, which is now part of London, and brought home sufficient "bog earth" to fill his box.

The cranberries thrived, flowering and producing ripe fruit in their first year, which proved a great source of delight. They "sent out runners somewhat resembling strawberries, but longer and less inclined to root when young." He observed that they rooted better in winter and sent out branches 10 in. (25 cm) or more in length during the following summer, which fruited the following year. By 1807 his cranberry beds occupied 326 sq. ft. (100 sq. m) of the pond and he harvested "5 dozen bottles of fruit" that fall. He had no problems with pests and diseases and was pleased with the consistent and heavy yields of fruit. One wonders what would happen if wastewater from a house was used for a cranberry bed nowadays.

In 1821 Robert Hallett, writing from Devon, England, in the Transactions of the Horticultural Society tells how he obtained some cranberry plants from Banks and was very successful with them in a small bed in his small pond. Having no more pond space he "resolved to grow them on a dry bed." For propagation he constructed six boxes 18 in. (45 cm) square and 4 in. (10 cm) deep and filled them "with peat earth," presumably taken from the moors nearby. He then took woody cuttings 1½ in. (3.8 cm) long in April and inserted them an inch apart in his boxes, which he placed in his heated melon bed, where they were "frequently watered." They rooted well and were planted out in his outdoor cranberry bed in June 1818.

This bed was "150 ft. long and 4 ft. wide," filled to a depth of about 6 in. (15 cm), with "peat earth collected from a dry hill where wild heaths flourished in abundance." The young cranberry plants were planted in a single row down the middle of the bed, 2 ft. (60 cm) apart. He knew, presumably from Banks's experience, that they would soon grow because he noted that "if planted 4 or 6 ft. (1.2 to 1.8 m) apart the shoots would soon meet." This confidence was borne out because by the end of the following year, 1819, his bed was covered by the young growth. The following spring Hallett noted that runners from the previous year had produced "a number of upright bearing shoots." These, he was pleased to note, subsequently bore flowers and fruit. He makes no mention of providing water but notes that his cranberry plants were free from pests and diseases and appeared to be tolerant of both cold and drought. He made some important observations, such as "dung is peculiarly injurious to the cranberry; it absolutely destroys it." Hallett also tells his readers that "peat earth is the only soil in which they flourish—nor can a supply of this very valuable fruit be expected except in situations where the plants will have a due enjoyment of sun and air." His pioneering spirit extended to the planting of "a double row of Bilberry or Whortleberry plants, which are thriving and full of blossoms" around the edge of his cranberry bed.

On the commercial front in the 1800s there was a thriving but relatively small-scale cranberry industry using *Vaccinium oxycoccus* in Lincolnshire in eastern England. The naturally peaty soil and abundance of water provided ideal conditions. All that remains today is the name "Cranberry Lane." Cranberry cultivation started in North America, using native plants from the surrounding countryside, either by managing them in situ or transplanting them into newly constructed "bogs." The main period of development of the industry took place in the middle of the nineteenth century in the East, in Massachusetts, New Jersey, Wisconsin, as well as in the coastal areas of Washington and Oregon in the West from 1883.

A document in 1816 (Cape Cod Cranberry Association) reported that Captain Henry Hall, a veteran from the American Revolution living near Dennis on Cape Cod, Massachusetts, had, in 1810, noticed that sand blown onto the marshes near his home seemed to encourage better growth and subsequent fruiting of the wild cranberries. He created the first recorded North American cranberry "bog" by draining an area near his home, which he covered with a layer of sand into which he then planted sods consisting of cranberry plants gathered from wild populations. Within ten years the yield from his cultivated cranberries enabled Hall to send cranberries to city dwellers in New York. He was even being taxed on his income, the first cranberry producer to experience this "privilege."

A new industry was born. Other pioneers followed, and a variety of observations and experiments were carried out to improve production. Notable was the observation that different wild populations had variable characteristics; some plants became known as "jumbos" because they produced extra large fruit. Cultivation in the northern area around Boston began in 1831, and Augustus Leland soon emerged as an innovator of great significance. He learned to control water flows to benefit his cranberry bogs, both as a means of frost protection and cranberry worm control. He was also the first to see the practical advantage of adding sand while his bogs were still frozen solid. He also identified the weeds found growing among his cranberries. Several growers in Massachusetts who were not fortunate enough to have property on lowland areas tried, with mixed results, to grow cranberries on upland sandy loams, land which was normally used to grow corn.

The southern part of New Jersey is the home of what were formerly known as the Pine Barrens, or the Pinelands, which is an area of marshes and peat bogs with pines growing on the drier land. Wild cranberries were abundant, but it was not until 1835 that Benjamin Thomas of Pemberton started to cultivate the wild cranberries. New Jersey's John Webb, known as "Peg Leg John," copied the Massachusetts system of transplanting sods from wild cranberry colonies and the method of sanding the bogs. He also observed that healthy, firm berries bounced down steps while soft, diseased or over-ripe ones did not reach the bottom. Having only one sound leg, he found it of considerable advantage to "pour" his cranberries down the stairs from his storage loft to his packhouse instead of having to carry them. The "bouncing principle" is used to this day in separating good berries from bad. This is an excellent example of a useful technique being discovered by accident.

Peg Leg John was not, however, the most influential of cranberry producers in New Jersey. Far more important were J. J. (Joseph Josiah) White and his father-in-law, Colonel James A. Fenwick. Fenwick bought nearly 500 acres (200 hectares) of land with many acres of wild cranberries growing on it. It was well supplied with water from a canal and a canal pond that had once supplied an old iron-smelting furnace. He proved very successful at cultivating the wild cranberries, as was White, who was given 100 acres (40 hectares) of land at the age of 20 by his grandfather and later acquired another 100 acres (40 hectares) from his brother. Three years later, in 1869, he married Fenwick's daughter, Mary, and within the first year of their marriage they wrote their manual for cranberry growers. (The first manual to be produced for commercial cranberry growers was written by B. Eastwood in 1856.) They took over the management of Fenwick's farm on his death in 1882.

White was also the first cranberry grower to actually construct cranberry bogs and to cultivate cranberries from scratch instead of cultivating areas where wild cranberries already grew, an innovative idea in those days and one mocked by others, who called his enterprise "White's Folly." White had the last laugh, though, because he became producer of the largest volume of cranberries in New Jersey. J. J. and Mary White had four daughters, the eldest, born in 1871, being Elizabeth. She was the only one who took an interest in the family business and she started working with her father in 1893. She went on to become among the most influential people in the blueberry-growing world.

In Wisconsin wild cranberries became an important part of the local economy and, as in New Jersey, a law was passed to try to stop the practice of picking unripe cranberries. The fine was $50 for picking or possessing cranberry fruit before 20 September. The first cultivation of the wild cranberry is recorded in 1853, and production increased so rapidly that by 1869 the main cranberry growing area had 1,000 acres (400 hectares) under cultivation.

Although the cultivation of cranberries continued to develop, peaking in the middle of the nineteenth century, the traditional harvesting of wild cranberries continued. Both wild and cultivated cranberries were on sale in the towns and cities, with Boston being the main market in the East and the port from which they were shipped to Europe and to wealthy cities in the southern states. The whaling fleets bought large quantities for their ships' crews to ward off scurvy and provide a welcome change from their monotonous, unhealthy diet. Many cranberry bog owners on the East Coast were also seafarers whose descendants still own portions of Cape Cod cranberry bogs.

As cranberry cultivation increased and some areas became highly concentrated with cranberry bogs, so the incidence of damage by pests and diseases grew, and management techniques to deal with them became more and more important.

Botany and Life Cycle

To cultivate cranberries successfully, whether commercially or in the garden, it helps to understand their annual life cycle as they all have well-documented requirements. Production of flowers, followed by fruit, must be preceded by the frame of vegetative growth upon which they develop. The vines must be encouraged to produce as many sturdy, vertical, lateral shoots (usually termed "uprights") from the main horizontal vines as possible, as it is these which bear the flowers.

Vaccinium macrocarpon is a low-growing, trailing woody perennial that forms a dense spreading mat. Horizontal woody stems or vines, also known as runners or stolons, sometimes reach 6.2 ft. (1.9 m) from the original small plant. Leaves on the horizontal vines are quite widely spaced and are produced spirally around the stems. In spring, buds in the axils of these leaves may produce new shoots that grow upward to form a short, $2\frac{1}{2}$ to 4 in. (6.4 to 10 cm) branch known as an upright. These young shoots bear closely packed leaves. Their terminal buds consist of tissue that will produce future growth and, one hopes, flowers as well. In the following year uprights may either continue to grow upward or bend over to become additions to the horizontal mat.

Leaves are $\frac{1}{4}$ to $\frac{1}{3}$ in. (5 to 8 mm) long, $\frac{1}{8}$ in. (2 to 3 mm) wide, round tipped, oval, usually flat and with rolled margins. The shiny leaves are midgreen above and paler and waxy below, where all the leaves' stomata or pores are. These pores may number an extraordinary 632 per sq. mm. The guard cells surrounding each pore are unusually erratic in their function so that whereas a normal leaf may quickly adjust to different conditions of light, temperature, moisture and wind, the cranberry pores do not. They act slowly or not at all, which means that when planning a cranberry bed, growers should know the climate in the habitats where wild *V. macrocarpon* thrives so as to provide a habitat which mirrors that as closely as possible. Young colonies are more vulnerable to climatic extremes than older ones where the "mat" formed provides a microclimate to protect the leaves and valuable buds in some of their axils.

During the winter it is normal for the leaves to become marked with brown or reddish coloring giving an overall reddish appearance to the vines. Leaves over two years old are naturally discarded and replaced by young ones.

Flowers are produced on short, 2 to 3 in. (5 to 7.5 cm), upright stems growing singly from May to June or even later in some areas. Up to five flowers (occasionally up to ten) may be produced in the axils of small bracts at intervals up each short upright. Each flower is borne on a slender 1 1/4 in. (3 cm) pedicel or stalk, initially appearing as a hook then opening to show four sepals and four reflexed, pale pink petals. These petals become sharply separated and curved back to reveal a "beak" of eight stamens surrounding a central stigma. The early settlers apparently noticed that the flower looked like the head and beak of the native sandhill crane, hence its former name "craneberry." The slender pedicels each carry a pair of tiny green bracts. The pedicels curve where the flowers join them, giving healthy flowers a nodding appearance.

Pollen is released from the tips of the anther tubes when the flower shakes. It is thought that cranberries are self-fertile, but as this pollen is ripe before the stigma appears through the anther ring, there has been some doubt about the effectiveness of this method. Wind pollination was thought to be significant, but the pollen is heavy and sticky so this method is no longer thought to be of great importance. Bees, especially bumblebees (*Bombus* spp.), are certainly active in their foraging for cranberry nectar, which has an attractively high sugar content.

After pollination the ovary and calyx fuse to form a true berry, which has a shiny, waxy surface. Inside are four loculi or chambers containing small seeds, which may be just a few in number or occasionally up to 50. The walls of the berry vary in thickness, but the air trapped in the loculi allows the fruit to float in water and is an important factor at harvest time in many commercial cranberry bogs. Berries deepen in color as they age, ranging from pale pink to deep red or even purple. They have a sharp flavor, especially when they are only just ripe. They sweeten slightly as they age, and some enthusiasts wait until November when they are quite soft and sweet before picking them.

Most commercial cranberry fruits are round, but five different shapes may be found: round, bell, spindle, bugle and olive. These may be different "forms" or different cultivars, or the different shapes could be the result of different management techniques in the bogs.

The upright stems continue to grow, adding 3 in. (7.5 cm) or so each year, until they drop and become horizontal. The uprights produce terminal buds, which contain tissue that will produce both next year's growth and next year's flower buds, while producing their own flower-bearing uprights as they become horizontal themselves. Thus the plant is built up over the years, and it should be possible to pick a commercial crop in the fourth year after planting.

A cranberry plant initially develops a taproot from which fine lateral roots emerge. As the plant grows, adventitious roots develop from the axils of leaves along the horizontal stems or stolons. In most terrestrial plants, a mass of root hairs provides a large surface area through which water and essential minerals may be absorbed by young roots. Cranberries, along with other vacciniums, have none.

What *Vaccinium macrocarpon* and other vacciniums do have is a mycorrhizal association with an endophytic fungus (a fungus that lives within the tissues of the plant). The fungus *Phoma radicis*, which is isolated in and around the roots, is present in significant quantities in soils rich in humus (such as peaty soils) and enters the roots of introduced new plants from this source. It is able to spread from living cell to cell in the cortical tissues and can reach most parts of the plant. It does not appear to be transferred from plant to plant, however, such as during vegetative propagation.

The mycorrhiza is a symbiotic association of benefit to both plant and fungus. It is believed that the fungus helps to improve the availability of nitrates and other minerals from the humus formed by the rotting remains of leaves and other vegetation around the plants. The plant, in turn, provides a host for the fungus, possibly supplying some carbohydrates manufactured during photosynthesis. There is no detriment to the plant; indeed some researchers found that the most vigorous plants contain the most fungal mycelium, a network of branched hyphae or stems that make up the body of the fungus. Recent work has isolated and cultured the fungus, and inoculation of the mycelium is now possible. It is likely that the mycelium actually add to the root surface area and act in the same beneficial way as root hairs do in other genera. In addition it is thought that mycorrhizae provide a useful filter for the roots by helping to prevent entry to harmful minerals and some harmful soil microorganisms.

Harmful root fungi kill their hosts mostly by invading and blocking the conducting tubes (xylem vessels) that carry water up from the roots, or sugars and other food substances (phloem vessels) down to them. Mycorrhizae merely occupy the nonconducting cortical cells and extend out into the soil by up to 1 in. (2.5 cm). They are not essential to the health of a plant but do seem to be of benefit.

Mycorrhizae are present in many virgin woodland or heathland soils and can be carried in the root systems of transplanted blueberries and cranberries already naturally inoculated with them. They are not found in soils previously cultivated with other crops or in highly fertile soils, and they do not thrive in very wet or very dry conditions. It is a factor worth considering when planning to plant blueberries or cranberries. Artificial inoculation of mycorrhiza has been tried but with only limited success so far.

Requirements for Cultivation

This book does not seek to be a handbook for commercial growers but our knowledge of *Vaccinium macrocarpon* is due in no small part to their work and that of the supporting scientists. This contribution has become an integral part of what has become, since the late twentieth century, a very important industry, with about 1,200 growers producing an annual harvest of around five million barrels with a market value of over $1.5 billion. About 90 percent of the crop is sold and consumed as fresh fruit within North America. Massachusetts is the leading cranberry-producing state, followed by Wisconsin, New Jersey, Oregon and Washington. Added to the North American market is the ever-increasing presence of cranberries in the diet of health-conscious people in other countries worldwide. More people are having a go at growing their own. Commercial cranberry production is being tried in several European countries as well as in Japan.

Many regard *Vaccinium macrocarpon* as the only species worth growing commercially, although the lingonberry (*V. vitis-idaea*) is being increasingly grown in Europe and in cold, upland areas of North America.

The capital investment needed to set up a commercial cranberry growing enterprise today is huge, and this, combined with the need for very acidic soil and plenty of clean fresh water, is a strong deterrent, especially as most of the land suited to this crop is now protected for conservation purposes. Those lucky enough to have in their possession an old, neglected bog may find it worth reviving but it is only worth the undertaking if there is a known market for the fruit, if the legislation affecting land use in that area has been thoroughly checked, if the soil is suitable and if the water supply is adequate. Many bogs, especially in Wisconsin, were abandoned because of pollution from mineral sources and are unlikely to be suitable again. Others have ceased growing because of an oversupply.

Growing cranberries at home can also be a rewarding experience, as Banks and his friend Hallett discovered about 200 years ago. Although they grew their cranberries solely for fruit production, cranberries do make good ground cover in an ornamental garden if the soil is sufficiently acidic. The basic requirements for cranberry cultivation are the same whatever the scale of the operation but, for the home gardener, Hallett's publication of his discovery that cranberries grow very well without the need for a bog is worth noting. The five criteria for good cranberry growing are as follows: acidic soil, the optimum pH being 4.0 to 5.5 (although they will grow in soils with pH 6.0); a source of noncalcareous sand available for topping; access to good clean water, whether the growing is done on a "dry" or "wet" system; awareness of the local climatic conditions, especially where low temperatures are concerned; and an ability to control invasive weeds, pests and possibly diseases.

Soil

Cranberries are not, as is often supposed, grown in water. Their roots require anchorage and oxygen in addition to minerals for growth, conditions which are provided by moist but not permanently saturated soil. For healthy growth, all plants need to have the vital macroelements of nitrogen, phosphorus and potash. Cranberries are no exception, although their requirements are low compared to most other fruit and ornamental plants. They also need calcium, magnesium and sulfur in smaller amounts, as well as trace elements or micronutrients, such as boron, chlorine, copper, iron, molybdenum and zinc in minute quantities.

In their natural habitat cranberries grow in soils that are always acidic, with the pH ranging from 3.5 to about 5.5. The optimum appears to be somewhere in the middle of the range, about pH 4.0 to 4.5. This is the range within which the minerals needed for healthy vegetative growth and subsequent fruit production are available to cranberries. Above or below this range, the availability of minerals becomes less efficient, and deficiency symptoms or symptoms of excess occur, resulting in less fruit being produced.

Ideally, soils are peaty, with moss or sphagnum peat being particularly common. These are termed organic soils and they have plenty of potential for nutrient release when conditions are favorable. Decomposition of the organic matter needs to take place for the nutrients to be released, which requires activity by bacteria, which in turn need moist conditions during the warm months of summer when they are most active, releasing nitrates when the plants especially need them for vegetative growth. In the wetter soils, such as those found in marshland or at the edge of lakes and ponds, these bacteria are less active, and decomposition of organic matter is slower but still sufficient to support some growth. Dry soil conditions not only reduce bacterial activity but they also have insufficient water available to conduct available minerals up into the plants. Mineral soils used for cranberry growing consist mostly of sand with a low or nonexistent organic content that may need to be added.

Relatively few traditional agricultural, horticultural or garden soils have a low pH. A good loam soil, which is traditional in most fruit growing areas, is not suitable for cranberries. It is possible, with the addition of powdered sulfur, to increase acidity. Professional advice is advisable before taking this step. Having access to a source of pure, clean, noncalcareous sand is useful, as the addition of sand, particularly to the surface of peat soils, is an accepted part of cranberry culture.

Water

Once a grower has determined that suitable soil conditions can be provided and that plenty of clean water is available to ensure that the correct level of nutrients is maintained, water comes into the equation. For most cranberry growers it is an important tool as it is used not only for irrigation but also as an aid for frost protection, insect control and harvesting. Commercial growers and gardeners growing cranberries "dry" will need clean water for irrigation in summer. Like their colleagues who grow cranberries under the wet system, these growers will use overhead sprinklers for summer irrigation. Cranberry plants are susceptible to desiccation when they are at their most active, which is in summer. It is difficult to rehydrate peat soils, and root damage is usually fatal.

Traditional commercial cranberry bogs are designed so that the plants are grown in low-lying rectangular fields surrounded by banks that are wide enough apart to allow tractor and truck access. The banks are made from the spoil (meaning soil, rocks and stones) excavated from the field during construction. These "bogs" are designed so that they can be flooded by opening them up to a surrounding system of dykes containing pure clean water, with the flood being drained off within 48 hours if necessary. The quality of this water is important; it needs to be of low pH and well oxygenated. It cannot come from stagnant, airless ditches. Water taken from an alkaline source is also not acceptable. Mineral pollution from any source is, of course unacceptable, whether it is from saltwater, industrial effluent, pesticides, roadside wash-off or natural phenomenon. In some East Coast areas of North America, a number of cranberry bogs that were flooded with sea water after severe storms remain polluted and unproductive even 30 or 40 years later.

Cranberry producers themselves have a responsibility to avoid polluting the surrounding rivers and streams with effluent containing excess fertilizer or pesticides. Many of the established cranberry producers, particularly in New Jersey, are located in "conservation" areas, which are tightly controlled by law. Fortunately, these producers need only low doses of mineral fertilizers, and they produce very little surplus runoff into the surrounding watercourses. This runoff is carefully monitored.

Climate

As evergreen perennial plants growing naturally in temperate climates in northern regions and often in quite exposed situations, it is natural to expect cranberries to be hardy. They are certainly hardy enough to survive harsh winter conditions, but this is the hardiness of survival, not the hardiness needed to flower, fruit and produce a rewarding crop for those growing cranberries solely for their berries. The plants do need a period of winter dormancy to complete their annual life cycle, but they are also vulnerable to damage from certain winter conditions. Research over the last 100 years shows that many wild plants of *Vaccinium macrocarpon* fail to flower regularly and many produce fruit in only one year in three, sometimes even less frequently. The reason is that factors other than just temperature are involved. Wind, sun and the state of maturity of buds and young growth are all affected by low temperatures. Low-lying cranberry bogs are often frost pockets, trapping the still, cold air in which frosts can be so damaging. Temperatures below 10°F (-12°C), even without desiccating winds, may cause damage to dormant flower and shoot buds. A combination of frozen roots and dry winds with a continuous day and night air temperature of only just below 32°F (0°C) for several days in succession will result in desiccation. Frost-damaged leaves turn brown and will drop off several weeks later, but as other leaves will replace them in the following summer, this is not the problem. The main problem is that damaged buds, which already contain the collection of cells that will be next year's flowers, will fail to develop.

Flooding or water sprinkler systems are used to prevent or reduce frost damage. Sprinklers, which are often controlled by sophisticated automatic systems, have replaced flooding as a method of frost protection in many areas. They can be quickly turned on and off as needed, whereas flooding is a much more cumbersome system.

Water sprinklers are also widely used for irrigation purposes and to cool vines during periods of high temperatures and low humidity in summer. Temperatures above 66°F (20°C), when combined with low humidity and bright sunshine, can be damaging, especially if it is also windy. Not only is there damage to the very tender new growth, especially the fragile flower stalks, more likely in early summer, but there is also damage to the newly formed cells of next year's shoots and flower buds. The size of the current year's fruit can also be affected if similar conditions occur in late summer. Early fall frosts can be damaging too to both developing fruit and the next year's flower buds.

As fall temperatures drop, the cranberry fruit ripens, gradually turning from white to red. The deepest colors are reached in the coolest areas, and a failure of the fruit to turn a true red sometimes happens, even in traditional cranberry growing regions, when there is a prolonged spell of warmer than average fall weather. Creative marketing has resulted in the sale of "white cranberries" as a desirable fruit crop in some warmer areas.

Cultivars

Most cultivars grown in the early years were originally selected from wild populations, and over 100 names have been allocated to them. Four, all selected in the nineteenth century, still form the basis for commercial cranberry production in North America, namely 'Early Black' (1845), 'Howes' (1843), 'McFarlin' (1874) and 'Searles' (1893). The first three were selected in Massachusetts and the fourth in Wisconsin. Since then a breeding program, supported by the USDA, has produced just seven commercially successful cultivars: 'Beckwith', 'Bergman', 'Crowley', 'Franklin', 'Pilgrim', 'Stevens' and 'Wilcox'. This seems an extraordinarily low figure considering the over 7,000 seedlings produced between 1929, the start of the program, and 1950, the first launch of the new cultivars.

Breeders continue to look for improvements in size, yield and color, as well as in the ability to withstand bruising during harvest and postharvest operations, to store well and, of course, to resist disease. One disease, false blossom disease, caused havoc in the first half of the nineteenth century but became more controllable once insecticide sprays were found to control the vector (the blunt-nosed leafhopper) responsible for its spread. Today, a greater awareness of both environmental and health issues has made the need for a reduction in insecticide use for pest control of great importance. Disease resistance has become a much higher priority for similar reasons.

The power of the market is also recognized as breeders seek to satisfy the demands of a wider range of customers. Varieties with less acid and more natural sweetness are sought. Such berries would reduce the amount of sugar added at the processing stage and may even lead to a wider market for the fresh fruit as more people become conscious of the need to reduce their sugar intake. Similarly, breeders are looking for varieties to extend the harvest season, the aim being to have early ripening in August.

Some varieties are more favored than others in different areas of a country, so there are those which are grown in commercial enterprises in the West Coast, for example, with others being more popular in the East. This difference in popularity is generally reflected in a variety's availability in nurseries in those areas. However, this should not deter home growers from trying to obtain any cultivar that seems appealing.

The following list of *Vaccinium macrocarpon* cultivars represents a range of cultivars available at the time of writing and contains those that not only span the season but also produce berries of different flavors, shapes, sizes and color depths. They are listed in approximate order of ripening.

'Beaver'. This cultivar originated at Beaver River in Nova Scotia, Canada. It was selected in 1940 by E. L. Eaton at Canada's Department of Agriculture Research Station in Kentville and was introduced in 1956. It came from seed selected from wild plants. Yields are moderate with large, good-looking fruit that stores well. Its particular advantage is that it ripens about a week ahead of 'Early Black', the standard early variety. The downside is that it is susceptible to false blossom disease.

'Early Black'. Cyrus Cahoon of Harwich, Massachusetts, introduced this wild selection, and it is still the most widely grown variety, especially in the eastern cranberry-growing areas of North America. It has been extensively used in breeding programs. Although the fruit is only small to medium, it ripens very early (as early as late August in some areas) and has good yields of shiny berries that turn dark red, almost black, when fully ripe. They are slightly pear shaped, being flat at the end and slightly pointed at the stem, and are firm in texture so they do not bruise easily, and they store well. They have a good flavor.

An additional advantage with 'Early Black' is that it is resistant to false blossom disease. It is an excellent choice for anyone growing cranberries for the first time, especially if ornamental value is wanted in addition to fruit. Its ornamental value lies in its small, light green leaves that turn deep red and provide attractive color for ground cover during the winter. It is among the most adaptable and easy to grow, doing well in gardens with slightly less acidic soils than are generally recommended, and it is more frost resistant than most.

'**Franklin**'. This cultivar, made in 1930 by H. J. Bain of the USDA at Whitesbog, New Jersey, is a cross between 'Early Black' and 'Howes'. It was tested at East Wareham, Massachusetts, and selected for introduction in 1961. It has a higher yield than either of its parents and ripens early, just after 'Early Black'. The medium to large berries keep well and are round and red to dark red. It takes time to establish as the vines are not very vigorous, but it does produce a compact plant with short runners and medium-length uprights so it is easy to control in a small area. It is also resistant to false blossom disease.

'**Stankavitch**'. This cultivar is the result of crossing a wild cranberry from Oregon with a selection from the eastern states, probably 'McFarlin'. It was selected some time between 1914 and 1917 in Bandon, Oregon, by Joseph F. Stankavitch and introduced in 1926. It ripens early, producing uniformly round, glossy, deep red berries averaging 1/2 to 3/4 in. (1.2 to 2 cm) in diameter. Yields are good and the fruit keeps well. The plant is of moderate vigor with tall uprights. It is best grown in cooler climates because it can, in milder areas, produce a second crop of flowers in the fall that do not, of course, produce ripe fruit and will reduce the yield the following year. Apart from its large fruit, it has the advantage of having a good sugar, low acid content. It is also resistant to false blossom disease.

'Wilcox'. Originated by Bain and tested at Whitesbog in New Jersey between 1938 and 1940, 'Wilcox' results from a cross between 'Howes' and 'Searles' and was introduced in 1950. 'Wilcox' is an early variety with medium to large, deep red berries of good quality that store well. The vines are vigorous with a mass of uprights, and it is resistant to false blossom disease. One reason for the increasing popularity of 'Wilcox' is its ability to become established very quickly after planting, producing heavy crops at an early age. It is particularly popular in New Jersey.

'Searles'. A cultivar that provides fruit in midseason from mid- to late September, it was selected by A. Searles of Wisconsin Rapids from a wild population and is still among the main varieties grown in Wisconsin. Berries are medium sized and deep red with firm flesh. They do not keep well in storage. The vines are productive, fairly coarse in habit and have tall uprights.

'McFarlin'. This cultivar is particularly popular in Washington and Oregon but is also widely grown in Wisconsin and Canada. It was selected and grown from a wild population by T. H. McFarlin of South Carver, Massachusetts, in 1874. Although the berries are not uniform in size, ranging from medium to large at harvest, they have an excellent flavor. They ripen in midseason and are quite distinctive, being deep red with a prominent calyx and a waxy bloom. They are either round or, quite frequently, elongated. 'McFarlin' is a vigorous grower, producing a mass of growth that tangles easily. It needs to be kept under control with regular pruning and is frost hardy and very resistant to false blossom disease.

'Stevens'. This cultivar is becoming increasingly popular with cranberry growers in Wisconsin and New Jersey. It is a cross between 'McFarlin' and 'Potter'. Originated at Whitesbog, New Jersey, by Bain, it was selected between 1938 and 1940 and introduced in 1950. The very large, deep red fruit is round or oval and flattened at both ends. It ripens midseason, and the flesh is firm and stores well. The vines are vigorous and productive. It is easy to grow and is particularly suitable for poor soils that lack organic matter. One drawback is that it is not as resistant to false blossom disease as some other cultivars.

'**Bergman**'. Another variety from Whitesbog, New Jersey, this plant was originated in 1930 by Bain and is a cross between 'Early Black' and 'Searles'. The seedling, introduced in 1961, was selected by F. B. Chandler and I. E. Demoranville of the Cranberry Station at East Wareham, Massachusetts, after being tested there. It is high yielding, and the short, red, pear-shaped fruit is large to medium sized and of good flavor. It ripens in midseason and stores very well. 'Bergman' is unpalatable to the blunt-nosed leafhopper and is therefore more resistant to false blossom disease. In addition, it holds its flowers—and therefore its fruit—well above ground, which makes it a good choice for both fruiting and ornamental purposes.

'**Beckwith**'. This selection came from Whitesbog in New Jersey and was originated by Bain and H. F. Bergman of the USDA. Introduced in 1950, it was selected between 1938 and 1940 as a result of a cross between 'Early Black' and 'McFarlin'. It produces good yields of deep red, medium to large, oval, elongated fruit. This fruit is of good flavor and stores reasonably well. Its harvest season is late. 'Beckwith' is prone to false blossom disease in New Jersey.

'**Pilgrim**'. A cross between 'Prolific' and 'McFarlin' made by Bain at Whitesbog in 1930, 'Pilgrim' was tested at East Wareham, Massachusetts, and introduced in 1961. It is a high-yielding cultivar with particularly large oval berries that are purplish red with a waxy bloom and cream-colored flesh. It ripens late and keeps well. The vines are of medium vigor with quite long uprights. It is not palatable to the blunt-nosed leafhopper so is not prone to false blossom disease.

'**Howes**'. A selection made from a wild population in 1843 by Elias Howes, 'Howes' was first cultivated at East Dennis in Massachusetts. The fruit is late ripening, of small to medium size, a good red color and normally round in shape or elongated if few seeds are present. The flesh is crisp with a high pectin content, which made it popular when canning was at its peak. It is an untidy grower, sending out a mass of uprights that tend to get tangled, which is not a desirable feature for either the commercial or home grower. 'Howes' is also not particularly resistant to false blossom disease but it is frost resistant and easy to grow.

Cultivation and Maintenance

Plants raised in the nursery are traditionally planted in the spring of the year following propagation when they have established a good root system and at least four branches. There is no hard and fast rule for planting distances, but 12 in. × 12 in. (30 cm × 30 cm) is about average. If peat blocks have been used they should be well soaked and put straight into the planting holes so there is no disturbance to the roots. Provided irrigation is available, they will establish quickly and grow into strong healthy plants which send strong, anchoring roots out into the soil very quickly before the following winter when they become dormant and have to withstand cold weather.

The roots of bog-raised cuttings may not be sufficiently developed to anchor the plants and prevent "lifting" by alternate freezing and thawing of the soil in their first winter. A well-sanded bog should not experience too many difficulties. Winter flooding solves this problem of lifting in commercial bogs, while small-scale plantings may be protected with horticultural fleece. With the arrival of warm weather and longer days, growth is rapid and the demand for water and fertilizer increases.

Propagation

The first cranberry farmers dug up sods bearing plants with desirable characteristics from the wild and transferred them to their own plots. This is no longer a sensible method, of course, as it is illegal for conservation reasons, and other plants which may be regarded as weeds are inevitably included too. Breeders propagate from seed when seeking new varieties, but seed propagation is otherwise not practiced as the results are so variable and few good varieties are produced.

Most important of all is the list of cultivars that breeders have produced. These cultivars have known qualities and are superior in so many ways because they are selected for all the attributes necessary to the regular production of good quality berries. The chosen cultivar is then propagated vegetatively by cuttings. It takes at least four years from the cutting stage to get a significant yield.

Established commercial growers use prunings collected after the mowers have been over the plants in early spring just before growth starts. Strong uprights are mown off and collected, preferably from a youthful bog, which is more likely to have vigorous, healthy growth that produces roots more readily. They may be stored in cool, moist conditions until the optimum time for inserting or "sowing" cuttings, which is in mid- to late spring when the dormant season is ending. Between one and two tons of cuttings per acre are scattered over the sand of the prepared new bog and then pushed into it using tractor-mounted vertical discs before being firmed in with a roller. Only about 2 in. (5 cm) of cutting should be visible above ground. Taller cuttings may be blown about by the wind which may prevent rooting. Reasonably high humidity and moist but not waterlogged soil should be maintained by using water sprinklers or by raising the water level of the bog until the roots are sufficiently established. Roots should form in about three weeks. This propagation method creates a bog with a randomly arranged planting, but no tidy rows are necessary as the aim is to produce a carpet of cranberry vines.

Cranberry cuttings root quite readily at home or in a nursery all year round, even in summer, especially if a mist propagator is available. However, it is best to take cuttings while they are still dormant, just before the buds break. This allows a full growing season after rooting. Cuttings from the previous year's growth are taken from healthy young plants. Their tops are removed, leaving a stem of $3^1/_4$ to 4 in. (8 to 10 cm) with 6 to 8 leaves near the tips. Purists remove the lower leaves; others do not bother. The removal of the tips encourages subsequent branching resulting from growth from the buds in the leaf axils. If the tips were not removed the terminal, dominant bud would be the only one to "break" and there would be little or no branching. The cuttings are inserted vertically and in pairs in peat or a 50:50 mixture of moist peat and sand in trays, cells, small pots or, better still, peat blocks to a depth of about 2 in. (5 cm). Peat blocks are ideal because they can be tightly packed on the propagating bench and are easy to handle at planting time. The cuttings should then be watered in and left to root. Bottom heat is not necessary. If mist is not used the containers can be put in a sealed cold frame, provided it is frost free if late spring frosts are expected, and some shade needs to be available when young growth starts.

Roots should appear at the leaf nodes under and at the surface of the rooting medium about three weeks after the cuttings are placed in their rooting medium. The newly rooted young plants should be kept moist and lightly shaded throughout the summer.

Rooted cuttings will need some minerals to encourage growth. Slow-release fertilizer granules that are specifically formulated for propagation and young plants are now frequently incorporated into the rooting medium of pots, cells or trays. They should gradually release their minerals in the summer months as the young plants need them and stop their release when temperatures drop and the plants no longer need feeding as they become dormant. High summer temperatures have caused excessive release in the past, but modern formulations are much improved and are now more suitable for such conditions. Liquid fertilizer with a high nitrogen content is usually applied at low doses to peat blocks every couple of weeks between mid-June and mid-August if the blocks are safely protected from frost for the coming winter. All these young plants need for their first winter is a cold glasshouse, frame or polytunnel. This is soft treatment compared with those cuttings inserted into the rigors of a commercial cranberry bog, but the resultant plants will be bigger and more likely to establish quickly and well when planted out in permanent beds.

Feeding

The objective is to produce vines with plenty of strong, sturdy uprights to carry a good crop of fruit, and while the fertilizer requirements of cranberries are low, applications are needed to encourage rapid vine growth in the first year or two to get the plants established. This provides a good framework for the future fruit-bearing uprights. Where possible, slow-release fertilizers, which gradually release their minerals as temperatures rise, are used, but two or three applications of granular fertilizer are traditionally given during these first two growing seasons to provide the low concentration of minerals the plants need at each application. One application of 200 lbs (90 kg) per acre of a 5–20–20 fertilizer in June and another of 100 lbs (45 kg) per acre of ammonium nitrate towards the end of July is one recommendation.

Once a cranberry bed is established, cranberry growers have a regular program of fertilizer application. It is necessary to replace the minerals taken out by the plants in producing each crop. The mineral requirements vary according to soil and climate, so local advice should be sought. Nitrogen, often in the form of urea, is frequently used to kick start growth once the danger of frost is passed.

Slow-release fertilizer pellets are increasingly used to provide additional nitrogen for the rest of the season, as well as phosphate, potash and even trace elements if deficiencies are indicated. These pellets can be scattered evenly in one application when growth starts. Alternatively, a granular fertilizer with a similar makeup is used and applied in two or even three doses between mid-May and late August.

Overfertilizing, especially with nitrogen, may lead to excessively vigorous growth with insufficient light being able to reach the vines to initiate flower formation. Additionally, where flowers are formed, flower stalks that are too long and slender to successfully bear fruit may result. Fungal problems, especially fruit rot, are more likely if growth is lush and overcrowded. The correct use of fertilizer, by contrast, provides an increase in the number of flower-bearing uprights, with more flowers per upright, followed by an increase in the amount of fruit set. Subsequent crops are therefore heavy with good-sized berries that have strong keeping qualities.

Small airplanes or helicopters are used in areas where commercial cranberry growing is concentrated. Fertilizer distributors mounted behind tractors fitted with large, partially inflated tires (these cause less damage to plants and soil) are also used. Small areas are fertilized by hand. It is a good idea to wash granular fertilizer off the vines by using overhead water sprinklers.

Liquid fertilizer may also be applied through sprinklers and washed off the vines with clear water after application. The objective is to produce vines with plenty of strong, sturdy uprights to carry a good crop of fruit.

Weed control

One of the downsides of adding fertilizers is that it encourages weed growth. Grasses, sedges and rushes are the main problems, but a number of perennial and woody, broad-leafed plants can also intrude. Many of the sedges and rushes are wetland plants; these can be deterred by keeping the water table more than 12 in. (30 cm) below the soil surface, a level that is sufficiently high for the cranberries but lower than what is required for the more shallow-rooting weeds.

Herbicides have been used extensively in the past, but in the environmentally sensitive areas in which many cranberry bogs are based, they are less acceptable now. As most weeds bear their flowers and seed heads above the level of the cranberry flowers and fruit, it is common practice to mow them off before the seeds can ripen and disperse.

Pruning

Pruning is carried out to keep plants producing strong, young growth. It is especially important when vines become old and woody and produce diminished yields, which is what happens when the fruit-bearing uprights become overcrowded resulting in insufficient light reaching them. Runners also become tangled and unproductive. Renovation pruning, which involves cutting all the plants to the ground by mowing or burning off in winter, results in the temporary loss of crop for a year or two. If plants are mown or burned off when the bog is not flooded but the water table is high, the roots will not be damaged. Clearing the vines in the following summer will produce strong new growth; of course, there will be no flowers and no fruit. In subsequent years, however, the crop should be much heavier than it was before pruning.

On a small scale, the vines of vigorous plants that are producing an excess of uprights are thinned annually using secateurs or pruning shears just before growth starts in spring. On a larger scale there are specialist mowers to do the job.

Water as a tool

Management of water is probably the most skilled part of wet cranberry growing. The water table needs to be maintained for optimum growth in the summer months, and the timing and level of flooding must be controlled. Research has shown that the best yields are from bogs where the summer water table (the upper level of water measured downwards from the soil surface) is kept at 9 to 12 in. (23 to 30 cm). The generally accepted level is 14 to 18 in. (35 to 45 cm) in pure sand soils. The water table needs to be at the higher level in more organic (generally peat) soils or in well-established bogs because the capillary action (the upward movement of water) is less efficient in soils rich in organic matter. These organic soils have usually developed alternate layers of organic matter and sand over the years. On the other hand, cranberry roots find it increasingly difficult to reach water maintained at deeper levels and will be deprived of the oxygen needed for healthy growth if the water level is kept too high.

The management of water in the commercial cranberry bogs is a skilled balancing act unique to cranberries. It takes knowledge and experience, together with a real "feel" for each individual bog, to use this tool successfully. Since it is also crucial to have the equipment to control the water levels to within a few centimeters, most commercial cranberry bogs are in areas where there is a plentiful supply of clean, running and therefore well-oxygenated water that can be used for repeated flood and withdraw operations throughout the year. The installation of sprinkler systems has not only reduced the amount of water used but has also made the job of water management a lot easier, especially where the sprinklers are automatically controlled to provide water when it is needed.

Flooding

It is the fascination with the wet harvest that draws tourists and television cameras to the cranberry growing areas in the fall, but flooding is also used at other times for less spectacular but nonetheless important purposes. The use of water to reduce frost damage, control pests and even reduce populations of competing weeds is less photogenic and very much less publicized, but each is every bit as important in the annual cycle of management in most of the cranberry-growing areas. The system of dykes and ditches surrounding the productive bogs needs as much maintenance as the bogs themselves, as do the pumps and pipe-work responsible for controlling the volume of water allowed in and out of them. The same network supplies the water for sprinkler irrigation. Once the sprinker is installed, the control of the water depends on the grower's considerable skill and diligence, especially in winter. Most cranberry growers live near their bogs as this allows them to keep a tight control.

Traditionally, once cranberry plants become dormant and winter begins to really bite (usually some time in December in the Northern Hemisphere), the sluice gates are opened and the winter flood begins. Water should reach sufficient depth to just cover the vines, the average depth being about 12 in. (30 cm). This keeps the plant temperature high enough (32°F or 0°C when the water freezes) to prevent damage. Some growers wait until sufficient ice has formed to carry the weight of their machinery before draining off any water remaining under the ice. This procedure allows air to circulate around the base of the plants so that they can respire while still keeping them insulated with ice. This method is particularly useful in areas where the bogs are likely to be covered with a deep layer of snow since snow excludes light and prevents the photosynthesis that enables plants to produce some of the oxygen needed for their own respiration.

If the ice in these bogs melts during the winter, leaving the vines exposed, more water is added to ensure that they are covered again before the next spell of freezing weather arrives. Many cranberry growers take the opportunity to sand their bogs while they are frozen as it is much easier to transport and scatter sand over a frozen bog than a wet one. Growers try to do this late in winter just before the ice is expected to melt so that the vines do not suffer from lack of light under their blanket of sand for too long. They may be dormant but they continue their normal physiological processes, including photosynthesis, at a level sufficient to sustain life.

The timing of spring drainage of the bogs is tricky, especially in areas where spring appears to come early, spurring growth, and then late spring frosts occur. Should the water remain over the vines until all danger of frost is past or should the bogs be drained early and then reflooded if low temperatures are forecast? It is known that the shorter the winter-flooding period the greater the volume of the subsequent crop is likely to be. The practice, therefore, tends to be to drain the bogs in April in areas where late frost is unlikely and to use the sprinklers for frost protection if necessary instead of reflooding. However, although the total volume of crop is greater when bogs are drained early, late flooding does tend to produce bigger, better quality berries with good color. Late removal of the winter flood is used when there is no reason to suspect that the vines are lacking oxygen from being submerged too long in poorly aerated water.

Another argument for keeping the bogs flooded even until late May in some areas is that it offers a means of controlling some insect pests. Pests will not be able to complete their life cycle under water and, instead of emerging from hibernation to cause damage to the cranberry plants, they are killed by drowning. Some sedges and grasses, which are potentially significant weeds, are also killed by prolonged spells spent under water in spring. After withdrawing the winter flood, reflooding (which involves completely covering the vines with water for about 24 hours) is sometimes used later in the season before flowering begins. Reflooding has been found to kill most emerging insect pests, which may have survived the winter. Reflooding again for about a week after the harvest flood has been withdrawn is also used to settle plants that may have been uprooted during mechanical harvest. Debris not removed at harvest will float and then be removed.

Flooding is, of course, a particularly important control method where a cranberry bog is being managed under organic systems that do not use chemical pesticides and herbicides.

Sanding

It was in 1801 that Hall discovered the benefits of sanding on a patch of wild cranberries that he harvested near his home on Cape Cod. When trees on a low sandy knoll nearby were felled, the sandy soil was exposed, causing erosion. It blew onto his cranberries and covered many of them. Hall noted that instead of being damaged, the vines grew up through the sand and produced bigger, better berries. Sanding has been an important part of cranberry cultivation ever since, not just before planting but also to provide a medium into which young plants or cuttings are inserted. Sand encourages better rooting of cuttings, produces better, more advanced fruiting, helps pest and weed control (to some degree), prevents the underlying peat from cracking in dry conditions and encourages rooting from the leaf nodes as the vines spread across the soil. Sand, applied evenly once every three to four years to a depth of between 1 and 2 in. (2.5 and 5 cm) also buries and encourages rotting of the dead leaves and other organic matter that tends to accumulate under the vines.

Managing pests and diseases

As with any horticultural business that involves fairly intensive cultivation and relies on a single, long-term crop, there can be pest and disease problems. These are less likely to be a problem for the small-scale grower or home gardener, especially if pest- and disease-free plants have been bought and if they are being grown outside the main commercial cranberry-growing areas. The pests and diseases I describe are all identified from cranberry bogs in the United States because relatively few are found in other countries or in areas where there is a lower concentration of cranberry plants.

Integrated Pest Management (IPM) is now widely practiced in all areas where cranberries are grown. As Gary Paulis of the USDA describes it, it is a "socially acceptable, environmentally responsible and economically practical" form of crop protection (personal communication). IPM is particularly important for cranberry producers because their bogs are so closely involved with the much wider environment. Their use of natural fresh watercourses and the proximity of many to environmentally sensitive areas means they are in a position to cause great damage to wildlife.

IPM calls for an initial knowledge of the possible problems that can be expected in a particular location. The first question must focus on what pests are present. Are they likely to build up to harmful levels, needing the expense of treatment, or is their presence at a low level and therefore tolerable? Knowledge of their life cycles and, in many cases, of alternative hosts of the various cranberry pests, is essential. An appreciation of the natural predators that help to keep a balance is also advisable since in the past some sprays have destroyed many of them. There is now a movement to identify and build up populations of these natural predators so that they can be used more, so that the use of chemicals can be reduced and because pests are becoming resistant to many of the chemicals that have been used over many years.

A mixture of control measures can help cranberry growers reduce the use of chemicals considerably. Such measures include one or more of the following depending on individual situations.

1. Using water. By flooding the bogs at critical times in the life cycle of certain pests, pests can be killed by drowning.
2. Destroying the habitat occupied by pests at some stage in their life cycle. In the case of cranberries, this destruction may involve sanding the leaf litter under the vines or controlling the weeds in the ditches and vegetation around the bogs.
3. Improving air circulation and reducing leaf fall. Trees that are too close to the margins of cranberry bogs can be felled, and this reduction in leaf fall will also reduce the build-up of leaf litter for hibernating insects. Some of these trees are alternative hosts for pests.
4. Controlling weeds. In particular, grasses within the bogs should be removed or at least mown before they form seeds.
5. Encouraging or introducing natural biological predators of the known pests in the area.
6. Spraying with chemicals. The chemicals must be approved specifically for cranberries by the appropriate department of agriculture and horticulture, and the spraying itself must be done when maximum control of the pests can be achieved with minimum disruption to beneficial insects such as pollinating bees.

Monitoring or scouting

Among the most common sights in a cranberry bog during the summer months is a sweep net being wielded by a human being with an intense look of concentration. Efficient scouts wield their nets with a certain panache. The objective is to catch insects and identify the individual pests present and track their numbers by systematic sampling. Sites are chosen across the whole area of a bog (typically one site per acre in a bog of up to 10 acres or 4 hectares) and are often marked with pegs. The scout goes in with two hands on the handle of an insect net 12 in. (30 cm) long and sweeps deep into the foliage of the vines, each sweep covering 180°. This deep sweep is repeated every step for 25 steps, all steps being walked in a straight line, before the scout moves on to the next site. The contents of the net are identified and recorded, and the average number of each pest present per 25 sweeps can then be calculated. Published tables for the use of control measures are based on the Action Threshold (AT), which is the level of infestation that indicates when control measures need to be activated.

Regular, daily scouting by day or night is of enormous benefit in keeping growers up to date with pest control needs. It needs to be started as soon as temperatures rise in the spring.

Insect traps are also sometimes used to monitor insect pest populations. They may be ultraviolet (UV) or pherome traps, which use insect sex hormones to lure moths.

Pests and diseases

Many of the most damaging pests are the larvae of insects, usually moths, which have developed some form of protection against natural predators. Many pests feed on young leaves, buds and shoots, destroying not only the current year's growth and buds bearing the current season's flowers but also next year's potential. The blunt-nosed leafhopper is not in itself particularly damaging, but it carries one of the most destructive diseases to affect cranberry vines, namely false blossom disease. Many insect pests of cranberry vines are also remarkably successful at avoiding the natural predators, which would otherwise keep their populations under control. For example, there are the fireworms that spin a protective web around groups of young caterpillars as they feed, the spanworms that are so well disguised they look like twigs and the distastefully hairy caterpillars of the gypsy moth. Then there are the cutworms which feed at night and hide in the leaf litter during the day, their only redeeming feature being that they have been known to eat each other. No wonder insects are the most successful family in the animal kingdom.

I list below those insects that are the most worrisome to cranberry plants.

Fireworms. A cranberry bog which appears as though it has been ravaged by fire in midsummer (the vines are covered with dead, brown leaves) has probably been attacked by the larvae of the black-headed fireworm moth, especially if there are fine, silky webs enclosing much of the debris.

The black-headed fireworm is a major pest not only because of the sheer destructiveness of its larvae but also because it can, and usually does, produce two broods during the summer. The eggs of this moth can also overwinter. They attach themselves to the underside of the upper leaves of the vines, even in the flooded bogs, and hatch in spring when temperatures rise, possibly as early as April. The tiny larvae burrow into the host leaf, eating as they go, then emerge to start work on the terminal buds. Having destroyed these buds, the larvae make a web to hold the upper leaves and upright stems together and then devour the young buds, leaves and flowers as they develop. After about a month of feeding the larvae have a black head and a dull yellow body that is about $1/3$ in. (8 mm) long. They pupate on the ground among the leaf litter and emerge a couple of weeks later as adult moths. The adults are at their most active in late afternoon, especially in dull, cloudy, windless weather, and they attract attention because of their characteristic jerky flight. They are small, only about $1/8$ to $1/4$ in. (3 to 5 mm) long, with dull brown bodies banded darker brown with the last band being a V shape. This first generation of adults then mate, and the cycle is repeated.

It is vitally important to control the first brood to prevent a second attack. A brief overnight flooding just after the first hatching has been identified, repeated again a week later to catch the last emerging larvae, seems to be effective. If these two floodings are not done, spraying with an approved insecticide should be carried out. Spraying is the only way to control the second brood as flooding in late summer can be damaging to the flowers or developing fruit.

The yellow-headed fireworm (*Acleris minuata*, synonym *Peronea minuata*) is capable of nearly as much damage as the black-headed fireworm, mainly because it can produce up to four broods a year, although three is more normal. It has other hosts, particularly other *Vaccinium* species such as blueberries, that support it in the land surrounding the bogs. Dull gray, adult female moths are able to live through the winter and emerge from hibernation to lay their eggs on cranberry plants when temperatures rise in spring, usually in late April. The young larvae grow to about $1/2$ in. (1.25 cm) long and are pale yellow with a yellow head. They make a web that enfolds a number of upright stems that they feed on. They then pupate within the web's protection. The pupa has a distinct knob at the head end, which distinguishes it from other fireworms.

Control of the yellow-headed fireworm is done partially by winter flooding, which kills the adults hibernating in the bogs, and by spraying with an approved insecticide, which kills the feeding larvae, many of which may be larvae from moths that have migrated from surrounding habitats. It is important to break the cycle otherwise the later hatchings will do great damage to the developing uprights, denuding them completely.

The hill fireworm (*Tlascala finetella*), spotted fireworm (*Archips parallela*) and the red-striped fireworm (*Aroga trialbamaculella*) are all of lesser general importance but should still be eliminated sooner rather than later as populations may build up and cause damage later.

Spanworms or loopers. These masters of disguise are often confused with twigs, especially when they are alarmed and anchor themselves to their host plants using the legs on the last section of their bodies, leaving their fore section upright and stationary in the air. Their characteristic looping movement enables these larvae to travel and to move from host to host; few are specific to cranberries.

Probably the most seriously damaging—and fascinating—spanworm is the chain-spotted geometer (*Cingilia catenaria*). It has many hosts including lowbush blueberries and gray birch. It overwinters in egg form and can survive the winter flood. Larvae hatch in late spring and feed voraciously, stripping all foliage as they travel, leaving the vines brown. Spanworms are inactive during the day, spending the daylight hours hanging upside down like dead sticks, and only become active as dusk falls.

The damage done to cranberry vines is similar to that done by the black-headed fireworm, but unlike that pest, this one makes no web. Larvae are yellow with round, black spots on the head and neck shield. They mature to about $1\frac{1}{2}$ in. (3.8 cm) long in mid-August when they pupate, emerging as adults a month or so later to lay their eggs in the leaf litter.

Another very damaging spanworm is the brown cranberry spanworm, which is found mostly in Massachusetts. Like the yellow-headed fireworm and chain-spotted geometer, it has many other host plants in addition to cranberries. It causes damage to all parts of the cranberry plant except the roots. The pupae spend the winter in the leaf litter among the vines and can survive the winter flood. The adult moths emerge in midsummer to lay their eggs, and the larvae hatch as the cranberry starts to flower. They grow to about 1 in. (2.5 cm) and are dull brown.

Controlling the brown cranberry spanworm is difficult, not only because populations can build up on hosts in the areas surrounding the bogs, but also because it is very difficult to use insecticides during the cranberry blooming time when pollinating bees are very vulnerable. Monitoring of the adult moths in flight in early June gives an indication of possible problems, and this should be followed by scouting with a net a few days later.

Cutworms. The larvae of these nocturnal moths can be extremely destructive because they destroy whole stems, cutting off leaves, buds, flowers and young berries as they feed. About six species affect cranberries, most of which feed at night. They can be difficult to identify separately, especially as young larvae. They are hairless and quite inconspicuous, usually gray-brown or dull green-yellow, and can reach 2 in. (5 cm) at maturity. An infestation is often first noticed because of the amount of severed leaves in the ditches surrounding the bogs. Control of these larvae is usually by insecticide, provided it is used while the larvae are small. Reflooding for 10 to 12 hours in mid- to late May is an effective biological control of young larvae.

Gypsy moth (*Porthetria dispar*). Occasional heavy and potentially very damaging infestations of cranberry bogs by the hairy caterpillars of the gypsy moth occur about once every ten years in the northeastern areas of the United States. During the time between those infestations, the numbers are not significant enough to do serious damage, and generations of larvae keep to their main hosts, which are the leaves of hardwood trees such as oak. Adult moths lay their clusters of light brown eggs in the crevices of the bark of these trees or, if in a cranberry bog, among the leaf litter. The eggs, which can survive -55°F (32°C), hatch over a period from mid-April until midsummer or even later. The bodies of the tiny gray caterpillars are covered with hairs, which enable them to be blown by the wind for 20 miles (32 km) or more. As they mature they develop spots, five pairs of blue ones on the front segments and six pairs of red ones on the rear end. They pupate in July, and the moths emerge two or three weeks later. The white female is so heavy she is incapable of flight and so she lays her eggs close to where she has emerged from her pupa.

Control of this pest can be achieved with a brief reflooding in late May as that will drown the small vulnerable larvae that are blown onto the bogs while they are young. Insecticides need to be used before flowering begins.

Cranberry girdler (*Chrysoteucha topiaria*). The adult moths of this insect are small, about $^1/_2$ in. (1.25 cm) long, silvery gray with light brown outer edges to their forewings. They emerge from their cocoons in the leaf litter in June. Adult females scatter their white eggs at random on the ground, where they turn orange or red before hatching in 10 to 12 days. The larvae feed on the roots and stems of cranberries between June and September, often girdling the bark, thus severing the plants' transport systems. Damaged plants have reddish brown foliage on affected runners so the plants are weakened and produce a poor crop. Their sawdustlike excreta are distinct signs of their presence. Larvae mature by September and cocoon themselves in a nest of silk and intertwined sand and leaves within which they over-winter.

Sanding with at least ³/₄ in. (2 cm) of sand over affected patches in the dormant season, coupled with regular sanding of the whole bog every four years, is effective in spoiling the habitat for egg laying. Removing dead stems and leaves between sanding also helps.

Fruitworms. The most serious pests in many cranberry bogs are fruit-worms. The cranberry fruitworm (*Acrobasis vaccinii*, synonym *Mineola vaccinii*) is a particularly serious pest in the maritime provinces of Canada, especially on early maturing varieties, but it is also common throughout the eastern United States and Canada. It is not specific to cranberries as it is also found on other *Vaccinium* species such as blueberries.

The adult moths are small, nocturnal and brown-gray with white bands on their forewings. They emerge from their pupae in the debris below the vines in June or July after the berries have formed. Eggs are laid within the cup at the top of the fruit that is formed by the remainder of the calyx. The tiny, pale green larva emerges four to five days later and migrates down the outside of the fruit to the stem end where it bores into the fruit. The hole that it forms is covered by a tiny silk web. It devours the pulp of the fruit unseen until the fruit is completely hollow, containing just the droppings or frass. The berry turns prematurely red, which may be the first sign of this pest that the grower notices. One larva may destroy up to four more berries before it matures, often webbing groups of berries together. Fully mature larvae may reach about ¹/₂ in. (1.25 cm). They build a protective cocoon around themselves in early fall and overwinter in the leaf litter below the vines in this form, eventually pupating in the spring.

Control is by insecticide spray that kills the larvae, although natural para-sites are being researched for possible use as biological controls. Determining the need for control measures is done by regular monitoring. If two or more berries from a sample of 100 carry live eggs, spraying may begin. Sampling is carried out every three to four days over a two-week period, and spraying may have to be repeated 10 to 14 days after the first application.

Sparganothis fruitworm (*Sparganothis sulfureana*). This pest produces two generations a year, the first emerging to feed on new tip-growth in spring, moving on to young blooms before maturing in June or July. The second generation of larvae feed on developing fruit, causing superficial damage to other neighboring berries as well.

Control is by insecticide spray, which is more effective on the first generation larvae before flowering begins. The choice of insecticide is a difficult one as many also destroy natural parasites of this pest.

The cranberry weevil (*Anthonomus musculus*) and the black vine weevil (*Otiorhynchus sulcatus*). These two weevils are significant pests, particularly in bogs that are adjacent to woody areas. Adults of the cranberry weevil make a tiny hole in the flower buds and lay their eggs into it. The resultant larva feeds on the internal parts of the flowers before pupating within the remains of the flower, emerging six days later as an adult. The adults eat buds, leaves and developing berries, leaving berries disfigured by dimples. Two generations of adults may be produced during the summer.

Sweeping with an insect net on calm, warm days from mid-May through mid-June will monitor the older generation of cranberry weevil adults that are responsible for the current year's reproduction, while sweeping after flowering will monitor the newly emerged generation. Like many weevils, adults of this species can lie motionless and apparently dead for a few seconds after being disturbed. Control by spraying is possible, but care needs to be taken with the timing because of possible damage to insects pollinating unaffected flowers. Biological control is being investigated.

The black vine weevil (*Otiorhynchus sulcatus*), a universal and highly successful pest, turns up in almost any horticultural situation, and cranberries are no exception. Vine weevils are particularly difficult to control in nurseries and gardens where there are so many alternative host plants. They are also a serious economic pest in some cranberry bogs although flooding will kill many larvae, especially in bogs in the colder areas that hold a full winter flood.

The adults are about 1/3 in. (8 mm) in length, brown with light speckling on their rough-textured wing cases. They are all female; no males are needed for fertilization. Adult feeding is nocturnal and limited to leaves. Damage to the leaves is characterized by circular notching, but it has no significant harmful effect on the plant. Adult females are active during the warm summer months, each capable of laying 1,500 eggs in the soil in this season. The eggs hatch into white grubs that feed on the roots. They sometimes girdle stems where they emerge from the soil, causing the plant to wilt and then collapse. When winter comes, the grubs burrow deeper into the soil to try to avoid being frozen, becoming active again in the spring. They develop a brown head as they mature, finally pupating for about three weeks in May or June before beginning the cycle all over again.

Adult weevils may be monitored by sweeping with an insect net at night during June and July. They are said to be most active in the two hours on either side of midnight and, like the cranberry weevil, are good at pretending to be dead. A number of biological control methods are available, including sprays containing thousands of microscopic nematode worms that, when added to water, enter the weevil larvae and release a baterium that kills the host larvae within two to three days.

Blunt-nosed cranberry leafhopper (*Euscelis striatulus*). This was a serious pest in the early twentieth century, particularly in bogs in Wisconsin where populations built up to a level where their feeding caused a loss of vigor in many plants. The introduction of organo-phosphate insecticides in the 1960s greatly reduced its population. The main damage, however, is caused by them being vectors for the very destructive cranberry false blossom disease. Eggs of this pest overwinter under the bark of cranberry stems, surviving the winter flood in this form. Wingless nymphs hatch from June through July. The only effective means of control of leafhopper is by spraying with an approved insecticide.

Beetle grubs. A variety of beetle larvae cause damage to cranberry roots. They are difficult to identify, so professional help should be sought if their presence is suspected. Hoplia, cranberry white grub and cranberry root grub are all significant pests.

Some diseases affect the whole or several parts of the vine, such as stem, shoot and developing flowers and fruit. Since many of these diseases are difficult to detect until their life cycle is well established, most growers have a routine spray schedule involving applications at intervals during the growing season to keep control.

Although nearly 70 fungal diseases have been identified on cranberries, only eight have proved to be of serious economic importance, with another 24 being of generally lesser significance but sometimes of local seriousness. Cranberries are therefore relatively disease-free, especially in a garden or small-scale planting situation where care has been taken to provide suitable growing conditions. For example, root rots are a problem where drainage is poor during the summer. Overfeeding, especially with a high nitrogen fertilizer, produces lush, soft plants that are vulnerable to rot diseases, especially of stems and shoots.

Diseases of fruit, both on the vines and in postharvest storage, are particularly damaging. Most of these problems are caused by fungal infections, but probably the most serious disease affecting the vines is not a fungus. False blossom disease causes deformity of the flowers from which no fruit will follow. It affects cranberry bogs in all North American cranberry-growing regions except the West Coast ones in Oregon and Washington.

False blossom disease. Unlike most cranberry diseases, this is not caused by a fungus but by a mycoplasma, a viruslike organism. It was a major problem in the first half of the twentieth century, causing many bogs to cease production, but is less of a problem now that effective insecticide sprays are available. First noticed as it was being spread by the blunt-nosed leafhopper from wild cranberry vines and other wild vacciniums surrounding bogs in Wisconsin in 1900, it was probably spread when growers in areas outside of Wisconsin bought vines from the infected area.

The disease initially causes damage to the pedicel, which fails to form a bent neck, thus making flowers stand erect. Flowers become red, then stunted and distorted, and they are, of course, infertile and unable to go on to form fruit. Leaves may be smaller and redder than usual, and a witch's broomlike mass of stem growth may develop.

There is no means to completely control the disease, although prompt removal and burning of infected vines from both the bog and the surrounds helps. The main method of control involves dealing with the carrier. The blunt-nosed leafhopper can be killed using approved insecticide sprays applied on the bogs and, with care, over the surrounding areas during the growing season. In areas such as those west of the Rocky Mountains where this insect is not found, the disease is not a problem.

Some cranberry varieties are less prone to infection than others, notably 'McFarlin' and 'Early Black', two of the older cultivars, and 'Stevens' and 'Franklin', which are slightly more recent.

Phytophthora root rot (*Phytophthora cinnamomi*). This universally distributed fungus is especially harmful where drainage is poor as it thrives in anaerobic or oxygen deprived environments. It initially causes root death, which then leads to stem dieback and generally poor growth and lack of yields. Plant death occurs in worst case situations. An olive-brown color under the epidermis of roots is an identifying feature of this fungus. Controlling it involves improving drainage, and sanding to raise the level of the bogs will help. Some fungicides have been approved for use.

Leaf spot diseases. Most of these are harmful but not of generally serious economic importance, probably because they are now controlled by routine spray schedules. They may, however, be of more significance in nursery or garden situations where plants are being grown to a large extent for their attractive foliage as well as their fruit. Microclimates in such places can sometimes produce still air and high humidity, perfect conditions in which most of these diseases thrive, especially when plants are grown "soft" with high nitrogen fertilizer feeds.

Red leaf spot (*Exobasidium vaccinii*). Bright red circular spots on the upper leaf surfaces of young leaves (the spots are paler on the lower leaf surfaces) and a dense bloom or powdery substance indicates the presence of spore-bearing hyphae. The disease soon spreads to the young shoots and stems, which turn bright red and become distorted. With the death of young shoots come the loss of potential flowers and fruit and the reduction of growth for the following year. Control is by improving the environment to keep plants from going soft and by ensuring good air circulation. Approved fungicide sprays are available.

Black leaf spot (*Mycosphaerella nigro-maculans*) may form in the lesions caused by red leaf spot, forming elongated black spots that may eventually surround the stems. Black, spore-bearing bodies form on dead stems and later release spores.

Fungicide spray that controls red leaf spot should prevent this secondary infection, but if it becomes established, all infected parts of the plants or even the whole plant should be removed and burned. An additional fungicide spray can be used repeatedly before the fruiting bodies form.

Rose bloom (*Exobasidium oxycocci*). This is a fungal infection that affects buds in the axils of leaves. It stimulates dormant buds into premature growth, producing lateral shoots with crowded pink leaves that look a little like a rose flower. It, too, is more of a problem among lush and overcrowded vines where there is decreased air and water movement. Improving cultural conditions will help contain the infection, and applying an approved fungicide spray as soon as symptoms appear in early spring gives good control.

Twig blight (*Lophodermium oxycocci*). This fungus occurs mostly in Oregon and Washington, where damp climatic conditions encourage its activity. Severe infections can result in vine death. Spores are released in summer, peaking in July and August, and become established on the young growth. The disease does not become apparent, however, until the following winter when infected leaves develop a bleached brown appearance and upright stems are killed. Shiny black fruiting bodies that are large and round appear on the underside of the dead leaves which are still attached to the vines. Old wood is not affected.

Control is by approved fungicide, the idea being to create a chemical barrier on the young growths of the vines to prevent the spores invading their tissues. The first application needs to be made before the first spores are released from the fruiting bodies, with repeat applications to take care of subsequent spore release.

Stem blight, blossom blight, early rot, fruit rot (*Phyllosticta vaccinii*). This fungus needs cool wet conditions for its life cycle and is particularly virulent where vine growth is over vigorous and where there is a high weed population. It can infect all parts of the plant except roots. Fruiting bodies, which are round, black, and circular (the bodies are the size of a pinhead) overwinter on leaf, stem and fruit debris. They mature in spring and release clouds of spores into the air. These spores are carried in the wind and may produce more black bodies on any aerial part of the vines if prolonged wet conditions prevail. A secondary infection can result if wet conditions continue, and this can become a severe infection can build up during the summer to infect the flowers and flower stems, which are then killed. If prolonged it can infect developing fruit.

Early rot, so called because it affects young fruit, appears first as a small "water spot" on developing fruit, which spreads in concentric rings until the berry becomes soft, shriveled and black. It is most severe in long hot summers such as those experienced in the cranberry bogs of New Jersey and Massachusetts. Spraying with a fungicide at intervals recommended by the manufacturer during the growing season is effective, and sanding to cover winter debris also helps.

Tip blight, cottonball, hard rot (*Monilinia oxycocci*). This fungal disease also affects both shoots (the tip blight phase) and fruit (the cottonball phase), especially in West Coast regions. The tip blight phase may only appear occasionally over a cranberry bog or bed so it is sometimes missed or confused with other problems. The tips of uprights may suddenly wilt and die without warning, just as blooming is about to start. An inverted V-shaped, light brown marking appears at the base of infected leaves, and leaf stalks, leaves, flower stalks and flowers become covered with a mass of gray powdery dust.

The cotton ball stage of the disease affects the fruit, which fail to turn red. They develop broad red bands, which coalesce, and the whole fruit becomes brownish yellow. "Cotton ball" refers to the inside of the berry, which contains the bunched white threads of the fungal mycelium. The mycelium spreads throughout the fruit. The mycelium and the berry surrounding it gradually hardens and shrinks, eventually becoming hard black "nuts" (sclerotia), overwintering among the leaf litter on the ground. In spring the sclerotia produce small cup-shaped "toadstools" from which ascospores burst into the air. They are distributed to new young growth, which starts the cycle all over again on the flowers and developing berries. Spraying with an approved fungicide should occur when the buds burst into growth and again 14 days later, a third application occurring when blooming starts, which may be 14 days after that.

Upright dieback, viscid fruit rot, twig blight (*Phomopsis vaccinii*). This disease initially affects the tips of upright stems before spreading downward. Leaves show mottled yellowing and become completely yellow before turning brown and dying. The more serious stage is when the disease progresses to the fruit, which causes significant losses in storage when it is known as viscid rot.

Storage rots. Sometimes a few berries in a package bought as fresh fruit will develop symptoms of rotting. Most storage rots result from a fungal infection of stems or other parts of the vine that has transferred to the fruit at or just before harvest time. Fruit that has been bruised or has lesions in which spores may enter are particularly vulnerable. When overripe berries are harvested, they are susceptible to rotting simply because of the natural physiological progress of things. Cold storage at around 17°F (17°C) with good ventilation will reduce rotting.

The Cranberry Harvest

Harvest time is the highlight of the cranberry growers' year, the culmination of the annual cycle of management. It takes place when the majority of the berries are at optimum ripeness, which is usually in the same week every year for each bog. Many owners are dependent on contractors who own the huge machines and provide the labor to do the job. Smaller bogs are still harvested by teams of traveling workers who wield the small machines that remove the berries from the vines.

Most cranberries are harvested under water. The harvest begins as early as the end of September, especially in states such as Wisconsin, when the water temperature has dropped below the required 55°F (13°C), and the bulk of the fruit has reached optimum ripeness.

Dry harvesting

During the nineteenth century and until the end of the First World War, the fruit was all "dry harvested." It was handpicked by whole families who would migrate to the countryside from the crowded cities with their poor living conditions, the growers providing the workers with basic accommodation for the duration of the harvest. Many were recent immigrants, including some from rural communities in European countries such as Italy and Portugal. It was, for many, a chance to make enough money to enable them to establish themselves in their new country.

The bog would be marked out in strips and an overseer or foreman would supervise the family groups allocated to pick the berries within their allocated strip. They were paid on a piecework basis that was based on the volume of fruit picked, a standard measure being the one-peck box. The natural tendency, therefore, was to skim over the bog, picking fast but missing fruit or including damaged berries. It was a backbreaking job that was also quite hard on the hands and knees, and most pickers wound strips of linen round their fingers to protect themselves.

The foreman's job was to make sure that the quality picked was good, while at the same time checking that sound berries were not left on the vines. The foreman also had to supervise the winnowing of the fruit in the field to remove remaining trash as well as the weighing and transport of berries from their picking areas over the vines to the pack house. In larger areas where fruit had to be transported over the vines, special barrows with large, partially inflated tires became popular because they did less damage to the vines.

As cranberry bog acreages increased and cheap labor became less readily available, growers devised means of speeding up the process with the help of various homemade mechanical devices. The first of these devices, which is still used today on small dry bogs and in areas where blueberry grows wild, is the handheld scoop. There were various designs, all based on the principle of a catcher with a handle, the outer edge having metal or wooden teeth set $1/3$ in. (8 mm) apart. They were used in a sweeping motion so that the berries were stripped from the vines and caught in the scoops, leaving the vine more or less intact as they passed between the teeth. The smaller scoops were used from a kneeling position, and different sizes were made to suit the size of the picker; even small children could help with the harvest. Extra large scoops were designed for two-handed use, and they would scoop the fruit up as the pickers walked steadily through the vines. Scoops were emptied into boxes as they were filled. If this was done from a height, much of the grass and leaf dross, which spoil the sample, was blown away before the boxes were removed by extra staff using specially adapted wheelbarrows to take the fruit out to carts waiting to carry the crop to the pack houses. It was important to make sure that scooping was always done in the same direction, from right to left, so that the vines became trained like well-combed hair, with the result that there were fewer tangles and therefore fewer torn or uprooted plants.

The use of scoops enabled the picking rate to be increased tenfold, making the harvest period shorter with fewer people needed. That in turn meant that the number of feet trampling the vines was also greatly reduced. The disadvantages were that berries were inevitably dropped or damaged; up to 30 percent of the crop was lost this way as compared with 10 percent from hand picking. Vines were also sometimes torn or uprooted as the scoop was swept through them, resulting in reduction of future yields.

Vines that were pruned to keep them relatively short were less prone to damage than untended ones, so pruning became more important. Shorter vines, it was found, actually produced fruit-bearing uprights at more frequent intervals compared to vines left to grow to 3 ft. (90 cm) or more, and over time their yields were increased.

In 1925 the first motor-driven harvester, the "Mathewson picking machine," was produced in Massachusetts. Based on the same principle as the combed scoop but designed so that the tines were mounted on a revolving drum that could harvest 15 sq. ft. (4.5 sq. m) in a single revolution, it had the capacity to harvest 3 to 4 acres (1 to 1.5 hectares) per day. Although it was heavy and expensive, it was widely used for 20 years. Other, more lightweight machines eventually followed using the same combing method, and the Darlington and Furford are still used today. They are small, capable of working a width of 2 to 3 ft. (60 to 90 cm), so an acre (0.4 hectares) per day is about their limit. All these machines made harvesting quicker than handheld scoops, but they all caused damage and loss of crop because of fallen or bruised fruit and torn or uprooted vines. Two factors justified their continued use, the fact that the Furford prunes the vines as it works and the increasing difficulty in finding labor. The traditional summer exodus from the cities largely came to a halt as better-paid and permanent jobs were created. About 75 percent of the cranberry crop was eventually machine harvested from the dry bogs, and much of it went to the canning industry that had grown up primarily during the 1930s. Dry harvesting is still carried out in about 15 percent of the commercial cranberry bogs with helicopters being increasingly used to lift the crop out of the bogs.

Wet harvesting

The natural ability of the air-filled cranberry to float was first used to the cranberry growers' advantage in Wisconsin, and by the end of the Second World War this method was used by over 50 percent of Wisconsin growers. It soon extended to all other areas, and since the 1990s, about 85 percent of the cranberry harvest is water harvested. The advantages of water harvesting are that cranberry growers can machine harvest, can do so quickly and with a limited labor force and that they can gather in virtually 100 percent of the crop. These advantages are, however, contingent on the machines being set so they can remove the fruit efficiently from the vines and on the berries being able to float to the water's surface.

An adaptation of the comb harvesters common in dry bogs that is used in some wet harvested bogs has a rotating head with retractable teeth. It is gentler than the flails and more suitable for harvesting berries intended for the fresh-fruit market.

A flail method is the standard method for wet-harvesting fruit that is destined for processing. Various designs have been tried, but the most popular is probably the Wisconsin water-reel harvester which was developed in the 1960s and is still in use today, especially in the smaller bogs. (Plate 2) A simple, lightweight piece of machinery that looks at first glance a little like a lawn mower with two bicycle wheels, it is easily transported and easily maintained. It is basically a wheeled, horizontally mounted open drum or reel driven by a bicycle-type chain from a small two-stroke engine mounted above water. The operator steers the harvester with both hands and controls the throttle using a cabled lever on one of the handles. Watching a team of harvesters working their way over a cranberry bog with these simple machines is quite an experience.

In the Pinelands area of New Jersey, rectangular bogs have been created in clearings in the pine forests by one of the biggest growers. The harvest takes place between September and the end of October. The water from surrounding dykes is used to flood the bogs to a little over 8 in. (20 cm), which allows the vines to float but means that harvesting staff have to wear extra long waterproof boots known as waders. Roadways that are sufficiently wide and sturdy to carry large, deep-bodied transport trucks surround each five-acre (2-hectare) bog. Machine operators who do much of the harvesting in this area are contracted to harvest as a team, and they move from one property to another as the season progresses. The way they move up the bog in a staggered row with their machines flailing the fruit from the vines is almost poetic in its appeal, rather like a skein of migrating geese! Their leader sets off up the bog, walking in a straight line, the other harvesters following a short distance behind and slightly to one side of him. Each reel works a strip about 3$^1/_3$ ft. (1 m) wide, just overlapping his neighbor's work. As the reels rotate, their horizontal rods shake or knock the berries from vines and a sea of red fruit is left floating in the water. It helps if there is a slight breeze to blow the fruit toward one side of the bog. A plastic boom is dragged around the sea of berries when the machines have finished to gather or corral the fruit towards an elevator or pump which transports them into waiting trucks.

In the 1960s the first of the much larger machines was developed for use on the bigger bogs with reels capable of working a 20 ft. (6 m) strip. One worker is mounted high above the bog in his weatherproof cab, replacing six to eight workers using the small machines. Barges carry 250 lb (113 kg) boxes into which the fruit is loaded, and cranes are used to lift these boxes off the barges into the 40,000 pound trucks that transport the fruit to the receiving stations for cleaning, grading and packing. The harvest is a hectic time for all, and the receiving stations often have water-filled concrete storage pits that act as temporary holding areas for fruit destined for processing.

At this stage in the harvest there is a considerable amount of dross among the cranberries: bits of vine, leaves, weeds (especially grasses) and some unripe, green fruit. The dross must be removed, and there are a variety of methods for doing this, most of which involve rubber belts that the grass and leaves stick to. They are removed when they reach the top of an incline. The berries roll down to another conveyor that takes them to a dryer. A typical New Jersey drier consists of a screen carrying the berries over first a hot-air and then a cool-air blower. They then travel down a series of wooden steps, the good, firm fruit bouncing to the end of the steps and the poor, damaged fruit falling into bins that are later emptied. Finally, the berries are checked for quality before being weighed and sent to the local cooperative depot for final packing and marketing. In some cases the fruit is stored unscreened and taken out for final screening and packing only as required.

Markets

There are two major national cooperatives in the United States, Ocean Spray and Northland. Ocean Spray was formed by growers in 1912 in Hanson, Massachusetts, and became a national company in 1930. It is owned by 750 cranberry growers located throughout North America's cranberry-growing regions. Northland is based in Wisconsin, which is the leading cranberry-growing state in the United States.

In 1999, cranberry production totaled 6.39 million barrels, which exceeded demand, and in 2000, 5.5 million barrels were produced that again exceeded demand. The result was that prices dropped from a 1996 price of $60 to $80 per barrel to $20 per barrel, causing great insecurity and financial crisis among growers. The Agriculture Secretary ordered a 35 percent reduction in the volume of cranberries which could be sold nationwide before the 2001 cranberry harvest to prevent this overproduction from happening again. Meanwhile, research has found that consumption of cranberry juice may inhibit the development of breast-cancer tumors, and further research has been commissioned into the health benefits of cranberries in the hopes of encouraging sales of juice and other cranberry products.

Storage and Processing

In the past, before the use of refrigerators, unscreened cranberries were stored in chaff in well-ventilated, insulated storehouses. The goal was to get the ambient temperature down and to maintain it at a constant level to avoid condensation and rotting. These storehouses kept the fruit until after the main Christmas market.

With the introduction of refrigerated storehouses, the life span of the stored fruit could be extended to a maximum of about 19 or 20 weeks, though a storage time of about 12 weeks produces the best results. The optimum temperature for storage is 40°F (4°C). Storage in bulk bins was also found to be more effective than storage in prepacked cartons. Berries that were prepacked after harvest tended to deteriorate after about six weeks but they had a longer shelf life if they had been cooled immediately after harvest. Some cultivars store better than others, with the popular 'Howes' and 'Early Black' being the best of the traditional varieties. Cranberries also freeze very well and, unlike most fruits, can be refrozen after thawing. The berries keep both their color and flavor well, and their vitamin and antioxidant content is unaffected.

Cranberry sauce has been an accompaniment to roast turkey or goose at both Thanksgiving and Christmas since cranberries were first harvested by the early Pilgrims, but it was the invention of the can that allowed cranberries to be extended to year-round use. The first canned cranberry sauce was produced in Maine in 1888, and it was soon realized that this was a profitable means of using surplus or poor quality crops. By the end of the 1930s, one quarter of the cranberry crop was being canned, and even small packing houses have a division devoted to canning.

By 2000 over 80 percent of the cranberry crop was processed, mostly into juice. The industry has, however, invested in a wide array of other cranberry products; one observer has listed 700 different cranberry products ranging from the traditional sauce to luxury juices (which may blend cranberry juice with other fruits such as raspberry, grape or apple) to cereals, muffins, salad dressings, salsas and even "craisins," which are dried, sweetened cranberries. The once famous "ruby phosphate," a concentrated cranberry syrup first marketed in 1885, was made by pressing raw cranberries to extract the juice and adding sugar and a little wine. This juice made a refreshing and vitamin-rich drink when diluted and carbonated. Cranberry wine is another product that many people enjoy. The need for bright red berries for these products with their high anthocyanin content led to premium prices being paid to growers for the reddest fruit.

Indeed, the stability of this coloring has led to cranberry concentrate being used as a natural food dye for enhancing color in other foods, including cherry pie. After the fruit has been processed to make juice, for example, the unwanted by-products have to be disposed of. The pulp contains seeds from which oil and wax can be extracted for use in cosmetics and salves that treat burns and cuts.

At the turn of the twentieth century, cranberries reached a plateau in terms of popularity, and the most widely sold product is still cranberry juice. It may be that efforts to popularize other products will result in cranberry growers enjoying prosperity again.

The Small Cranberry

The small cranberry (*Vaccinium oxycoccus*) with its many common names including mossberry, spiceberry, buckberry and moorberry is described as an evergreen creeping shrub with fine woody stems and young growth that is reddish brown. The short upright shoots, which may be up to 1 1/4 in. (2 to 3 cm) high, tend to have only one growth spell, particularly in more northerly regions. Ovate-elliptic leaves are about 1/4 in. (5 mm) long on average and 1/8 in. (3 mm) wide, glossy dark green on the upper side and pale and very waxy underneath with a curled margin that is very pronounced. They develop reddish hues as cold weather approaches in the fall.

Flowers are sparse. In lower latitudes they are produced singly in the axils of small leaves at the base of the current year's shoots. In latitudes north of 50°, the leafy part of the flower-bearing shoot does not grow, so it appears as if the flowers are produced on short stalks bearing one to four flowers on slender pedicels 3/4 to 1 1/4 in. (2 to 3 cm) long. The blooms emerge between red, scaly bracts that are less than 1/8 in. (3 mm) long. They are white or pink and have a very strongly reflexed corolla. The fruit is glossy, 1/4 to 1/2 in. (5 to 12 mm) in diameter and deep red when ripe.

Vaccinium oxycoccus is much more widely distributed than *V. macrocarpon*. It is found in upland areas throughout Canada, the northern states of the United States, northern Europe, western coastal areas of Greenland and in northern Asia into Japan. It is more cold tolerant than *V. macrocarpon*, growing as it does in more northerly subarctic and alpine conditions. Its hardiness is probably the result of it growing low to the ground, usually among moss, which gives it shelter especially from desiccating winds. In areas where it is common there is usually a protective blanket of snow during the coldest months of the year. *Vaccinium oxycoccus* is found in moist acidic soils with a pH between 2.9 and 3.8. Although it offers no competition to *V. macrocarpon* in terms of large-scale commercial value, it is picked and has economic importance in areas where *V. macrocarpon* is not grown.

Vaccinium oxycoccus var. *microcarpum* (formerly *Oxycoccus microcarpus*) is similar to *V. oxycoccus* but has slightly longer flower stalks, elongated fruit and smaller leaves. It seems to be confined to northern Europe as far west as Scotland and into Siberia in the east. It is commonly known as the small or European cranberry.

Vaccinium oxycoccus 'Quadripetala' is now said to be either a form of *V. oxycoccus* or possibly a hybrid between *V. macrocarpon* and *V. oxycoccus* as it has large fruit like the former (although the fruit is lighter in color) and the small leaves and stems of the latter. It is not as cold hardy as *V. oxycoccus* 'Microcarpus'. It occurs in the Pacific Northwest, in peat bogs in coastal regions and in meadows in the Cascade Mountains.

Vaccinium oxycoccus var. *ovalifolium* is another form of *V. oxycoccus* or a possible hybrid. It has large leaves, dark brown stems and large fruit that, unlike other cranberries, which are glossy, has a "bloom" like many blueberries. It is found in eastern Asia and in western areas of North America.

Vaccinium oxycoccus 'Gigas' is recognized by some but not all botanists. It is described as being vigorous and both shade and drought tolerant. It produces a few large berries that have sterile seeds. It is only found in a few areas in North America, Europe and northern Asia.

Chapter 2
Lingonberries

The lingonberry (*Vaccinium vitis-idaea*) is known in North America as the northern mountain cranberry, partridgeberry, foxberry, cowberry or wolfberry. Interestingly, it also carries the names "dry ground cranberry" and "rock cranberry." In parts of the United States and in most of Scandinavia it is called ling berry or lingonberry, and in other parts of Scandinavia it is known as tyttebaer. In Britain it is called a cowberry and in Germany a preisselbeere. "Lingonberry" is probably the most widely used name in common use. Regarded by devotees as having a richer, less astringent flavor than the commercial cranberry (*V. macrocarpon*), lingonberries are being grown in increasing numbers in northern areas, both commercially and in gardens.

Geographic Range

Vaccinium vitis-idaea is very widely distributed but occurs only in cold climate areas of the Northern Hemisphere. This areas includes Newfoundland, and in the northern United States it ranges from subarctic Alaska, Washington and Oregon and in the East as far south as about 42°N. It is also native as far north as northwestern Greenland (77°N), in much of northern Europe, especially in northern Germany and Scandinavia, in the mountainous regions of central and southern Europe and in Asia. Patches of wild *V. vitis-idaea* have been "cultivated" by the locals for centuries in all these countries and the fruit harvested to make sauces, jams and other food stuffs. The habitats where *V. vitis-idaea* is found vary from quite densely wooded areas, especially near the edges of pine forests, to heath, grass moorland, raised bogs, rocky exposed cliffs and even mountain summits. It is sometimes known as the "dry cranberry" because it prefers drier conditions than its relatives.

Vaccinium vitis-idaea has been of great importance in the diet of human populations in all the areas where it is found and the berries are still gathered from the wild by people living in the more hostile and remote northern upland areas of the United States. In Sweden, an estimated 200,000 tons of berries are picked in a good year, but because yields are variable from year to year, a poor year may yield considerably less.

Probably less than 10 percent of the wild crop is actually harvested, and they are apparently best picked after a sharp frost. The berries store well for consumption during the long winter months when the high vitamin C content is most appreciated. In some areas where there are dense colonies of *Vaccinium vitis-idaea*, such as in Newfoundland, they are regarded as a commercial crop, but it is not anywhere near the scale of modern cranberry production further south. However, in Scandinavia (especially Sweden and Finland), Germany, Austria and Switzerland, *V. vitis-idaea* is being increasingly cultivated in planted fields, and countries such as Latvia and Lithuania, others from the former Soviet Union and some in central Europe such as Bulgaria and Poland are also increasing production. Yields from Europe are currently about 80 million lbs (about 36 million kg) per annum.

There is also an expanding industry in some of the colder areas of Canada and the United States, which is partly the result of increased demand. Production and harvesting from the wild plants can no longer keep up with this demand.

In Newfoundland, which has a long history of appreciation of the small red berry, 212,750 lbs (96,500 kg) are harvested as wild partridgeberries. Descendants of both Native Americans and the early settlers guard their partridgeberry patches jealously. Efforts to control the harvest and thus to market the berry more efficiently have proved as difficult as in the cranberry growing areas in the East, where the tendency to jump the gun and gather the fruit before it is fully ripe was a big problem. However, the Newfoundland government evidently appreciated the value of their native partridgeberries and launched a publicity campaign, which boosted sales and added to the crop's value.

A further step has been taken in the United States, where research has begun into the potential of European-raised cultivars for commercial cultivation on some of the farms where the poor sandy soils do not lend themselves to traditional corn or cattle production. Lingonberries show great promise as an alternative crop in parts of Wisconsin. The Lingonberry Corporation of America was founded in Wisconsin in 1993 by Hiram

Anderson, with technical support and a supply of 5,500 plants from Dr. Elden Stang, Professor of Horticulture at the University of Wisconsin-Madison. Six years later, 20 acres (8 hectares) were under production and techniques were being developed to mechanize the whole operation.

Small quantities are harvested commercially in Nova Scotia (there they are known as foxberries) and Labrador (known as redberries). The yield from wild plants is between 1,100 and 5,500 lbs (500 and 2,500 kg) in Saskatchewan (where it is known as a cranberry) and are harvested mostly by First Nation peoples. In Alaska the lingonberry is called a lowbush cranberry, and in Maine small quantities are produced for home use.

Lingonberries are used to make a large range of products, including juices and syrups, jams and jellies, wine and liqueur, pickles and sauces, candy and ice cream. One excellent recipe turns lingonberries into a good accompaniment to roast beef. Lingonberries are also a component in syrups for coughs and colds. The medicinal properties of this berry, which is rich in magnesium and vitamins A and C, and their use as extracts for the treatment of blood disorders and urinary tract infections is well known. As is the case with their relatives, the main market for lingonberries is still in juice and sauce production.

Botany

Vaccinium vitis-idaea is a low-growing, semiwoody evergreen shrub. Bright green, oval and alternate leaves 1/4 to 3/4 in. (5 to 20 mm) long and 1/4 in. (5 mm) wide are glossy on the upper surface and matt below with small black dots. Broader toward the tips than the bases, the leaves may sometimes have a slight point at the tip. The margins are entire, revolute and sometimes wavy, but not as wavy as those of *V. oxycoccus*. The petioles are less than 1/8 in. (3 mm) long and bear fine hairs. New growth is covered with fine hairs, and mature twigs often appear to have a burgundy or brown cast to the basic green color. The older bark is dark, hairless and often peeling. Plants gradually spread outwards for 3 ft. (0.9 m) or more via runners or stolons that spread just below the soil surface and root from the nodes, forming mats with uprights reaching up to 8 in. (20 cm).

Flowers have four petals, are very pale pink to white and are held in clusters or corymbs from the lower sides of the uprights. They are bell shaped and 1/4 in. (5 mm) long. There may be two flowering periods, the first when average temperatures reach about 25°F (-4°C) between April and June, and the second between late July and September. Fruit ripens in July and August and again from September into November if there are two flowering periods, and in late August through September if there is only one. Later crops in climates of more northern countries such as Sweden frequently fail to ripen properly before winter sets in.

The berries of wild lingonberry plants are bright glossy red and they vary in size from ¼ to ½ in. (5 to 12 mm) in diameter. They have an aromatic flavor similar to those of *Vaccinium macrocarpon* but are not as tart.

Among the reasons for the sharp rise in interest in lingonberries as a commercial crop is that they have, like their cranberry relatives, a high benzoic acid content, which gives them good keeping qualities. Picked fruit has a long shelf life of eight weeks or more in a refrigerator and of several years in a freezer. If unpicked, fruit remains on the plants long after ripening and even into the following spring, birds permitting.

Cultivation and Maintenance

Cultivated lingonberries require acidic soil with a pH of 4.5 to 5.0 and a low level of nutrients. Poor, sandy soils with about 2 percent of organic matter are ideal. Thriving in the wild as they do in subarctic and even arctic regions in Scandinavia, lingonberries are incredibly tough and can stand low temperatures in winter, high temperatures in summer and exposure to wind in both seasons. However, they do prefer to be covered by insulating snow during the arctic winter.

The favored method of cultivating lingonberries is to grow them in beds or rows. Plants are spaced at 18 in. × 18 in. (45 cm × 45 cm) in beds or, if planted in rows, at 12 to 18 in. (30 to 45 cm) in the rows with 60 to 65 in. (152 to 165 cm) between them depending on what mechanical equipment is used for cultivation. They soon spread outwards as they produce runners. Peat, leaf mold, sawdust or finely shredded pine bark may be incorporated into the soil to a depth of 3¼ to 4 in. (8 to 10 cm) before planting if the soil is lacking organic matter. These additions not only supply minerals gradually over several years but also helps to retain moisture in dry weather. Mulching with any of these organic materials to a depth of about 2 in. (5 cm) also protects the young root systems from frost damage and, if the snow cover is insufficient to act as an insulating blanket, from the effects of "frost heave" in winter. As they are shallow-rooting plants, lingonberries need additional water in the dry summer months. Drip irrigation is suitable, especially if the row system is used, preferably from an acidic water supply.

Additional fertilizer is not usually required and can even be harmful, producing excessive vegetative soft growth and a lack of flowers. However, in poor mineral soils where the available nutrients, especially nitrates, are missing, or if the incorporated organic matter or mulch is not sufficiently rotted, extra nitrate may be needed at the rate of about 300 lbs (136 kg) per acre. Magnesium deficiency also sometimes needs correcting in poor soils.

Approximately 40,000 plants are required to plant 2.5 acres (1 hectare). Cross-pollination produces a better fruit set and bigger fruit, so two or more different varieties are planted. One-year-old rooted cuttings planted in the spring will grow away quite quickly during their first season and gradually start to form runners that root as they extend out to form a mat. They should produce a few flowers and fruit in the second summer and a more generous crop in the third season after planting. Larger plants, which can yield in the summer following planting, are suitable for small areas but are expensive and uneconomical for larger areas.

Propagation

Owners of established plantations where lingonberries are grown in long, narrow beds slice off runners that extend out from the rows and use clumps of these to extend their plantations. They are able to get a crop from these runners within two years. The most usual nursery method of propagation is by stem cuttings, which are taken when the current year's growth has become firm, usually in late summer. They may be rooted in a mix of 50 percent peat and 50 percent sand in beds with raised polythene covers or mist to maintain humidity. No bottom heat is necessary, but the beds under polythene should be shaded in hot sunny conditions. The cuttings should be rooted by fall or early winter and may be overwintered in their propagating trays and potted into $1^1/4$ (3 cm) pots in a peat, sand and grit mix in the spring. A very small amount of slow-release fertilizer may be incorporated. Cuttings incorporated into the soil with agricultural discs like those used in commercial cranberry-growing areas work well, provided there is a good water supply to provide overhead irrigation or misting until the cuttings are well established in their first summer.

Pollination

Wild colonies consist of entangled masses of different seedlings that vary in characteristics. It is thought that pollen is transferred by insects, mostly bees, from one seedling to another and that there is cross-pollination between different seedlings. Some growers and their advisers therefore assumed that cultivated lingonberries needed to be cross-pollinated and that commercial growers, using named varieties, should plant them in alternate rows. This method was recommended for cultivated blueberries, but with the advent of larger mechanical harvesters in the 1980s, these are now planted in half-acre (0.2 hectare) blocks of a single variety with no detriment to pollination and subsequent yields. It may be that lingonberries are as self-fertile as many highbush blueberries have turned out to be.

Managing problems, pests and diseases

Weed control is the main problem. Few herbicides have been approved for use on lingonberry plantations as this is a new, minor crop, so commercial growers have to consult with their local agricultural offices. Generally, approval is given if the herbicide or pesticide has been approved on cranberry crops since the two are so closely related. The best solution is to plant the lingonberries in soil that is "clean" and free of perennial weeds and to control annual weeds by mechanical cultivation between the rows. Growers often welcome annual weeds within the rows in the early years, provided they are not too invasive and or competitive, as they shelter young plants from desiccating winds.

Few pests or diseases appear to cause serious economic problems in Europe or indeed in the United States and Canada, although dieback diseases (*Phomopsis* spp.) have been identified in some crops in Oregon, causing progressive twig dieback and eventual death of stems. *Exobasidium vaccinii* is also seen on some plants both in cultivation and in the wild, which causes the distortion of shoots and produces a fleshy growth. A rust (*Pucciniastrum vaccinii*) that may affect lingonberries is identified by its yellow reddish coloring on the underside of leaves.

Varieties

In 1969 in Holland, H. van der Smit first brought lingonberries into cultivation as ornamental plants for ground cover in the garden with the introduction of the wild selected clone 'Koralle'. It was not until 1984 that 'Koralle' was introduced into commercial production by Zillmer in Germany. It is still the main cultivar for commercial production, although others have since been selected and are showing promise. The following are some of the more widely available cultivars of *Vaccinium vitis-idaea* at the time of writing.

'Erntedank', which translates from German into English as "thanksgiving," is one of three clones found on a German heathland by Albert Zimmer in quite hostile, exposed conditions. The others are 'Erntekrone' and 'Erntesegen'. (Plate 3)

'Ida' was introduced in August 1997 by the Swedish University of Agricultural Sciences at Balsgard, Sweden. It has very large berries, probably the largest ever produced, with each weighing up to $1^3/4$ ounces (50 g). Growth is vigorous and upright.

'Koralle' was released in 1969 in Holland as an ornamental ground cover plant but later was taken into commercial production for its fruit. Light red fruit of moderate size remain on the vines without deterioration for several weeks. This cultivar bears well from a young age and has a bushy upright growth to 12 in. (30 cm). It does not produce many runners but can be demanding in its soil and site requirements. (Plate 4)

'Linnea'. Introduced in August 1997 by the Swedish University of Agricultural Sciences at Balsgard, this cultivar has smaller berries than 'Ida' but it produces a heavier crop. The fruit has an excellent aroma, and the growth is vigorous and upright.

'Red Pearl' was introduced in Boskoop, Holland. A fast-growing variety, it is a compact, highly attractive plant with uprights to 13 in. (34 cm). Since the soil requirements for this lingonberry are less critical than those of other lingonberries, it is the one to choose if soil conditions are not ideal. Its ornamental use is outstanding as the young growth is an attractive bronze that is visible at almost any time of the summer and into fall. The leaves then turn a glossy green. 'Red Pearl' regularly has two main flowering periods in all but the most severe climates, one in spring and another in summer, and it produces berries in both summer and fall. It tends to produce both flowers and fruit together until late fall when frost destroys the latest blooms. Berries average $1/3$ in. (8 mm) in diameter, are dark red and of excellent quality. (Plate 5)

'**Regal**'. Introduced by the University of Wisconsin-Madison in 1994 from seed obtained in southwest Finland, this cultivar is vigorous, moderately spreading and produces uprights 7 to 8 in. (18 to 20 cm) at maturity. Berries average $1/3$ in. (8 mm) in diameter and weigh $1^{1}/3$ ounces (37 g), yielding well in the third year. In Wisconsin it has two blossoming periods, the first beginning in the last week of May and a second, more profuse period in approximately late June to early July. The main harvest period is in late September or early October.

'**Sanna**' is a Swedish cultivar that was released and patented from Balsgard in 1988. It spreads moderately, growing to 12 in. (30 cm), but is a very heavy cropper and produces top quality berries. Yields of $1^{1}/4$ lbs (1.2 kg) per bush, which is about six tons per acre, have been recorded. (Plate 6)

'**Splendor**', which was introduced in 1994 with 'Regal' by the University of Wisconsin-Madison, is from the same original source as 'Regal'. 'Splendor' is vigorous with a moderate spread. It reaches 6 to 8 in. (15 to 20 cm) at maturity, flowers in the second year and may produce a moderate crop in that year too. It produces heavy crops from year three onward. Brilliant carmine red fruit is of medium size, $1/3$ in. (8 mm) in diameter and weighs $1^{1}/2$ ounces (43 g). Its harvest period is much the same as for 'Regal' but may be a day or two earlier.

'**Sussi**', released in 1986, is another patented Swedish variety from Balsgard. It spreads readily but has shorter uprights that are 6 to 7 in. (15 to 18 cm) in height. Its yields are heavy and it produces medium to large berries of excellent quality.

The Lingonberry Harvest

A mature plant can produce about $2^{1}/4$ lbs (1 kg) of berries that, if translated into commercial terms, produces yields from 4.5 to 10 tons per acre, depending on variety and cultural conditions. Lingonberries tend to be a little inconsistent, with yields in some years being better than others. Two possible harvesting periods a year are possible for most varieties. In Wisconsin, heavier yields are taken from the second crop in the fall. The first crop of berries, which is only light, has to be ignored, especially when any form of mechanical harvesting is used, as it damages or removes the blooms that produce the second, more valuable crop. In Sweden the earlier crop is the important one.

Even on a small commercial scale, some form of mechanical aid is useful to remove the berries, be it a hand-held scoop (such as one traditionally used for harvesting dry cranberries or wild lowbush blueberries) or a more modern mechanical harvester like those used for dry harvesting cranberries.

Part III

Blueberries

The word "blueberry" conjures up strong emotions of both loyalty and confusion in the different areas where "blue" fruited vacciniums are grown. Talk to people from Maine or Nova Scotia, Canada, and they will tell you firmly that the only blueberries worth mentioning are the "lowbush" blueberries, which grow wild in their states and are cultivated to produce a valuable commercial crop. Speak to people from the Pinelands in New Jersey and they will talk proudly of their native "highbush" blueberries which grow wild in the clearings and on the fringes of the pine forests, though they are more likely to be noticed growing in huge plantations owned by commercial growers. In the southeastern states, the talk is of rabbiteye blueberries growing 10 ft. (3 m) or more.

The blueberry story is further complicated if you travel to somewhere like New South Wales in Australia, where most of the blueberries grown are southern highbush. These are hybrids that carry the genes of both northern highbush and rabbiteye blueberries. On the North Island of New Zealand, growers plant northern highbush, southern highbush and some of the rabbiteyes. In Europe a different confusion abounds in that the native "blueberries," although very similar to the wild blueberries of North America, have been given a variety of local names to identify them.

Chapter 3

The "Wild" or Lowbush Blueberries of North America

Two Kinds of "Wild" Blueberries and their Geographic Range

There are two kinds of "wild" or lowbush blueberries to consider, *Vaccinium angustifolium* and *V. myrtilloides*. In North America most are *V. angustifolium* Aiton, but *V. myrtilloides* also occurs in some areas, often near or among *V. angustifolium*. *Vaccinium angustifolium* is known as sweet lowbush blueberry, though when it is being marketed it is called "wild blueberry" to avoid confusion with the cultivated highbush blueberries. It is a dwarf, woody, usually deciduous shrub that is found growing in a wide range of areas such as high moors, exposed rocky outcrops, abandoned pastures and bogs and among pine or oak trees. The soil pH where it grows ranges from 2.8 to 6.0 and may be peaty or sandy. It is a species that tolerates a wide range of temperatures.

Vaccinium angustifolium forms a spreading mat from underground rhizomes that can spread for up to 35 ft. (10.5 m). Uprights 12 to 18 in. (30 to 45 cm) high grow at intervals from nodes on the horizontal rhizomes. The twigs bear elliptic or narrowly elliptic leaves that are ¼ to ⅔ in. (5 to 17 mm) wide to ⅔ to 16 in. (17 to 40 mm) long, usually with toothed or serrate margins. Their summer color is green, sometimes with a bluish or glaucous cast, and they change to a vivid red or orange in the fall before dropping. Flower-bud initiation occurs in midsummer of the previous year with flower parts undergoing initial development within flower buds, which can be identified by the end of August. The buds rest through the winter until activity starts inside them, unseen, as temperatures begin increasing in March. Active growth becomes obvious in April.

Bell-shaped flowers are borne in loose clusters. They mature in May and are typically white, though sometimes tinged pink. They are about ¼ in.

(5 mm) long, with a glaucous or glabrous calyx and pedicel and very occasionally pubescent or covered with a soft down. The fruit, which is quite variable in color and size, may be a dull or glossy black, although those with a good bloom appear blue. The berries may be ⅛ to ½ in. (2 to 12 mm) in diameter. They ripen from late July in southern Maine, with the last ripening occurring in late September in Newfoundland. (Plate 7) Individual plants are produced from seedlings germinated naturally from within the population, so each blueberry "patch" in fact consists of thousands of different clones that have developed over thousands of years as a natural process of evolution.

The wild blueberry industry extends from New Hampshire up into northeastern Maine (this is where the greatest concentration is) into New Brunswick, Nova Scotia and parts of Prince Edward Island. It also includes a small area of eastern Newfoundland and the Lac-Saint-Jean area of Quebec, northern Michigan, Minnesota and Wisconsin. *Vaccinium angustifolium* is also found in the uplands of West Virginia.

Vaccinium myrtilloides, the sour-top blueberry or velvet-leafed blueberry, is picked as part of the wild blueberry harvest, particularly in the Maine and New Brunswick blueberry barrens. It is also found in several isolated uplands of the Appalachian Mountains and further north in populations in central Labrador, the Northwest Territories and on Vancouver Island. Colonies are usually not as large nor as dense as those of *V. angustifolium*. Uprights are 4 to 46 in. (10 to 117 cm) high, and it is a much more hairy plant with a soft down or pubescence on the twigs and leaves. Long, green, elliptic leaves are ⅓ to ⅔ in. (8 to 17 mm) wide, ¾ to 1½ in. (2 to 3.8 cm) wide and downy on both sides with an entire, untoothed margin. Flowers are white or pale pink, often smaller than those of *V. angustifolium*, with a green, glabrous or smooth calyx and pedicel. The fruit is glaucous, blue and ¼ to ⅓ in. (5 to 8 mm) in diameter. It has hairy stems.

History of Human Use and Early Cultivation

Modern growers of European origin are not, of course, the first to "cultivate" wild blueberries in North America. Indians have gathered the fruit for centuries and still contribute considerably to the harvest. It was they who introduced the practice of burning to control encroaching shrubs, trees and other unwanted "weeds" and to kill the pests and diseases that invade the blueberry patches. This method was not very discriminating, and the

European settlers arriving in Maine found a wild, desolate landscape, often with many thousands of acres charred and apparently barren. In Washington County, Maine, the first area of land was officially designated a "barrens" in 1796. This term is now widely used to describe such wild, open spaces, and "blueberry barrens" refer to areas with large patches of lowbush blueberries. It was soon apparent that blueberries thrived under these burning practices and anybody who wanted to could descend on the barrens to harvest the berries for their own use and later resale. By the end of the eighteenth century, most of the land was owned by settlers but others could still freely access it. The freeloaders continued with their indiscriminate burning, which not only increased the area where blueberries thrived but also did considerable damage to the land.

It became obvious that burning the land not only destroyed valuable timber but that the shelter that had previously been created by stands of trees was now gone, resulting in barrenness in some years since the protective blankets of snow were being blown away. Without this snow cover to protect the plants in winter, there resulted both scorch damage and a loss of fruit in the following summer. A stumpage fee was introduced in 1871, a levy that was collected from anyone gathering wild blueberries and that was designed to compensate landowners and to reduce indiscriminate burning. Larger landowners began to lease out areas of land to control production and harvesting, and that was the beginning of modern management of wild blueberries. Leaseholders or landowners continued to burn off about one third of their blueberry acreage each winter, but those whose land was more level started to use mowers.

Two innovations that occurred in the mid- to late 1800s stand out. The first was the introduction of canning, which began in the 1860s out of the need to feed Federal troops of the Union Army during the Civil War. Companies in Washington County, Maine, which produced canned fish and lobster for this market, started to can wild blueberries also. They cooked the berries in kettles over a fire and filled and sealed the cans by hand. Canning undoubtedly helped to increase the demand for wild blueberries, and many tons were shipped out by boats from small ports along the Maine coastline. The building of the railways changed that, however, and by 1899 the Washington County Railroad transported virtually all blueberry fruit and blueberry products out of the area. Maine continued to be the primary producer of canned blueberries in the 1920s with four canning cooperatives in operation. The Washington County Commissioner stated in 1926 that "Maine packed 70 percent of all commercially prepared blueberries in the United States or in the world."

The second innovation occurred in 1883. As can be appreciated, picking the small berries individually and by hand is a lengthy and tedious business, and one that becomes increasingly uneconomic. The blueberry rake, invented by Abijah W. Tabbut, revolutionized the whole business of wild blueberry harvesting. This simple tool is still in wide use today and it is still manufactured by a descendent of its inventor.

Blueberry rakes look very much like deep dustpans with between 25 (for a small rake) and 60 (for one that is man-sized) closely set teeth. They are usually made of galvanized iron and are of different sizes to suit pickers, from children to adults, with varying arm strengths. The single handle is fixed on the inside to give leverage as the picker scoops through the bushes with a forward and upward sweeping motion. After several sweeps the scoop is filled. Traditionally the scooper then quickly removes any obvious debris with his spare hand before holding the rake several feet above a box or bucket, allowing the wind to blow leaves and other light debris away, leaving the fruit and a small amount of trash to go to the packing shed. Further winnowing was done here before the fruit was sent to market using fanning machinery originally adapted from wheat millers.

As the wild blueberry industry developed, customers became more conscious of quality and the presence of insect larvae among the berries. The blueberry maggot was not entirely controlled by regular burning of the plants. Dusting the ripening fruit with the insecticide powder DDT became a routine operation. This controlled the pests but probably did not do the consumers much good. DDT is of course now banned, and safer insecticides are used instead.

The recession of the 1930s affected the industry because customers were unable or unwilling to pay a fair price for processed fruit. This forced growers to sell as much as they could as fresh fruit, but many neglected their blueberry fields and the industry slumped.

Since the Second World War there has been enormous progress, due, in part, to the evolution at this time of the highbush blueberry industry in New Jersey and Michigan. The industries there stimulated a general demand for blueberries, but they also established the superiority of the larger fruit for the fresh-fruit trade. Wild blueberry growers where thus forced to concentrate their efforts on production and marketing for processing. This they have done with considerable success, especially since the development of storage and transport of frozen fruit became universal. (Freezing as a method of storage was first used in 1928, but not widely adopted until much later.) The small, tasty berries of the lowbush or wild blueberries can now be found all over the world, from the United States and Europe to Japan and Korea, processed into cakes, muffins, pies and a wide range of other products. Bakers appreciate the small size of the berries because that allows for good distribution throughout goodies such as muffins and cookies, and the firm skin of the berries means that they keep their shape during cooking. These small berries also have their own intense blueberry flavor and have a very high level of antioxidants.

The Annual Growth Cycle

The annual growth cycle is usually based on biennial cropping of a given area of the operation. In late fall or early winter, as soon as the blueberry plants are dormant, the chosen plots are "pruned," either by mowing or burning. These areas will not yield fruit the following year, but the process is meant to encourage healthy vegetative growth, to help control competing weeds and to kill harmful pests and diseases.

Tractor-drawn flail mowers are useful on level, rock-free land, which allows the rotating blades to chop all growth down to about 1 in. (2.5 cm) above the ground. Mechanically operated flails are favored by growers of the larger, flatter, rock-free areas because there is minimal risk of damage to underground rhizomes and because operating costs are lower. However, many wild blueberry growers do not have sufficient acreages of suitable land to be able to use this method.

Most growers have small areas that are frequently on hilly land that is often also rocky, so burning is the only option. Straw or hay is spread over the field either with a tractor-drawn straw layer or by hand if the area is not accessible by tractor. The straw or hay is then set on fire with the intention of burning both it and the aerial parts of all plants growing in the area. Tractor-drawn burners are used to control burning where possible. These burners are basically tanks of oil that feed the flames from a couple of long pipes extending several feet behind them. The driver can lower or raise the "flame throwers," and a skilled operator can prevent heat from going too deep and damaging the underground rhizomes. In areas with a high risk of fire, the grower must not only have fire-fighting equipment at hand in case the fires spread but must also notify the local authorities when a burn is

91

scheduled. (This latter precaution generally avoids panicked phone calls from the uninformed!) Areas not due for burning will be left untouched at this time, though they will receive a general tidying and removal of debris left behind after harvesting. Growers hope that all areas will be blanketed by a good covering of snow since it provides insulation from severe frosts. This hope is especially strong for plants that have not been pruned and are carrying the dormant flower buds that are responsible for the following year's harvest.

Controlling weeds using chemicals is very widespread. The introduction of the herbicide Velpar in 1982 (in Canada) or 1983 (in the United States) is credited with being the single most important reason for the increase in yields of wild blueberries during the second half of the 1980s. Applied in the spring following pruning, it proved very effective in killing almost all the weeds competing with the crop, including those that bear berries that would become mixed in with the blueberries and spoil the picked product.

In addition to reducing competition and allowing the wild blueberries space to gradually spread into spaces formerly occupied by weeds, chemically-based weed control has also meant that fertilizer can be used more effectively. Instead of encouraging the weeds to flourish above all else, the minerals go exclusively into the roots of the blueberries, which in turn increases the plant's growth in this first year of the biennial cycle. It is in the first year that the framework for the production of flowers—and therefore the fruit in the following year—is established. Growth starts in April and if a balanced fertilizer is used, it is applied just before then. Blueberries that are left unpruned are in the second year of the cycle. They will yield fruit provided there has been no damage to the dormant buds at the tips of the previous year's growth during the winter, and provided late frosts do not damage the potential flowers as they develop from those buds.

Once blueberries start flowering in early May, many growers put hives of honeybees into the area to help pollination. However, as with highbush blueberries, it is the wild, solitary bees that are most active as pollinators. Some growers are able to provide irrigation for their wild blueberries during spells of dry weather to allow the fruit to keep swelling.

As might be expected, pest and disease problems occur in areas where there is a concentration of a single species. Mummyberry may appear, and this can be controlled using an approved fungicide as the blueberry buds break into life in spring on the areas due to crop. Blueberry spanworm can be a problem, and this pest is controlled by using a biological method. A spray containing a bacterium (*Bacillus thuringiensis*) destroys the moth "worms" or larvae. Unlike most insecticides, it is harmless to bees. If the larvae of the blueberry fruit fly is burrowing into the fruit and spoiling its quality, then an insecticide spray may have to be used. The timing of the application of this spray is crucial because it has to kill the pest while leaving no residue by the time the fruit is ripe and ready for harvest.

Other animals compete with humans for the berries. Pickers have been surprised by 300-pound black bears that have traveled 10 to 15 miles (16 to 24 km) a day to feast on their favorite wild blueberry fields. Seeds have also been found in the feces of red foxes and raccoons. Birds such as robins, thrushes and grouse all enjoy a good feed from ripe blueberries.

The "Wild" Blueberry Harvest

August into September is a special time of great activity. The season lasts from four to six weeks, and the berries must be harvested during fine weather while they are dry. It coincides with the school holidays, so many school children and students are able to work on the blueberry fields and earn a good wage. Plenty of blueberry farms still rely on hand rakers who are paid for piecework according to the weight or volume they harvest. Some pick into a standard box or basket, and this is the unit by which they are paid. Crew bosses supervise the operation in the field and are paid according to the weight picked by the rakers under their charge.

Machine harvesting has become the norm on blueberry barrens or large, relatively level fields with sufficient acreage to justify the capital expenditure. This has only been possible since the 1980s when the removal of weeds using herbicides became de rigueur. All sorts of machines have been tried, ranging from simple hand-controlled, self-propelled harvesters similar to those used in the cranberry bogs in Michigan to huge, ride-on harvesters inspired by the combine harvesters of wheat farmers. (Plate 8) One of the most successful and widely accepted of these larger machines is the Bragg harvester. Mounted alongside a tractor, this harvester operates on the same raking or combing principle as the hand-held rakes. It needs just one skilled tractor driver to operate it. These harvesters enable blueberry growers to harvest their crops more economically and are invaluable where it is difficult to find sufficient people willing and able to harvest the crop by hand for a mutually agreeable rate of pay. These machines have, however, left a large number of Native American workers without their traditional summer jobs.

Most wild blueberries are grown in areas that also rely heavily on tourism, especially in Maine. The harvest provides a time of celebration for tourists and local communities alike. There are blueberry festivals, which have a carnival atmosphere with games, processions and other entertainments. Local papers carry reports of the harvest's progress and of awards given to workers who have won competitions for harvesting the most fruit that season. Many blueberry growers encourage the public to buy from their premises and have small shops selling a host of blueberry products in addition to their fruit.

The Allen family is one example. They have been farming wild blueberries in Maine near Blue Hill since 1912 and are now responsible for around 1,200 acres (485 hectares), most of which they own but some of which they manage for others. (Plate 9) A small gift shop, which is run very successfully by the women of the family, stocks a fascinating range of products bearing blueberry images, including stationery, aprons, bags and candles, as well as products made from blueberries such as preserves, cookies, teas and so on. The large, modern packhouse near the shop contains all the machinery needed to process the fruit from harvesting to storage. (The Allens take fruit for other growers too.) There is machinery to separate trash, wash and dry the fruit and convey it to the packing line, where it is checked to make sure it is clean and free of "foreign bodies" before moving on to whatever processing method is chosen. Large quantities of fruit used to be canned but this aspect of their business has been largely replaced by freezing. Freezing is usually done within 24 hours of harvesting.

Individual quick-frozen (IQF)) berries are frozen as they pass through a tunnel through which freezing air is pumped as the berries are blown through. By the time the fruit reaches the end of the tunnel it is frozen. From this stage the fruit is either packed ungraded or it is color sorted to remove those that are unripe or other impurities. Modern laser technology is being used to remove over 99 percent of unwanted material and can cope with more than 8,000 lbs (3,600 kg) an hour passing down the line. Rejected fruit is blown out by a stream of air from a jet ejector, which is activated as the laser detects it.

IQF fruit has a shelf life of two years when stored in a suitable freezer. Bulk freezing of clean-washed, air-dried fruit without using IQF methods results in a pack with mixed quality fruit, much of which has frozen as a mass instead of as individual berries, but it is suitable for sale to some processors for juice production.

Yields

Wild blueberry yields depend on several factors. They are reduced if the ripening berries get insufficient water in summer to swell properly. Winter damage, both in the nonbearing year and to the fruit-bearing plants in the second year of the cycle, happens quite often if there are low temperatures and a high windchill when plants are unprotected by a good snow cover. Late spring frosts are also lethal to buds that have broken dormancy and started to develop. Competition from weeds used to be a problem but it has largely been eliminated through herbicide use. Weeds can, however, still affect yields on plots that do not use chemicals and where owners fail to remove weeds manually. In general, yields of wild blueberries in the 1990s from the northeastern United States and eastern Canada doubled those of the 1980s, rising from about 2,000 or 3,000 lbs per acre to 5,000 to 6,000 lbs per acre. This increase is attributed to both better cultivation, which results in better productivity, as well as to better harvesting techniques.

Markets and distribution

With a very large number of independent producers trying to market a product from an area relatively remote from large human populations, marketing used to be a major problem. The method of marketing depends to a great extent on the size of the business. At one end of the scale there are the "hobby farmers" with an acre or two (less than a hectare) attached to their homes. At the other end are the "big business boys," the blueberry barons of the blueberry barrens. Many producers fall somewhere in between, and they are the small commercial farmers who have blueberry fields as part of their mixed farms of 50 to 100 acres (20 to 40 hectares).

Many people moving into the countryside in Maine (or any of the other areas where wild blueberries grow) may find that their property has an acre or so (0.4 hectare) of the plant on the land, providing too much fruit for personal use or for friends. They usually manage to sell most of their fruit locally, bringing in sufficient money to settle a few bills, and are quite happy with this new interest and extra income.

Small farmers with less than 100 acres (40 hectares) have to be more commercially minded. Some who have blueberries as part of their overall farm income may make enough money to live on, while others need an alternative, additional source of income. Forestry, fishing and tourism all provide possible sources. Some manage their own blueberry fields and harvest their own fruit, then sell it to a larger grower with modern sorting, packing and processing facilities or to a local cooperative or agent who takes the fruit to the next stage. Others, particularly older owners or those who need to spend their time and energy doing other things, carry out some of the work themselves but have a contract arrangement with larger growers who do the rest. In some instances, contractors both manage the fields and take care of harvesting, packing, storage and marketing. Large growers with hundreds or even thousands of acres carry out all the growing, harvesting, processing, packing and storage themselves and act for others where required.

In most years, less than 1 percent of the wild blueberry crop is sold fresh, mainly to local hotels, restaurants and other bulk users, with some being sent to the fresh-fruit markets in the cities. The remainder of the crop is processed and sold on, mostly as a frozen product in 30 lb (14 kg) boxes. A market still exists for canned wild blueberries, but it is limited. In addition to markets within and between the United States and Canada, an increasingly large volume of the fruit is being exported. Exports started in the 1920s when fresh wild blueberries were first sent by ship to England. Although the journey took a month and much of the fruit deteriorated, it nevertheless—and somewhat surprisingly—sold.

With the development of effective methods of freezing and transporting frozen fruit in the 1970s, the market began to expand. At first the fruit carried a 20 percent tariff when exported to European Community countries, but it was lowered to 4 percent in 1973, which helped increase sales considerably. Germany, with an established interest in wild blueberries from its own sources and from central European countries, especially Poland, became the main importer in the early 1990s with 30 million lbs (453,600 kg) per year being sold within the country.

From 1979, when trade restrictions were lifted, Japan became an increasingly important market. This might seem strange because blueberries, either wild or cultivated, had been unrecognized as a food in Japan. However, blueberries, with their distinct visual appeal and association with American folklore, soon caught the imagination, and although the trend has turned in favor of the bigger cultivated blueberries, Japan is still a major buyer of wild blueberries for processing and pharmaceutical use.

In the 1970s, 5 percent of the million or so pounds of fruit produced was exported, but during the 1980s, wild blueberry production increased to 35 million lbs (about 15 million kg), 18 percent of which was exported. At the turn of the century a production figure of well over 120 million lbs

(54 million kg) was recorded, and this figure is rising. The export market for wild blueberries is affected by the production of and demand for two related vaccinium crops, the wild bilberry (*Vaccinium myrtillus*) in Europe and the highbush (*V. corymbosum*) in North America and Europe. (Plates 10, 11, 12)

Cheap, imitation blueberries made from other colored and flavored sources and used in cake mixes and other products have been a source of complaint because they do nothing to enhance demand and only give a poor false impression of the genuine article. The WBANA, formed in 1981, is a voluntary trade association based at Bar Harbor in Maine that works to promote the blueberry on behalf of all the wild blueberry growers of North America. It is incorporated under both United States and Canadian laws and operates bilingually in both English and French. Funding comes from levies collected by the state of Maine and in Canada from growers and processors. WBANA is undoubtedly the most effective promoter of wild blueberries both within North America and now worldwide. It has established a powerful image for wild blueberries and works to maintain it by intelligent advertising and promotion in many languages and by attending food fairs in Europe and in Japan.

The North American Blueberry Council (NABC), formed in the 1960s, covers all blueberries, both wild and cultivated in North America. Its main function is to gather and distribute market data for its members. It is funded by voluntary assessment from growers, processors or blueberry associations. It also carries out promotional work within North America.

Research

Some superior clones of wild blueberries were identified as long ago as 1910 and 1921 by Dr. Frederick V. Coville of the USDA, who selected 'Russell' from a wild population in New Hampshire. It is still in cultivation, but there is doubt about it remaining available as 'Russell' because it is thought to be a hybrid, *Vaccinium angustifolium* being one of the parents. The Kentville Research Station in Nova Scotia introduced 'Augusta', 'Brunswick' and 'Chigneto' in 1978 from more than 800 wild-collected clones.

The University of Maine at Orono also does valuable work and has its own blueberry farm at Jonesboro, where trial grounds are established to identify improved clones, among other work. In addition to looking for the fairly obvious characteristics of good blue color, good flavor, late blooming, disease resistance, uniform ripening, heavy yield, vigor and easy propagation, researchers look for the ability of plants to self-fertilize. This characteristic is important in wild populations, which may not have an abundance of insects to carry out the job. Upright, vigorous, tall stems that carry the fruit above the main body of the plant are obviously desirable, especially for mechanical harvesting.

Tourism

Apart from being an attraction during the harvest, the wild blueberry areas are a huge draw in the fall. The acres and acres of brilliant red blueberry fields in Maine or Nova Scotia in October are a sight never to be forgotten. They attract thousands of tourists a year who boost the local economy. Walkers taking the northern section of the Appalachian Way passing over Blue Hill are, as in other areas where the interests of tourists and farmers may clash, warned to keep to the path—the urge to stray onto the concentrated areas of wild blueberries is understandably tempting but not welcomed!

Chapter 4
Northern Highbush Blueberries

"Highbush blueberry" is the name given to cover the taller species of shrubby *Vaccinium* species that are grown mainly for their fruit crops and it includes the northern highbush, rabbiteye and southern highbush blueberries. The latter are relatively recent hybrid introductions that should not be confused with selections of northern highbush suitable for some of the warmer climate areas of the southern states and that are occasionally called southern highbush blueberries. I discuss the propagaton of all cultivars and species of the highbush blueberries (the northern highbush, rabbiteyes, hybrids such as the southern highbush or half highs) in chapter 5.

Geographic Range

As the name implies, highbush blueberries are borne on bushes taller than the lowbush blueberries I describe in chapter 3. Their cultivars are grown in all the commercial and garden-planted blueberry fields or plots around the world where climate and soil conditions are suitable. There are cultivars that suit climates where winters are long and cold, cultivars that suit much warmer, subtropical regions and others, of course, that suit areas in between these two extremes. Suitability basically boils down to the "chilling requirements" of the different blueberry groups.

Blueberries require a period of winter dormancy or rest before they will break dormancy and come into growth. The number of accumulated hours of chilling varies considerably from species to species and cultivar to cultivar. It is fairly common for plants to receive their requirements met by midwinter, but normal winter temperatures keep the plants dormant until spring. Sometimes buds may start to develop if there are several days of temperatures over 46°F (8°C) in winter, which makes them vulnerable when normal winter temperatures resume.

Northern highbush blueberries require the greatest number of winter chilling hours and are therefore most suitable for areas with long, cold winters. Rabbiteye blueberries need a shorter period of winter chill—only 400 to 500 hours—and so are suitable for milder climates where winters are shorter and spring comes early. Those cultivars that bloom earliest (meaning they have the lowest chilling hour requirements) are generally, but not always, more prone to frost damage than the later blooming cultivars. Southern highbush plants are bred to have low chilling requirements; some need as little as 150 hours, but most require around 450 hours. Where the climate is not too extreme, as for instance in the Rotorua area of New Zealand's North Island, it is possible to grow all three types. In New Zealand, the first to ripen is the southern highbush, then the northern highbush, followed by the rabbiteye.

Virtually all cultivated blueberries carry mixed genes derived from more than one species, each introducing characteristics which provide benefits for the particular areas where they are grown and harvested. These areas are not clearly defined; in marginal climates where the chilling requirements overlap, some cultivars of northern highbush are grown alongside rabbiteye cultivars. Southern highbush cultivars offer a further choice in these marginal areas.

The hardiness of a plant is a factor that should be considered separately from its chilling requirement. Virtually all blueberries, wherever they are grown, are subjected to frost during winter. Many rabbiteye blueberries in the upland areas where they are grown are particularly prone to spring frost damage because of their need for relatively few chilling hours before breaking dormancy. Provided temperatures do not drop below 21°F (−6°C), highbush blueberries are unlikely to experience damage while they are fully dormant. As with cranberries, the most dangerous time is in the spring with the flowers receiving the worst damage. While they are still enclosed in their buds, flowers can tolerate temperatures down to 23°F (−5°C), but when the flower clusters open a little further and individual flowers are distinguishable, they are killed at 28°F (−2°C). Fully opened flowers may be killed or at least severely damaged at 28°F (−2°C).

Botany and Life Cycle

Vaccinium corymbosum, which makes up much of the genetic material of the northern highbush blueberry, belongs to the section *Cyanococcus* ("cyano" means blue and "coccus" means berry). *Vaccinium angustifolium*, *V. myrtilloides* and six other species (*V. boreale*, *V. darrowii*, *V. hirsutum*, *V. myrsinites*, *V. pallidum* and *V. tenellum*) also belong to this section. *Vaccinium corymbosum* was first named by Linnaeus and is probably a combination of three or more species that evolved long ago and produced the variable "combination" species we have today.

Vaccinium corymbosum grows wild in eastern North America from Nova Scotia and Quebec in Canada as far west as northeastern Illinois, northern Indiana and the more southerly parts of Michigan. Its range also extends eastwards to the coast and south into North Carolina, the greatest concentration being in New Jersey. Here, wild plants grow by the roadside in the federally protected area of the Pinelands, east of Philadelphia and inland from Atlantic City. They thrive in the dappled shade provided by the pigmy pines and Atlantic white cedars. They have formed colonies in clearings created by logging and for farming. *Vaccinium pensylvanicum*, a lowbush blueberry, also grows here, and there is evidence of natural hybridization between the species. *Vaccinium corymbosum* extends south into the Carolinas and as far as Florida, where the picture becomes somewhat blurred since *V. ashei* (formerly known as *V. corymbosum* var. *ashei*), the rabbiteye blueberry, takes over.

Vaccinium corymbosum is a very variable deciduous shrub that is typically 4 to 6 ft. (1.2 to 1.8 m) tall, occasionally 10 to 12 ft. (3 to 3.7 m). It typically forms a fairly compact base or crown of branches. Sometimes, however, it sends out suckers from adventitious buds on the roots up to 3 ft. (90 cm) away from the main plant, particularly if disturbed by burning or damaged by animals or humans.

The highbush blueberry has a fibrous root system with pencil-thin roots that anchor the plant in the ground and store nutrients. They have a bigger root system in relation to their aerial growth than the rabbiteye blueberry but are less efficient at absorbing nutrients. A mass of fine threadlike roots is responsible for absorbing water and nutrients, and as with other *Vaccinium* species, there are no root hairs. The root system tends to be spreading and shallow, but this depends on the soil texture, soil drainage and availability of oxygen, as well as the availability of water and nutrients in summer. This system may extend to a depth of 2 to $2^1/_2$ ft. (60 to 80 cm) in well-drained sandy soils but the greatest bulk of the root system is found in just the top 10 to 12 in. (25 to 30 cm) of soil. The lateral distribution of the root system provides useful information regarding irrigation and fertilizer supply. Roots from the average mature bush can extend well over $3^1/_3$ ft. (1 m) from the emerging stem or stems, the area where the root and shoot systems differentiate and that is known as the crown of the bush. About half of them are within 12 in. (30 cm) of the crown and most (84 percent) are within 2 ft. (60 cm) (Gough 1995).

The shoot system, which arises as a highbush blueberry plant develops, shows variation from cultivar to cultivar. Some, such as 'Berkeley', develop a small number of shoots (or canes) from the base or crown of the plant, and then go on to produce most of their branches from these. Others such as 'Bluecrop' produce a mass of shoots from the crown and tend to continue doing so throughout their life. Buds can remain dormant on the crown for several years and may be stimulated into growth by hard pruning. This pruning also stimulates vegetative buds to develop from old wood, as anyone who has taken a chainsaw to an unproductive old bush will testify.

Twigs vary greatly in color, from green through yellow to red according to the time of year. They may either be covered in down or completely hairless. Young stems have a green appearance (this is due to the presence of chlorophyll) and they redden as cold weather approaches in fall. Many stomata are dotted all over the young stem, and they become more visible as their guard cells become corky and lenticels are formed. The red coloring of young stems is one of the ornamental attractions during the winter months. The stems thicken as they age, becoming woody and gray-brown with bark that tends to flake vertically. Older bushes form a crown of growth with mostly woody, bare, grayish brown stems that have a flaky bark.

A productive, mature bush that is well cared for should have a structure built up to include a framework of stems of different ages and diameters. It should not, in theory at least, carry wood that is older than six years and about $1^1/_2$ in. (3.8 cm) in diameter. Older wood is less efficient at conducting water and nutrients, and an older bush with more than about ten canes is also less efficient because of the overcrowding that results in insufficient light and air reaching the center of the bush.

Vigorous shoots reaching possibly $3^1/_3$ ft. (1 m) in length in one season tend to grow in the second flush of growth in late summer. They have multiple flower buds near their tips, growth buds just behind them (they are capable of producing vigorous shoots) and growth buds a little lower down that produce shoots of moderate vigor and a few flower buds. Below these growth buds are widely spaced vestigial buds. These buds seldom break dormancy, remaining inactive and useless unless stimulated into growth in the following spring by pruning cuts made just above them. If the growing season is too short for the tips of these long vigorous shoots to mature sufficiently before winter sets in, they are aborted and the fruiting buds at the tips are lost.

As can be appreciated, shoots that are 3 ft. (90 cm) or more in length tend to encourage bushes to grow too tall, especially when they develop from a point high in the bush. A heavy canopy of leafy shoots near the top of a bush results in bare stems below and fruit only near the top. I discuss this topic further under the section on pruning later in this chapter.

Dormant buds that are small, narrow and pointed in the fall or in winter will remain vegetative, while those destined to become flowers are considerably bigger and broader. (Plate 13) These flower buds are formed during late summer and early fall with most being produced on healthy, medium-sized lateral shoots growing from the larger, two-year-old branches. On average, the top five or six buds near the tip of these shoots are capable of producing flowers. The topmost buds, which are initiated first, contain the largest number of flowers (possibly ten per bud) in highly productive cultivars such as 'Bluecrop'. 'Toro' can produce even more than ten. Numbers decrease the further down the stem they are because they have less time to complete development before the growing season ends. The actual number of flowers per bud depends on the cultivar, while the number of flower buds produced depends on the vigor and thickness of the shoot. Single flowers are produced from some buds, especially on thin, twiggy stems.

The ovate to narrowly elliptic leaves are $2/3$ to 1 in. (17 to 25 mm) wide and $1^{1}/2$ to $2^{1}/4$ in. (38 to 54 mm) long on average. They may be longer in some cultivars with margins that vary from entire to slightly toothed and some that are sharply serrated. They are smooth on the upper surface and vary between being glabrous to pubescent. Young growth is often greenish yellow but may be bronze or reddish. Some have a definite, powdery gray bloom on the lower surface while others are just pale green. A notable characteristic of the species and its cultivars are the bright fall colors of the foliage, which range from gold through orange-red to deep red and, in some cultivars, almost purple. (Plate 19)

Flowers are borne in clusters and have green or glaucous young pedicels that grow from a larger stalk or peduncle. The first flowers are produced before vegetative growth begins, while later flowers are accompanied by the emergence of young leaves. The calyx is green or glaucous with cylindrical corolla tubes of five fused petals that range from white through various shades of pink and very occasionally red depending on the variety and stage of opening of the bloom. The ovary, containing on average about 65 ovules, is inferior, meaning it is below the calyx. Their sweet scent is evident when a number of plants are present to contribute. (Plate 15)

The fruit is a berry with five loculi containing small seeds. The mature berries may be dull black, shiny black or blue, and they range from 1/8 to 3/4 in. (3 to 20 mm) in size according to variety. They vary in shape and in skin texture, again according to variety. The glaucous bloom is an asset that is prized in cultivated varieties. The remains of the calyx leave a five-starred scar at the tip of the berry.

Winter

As winter approaches blueberry plants gradually "harden" in readiness for the cooler temperatures. By this time their buds are clearly differentiated into those that are flower bearing and those that are vegetative. Northern highbush blueberries, being naturally deciduous shrubs, have a long period of apparent dormancy during winter. This period extends from leaf fall to shoot growth, and the whole plant appears inactive. This time of chilling and rest is essential for the future performance of both vegetative and flower buds. Varieties vary in their chilling requirements. Northern highbush cultivars, which are regarded as "high chill," need an average of 750 hours of temperatures below 45°F (7°C) before growth can begin. Many appreciate 1,000 hours or more to produce good strong growth and fruit development. In general, the more chilling hours the better, and temperatures that range from 36° to 48°F (2 to 9°C) are the most effective in promoting good strong growth and therefore abundant fruit in the future. Temperatures below 35°F (1.7°C) or above 54°F (12°C) have little effect. Year-round temperatures above 61°F (16°C) do not encourage dormancy at all. When plants do not become dormant (namely those in warm climates) they continue as evergreens, producing continuous light flushes of growth and both flowers and light crops of fruit all year round. This growth pattern is fine in a home garden but can cause problems for commercial growers, especially for those who use machine harvesters.

It is important to investigate winter temperatures and their duration before planting northern highbush blueberries. Where there is doubt about their suitability, an alternative choice may be the relatively recently introduced southern highbush cultivars as they only need 400 to 660 hours below 45°F (7°C).

Blueberry roots remain active below ground level even during the apparently dormant season and at least up to midwinter when soil temperatures are several degrees higher than air temperatures. As temperatures drop below 45°F (7°C), winter roots become brown. This browning is the result of secondary thickening (it indicates the formation of lignin, which makes cells "woody"), with just the tips of some remaining white and able to absorb water. Secondary thickening happens near the soil surface first, with roots deeper in the soil or deeper within the root system thickening last, and it is evidently a means by which the roots protect themselves from frost damage. It is therefore a mistake to assume that the visible root system in a container is dead because it shows no sign of white roots; the chances are that it is either dormant or has active roots deeper in the system.

Root death may occur, however, if plants are subjected to prolonged periods of freezing soil temperatures where the soil becomes deeply frozen down to the depth of the roots. This is most likely to occur in container-grown plants that are surrounded by freezing air for prolonged periods or where blueberries are grown in clean, cultivated soil with no mulch and at the more northern extremes for northern highbush blueberry cultivation.

Any late terminal shoots that have not "hardened" or matured soon die back since low temperatures kill immature cells. Sometimes, when a short cold spell is followed by several weeks of warmer weather in late fall, the odd flower may appear before midwinter on some varieties, especially those that have a high proportion of lowbush blueberry in their genetic makeup. This is not the same as a true break in dormancy, which will occur only after the chilling requirement of the particular variety has been met. In England, 'Berkeley' is particularly prone to this, and in New England, 'Bluetta', 'Collins', 'Darrow', 'Earliblue' and 'Patriot' are apparently prone (Gough 1995). These flowers do not, of course, survive, and they constitute a loss of fruit for the following season.

In the North American climate where wild *Vaccinium corymbosum* and the other species with which it hybridizes to produce the northern highbush blueberry grow, fall climatic conditions tend to be dry and sunny, with gradually lowering temperatures. Vegetative shoots, branches and flower buds are able to fully mature before winter sets in. Once dormant, some cultivars have been known to withstand winter temperatures down to −40°F (−40°C) when low humidity conditions are also experienced. It has been suggested (Gough 1995) that this is because a dry atmosphere draws water out of the tissues, leaving insufficient water in them to form damaging ice crystals. However, with the usual fluctuation of winter temperatures, the result is a partial reduction in but not a breaking of dormancy when temperatures rise, making the plant more vulnerable when temperatures fall again.

Northern highbush blueberries are not grown successfully where winter temperatures fluctuate wildly or regularly drop below −20°F (−29°C) during the course of winter. Snow cover is accepted with mixed feelings; on the one hand the snow acts as a good insulator against the effects of cold winds and low temperatures, but on the other its weight can do a lot of damage to the branches by splitting them.

In climates such as those in Britain and much of coastal continental Europe where northern highbush blueberries are grown, low temperature extremes are seldom experienced. The problem in those climates is that the bushes tend not to become fully dormant and are vulnerable on the few occasions when temperatures drop below 0 to −4°F (−18 to −20°C), especially if accompanied by strong winds. In Britain and other areas where winter humidity tends to be high, the lack of winter hardening can cause considerable damage. In central Europe the climate is more similar to the northern highbush areas of North America.

Spring

Roots become active and start to absorb water when spring arrives, provided the plants have had their required period of rest and that soil temperatures have risen above 45°F (7°C). As spring gets underway and both soil and air temperatures rise, plant hormones trigger root growth, and activity increases steadily. This activity allows increasing absorption of water and minerals, which, together with increasing light levels and day length, as well as rising average air temperatures, triggers plant hormones in the shoot tips to be activated. Shoot and leaf growth begins about two weeks after the start of root activity. Flower buds need fewer hours of chilling than vegetative buds, so they often precede leaf growth. Bushes are covered in flowers (their presence can be detected as much with the nose as the eye) and there are only a few leaves to be seen. Leaves on older, spindly wood often break into growth earlier than those on the more vigorous shoots for the same reason as the flowers do.

Once dormancy has been broken and active growth begins, there follows a nail-biting period when damage from late spring frosts can be increasingly severe, particularly as the flower buds develop. Fully opened flowers with mature sexual parts are most vulnerable, with some damage likely at 28°F (−2°C). Since flowers develop over several weeks, there will be flowers at all stages of maturity at any given time. It is therefore unlikely that a temperature drop to lower than 28°F (−2°C) will damage all the flowers on all plants of a particular variety. In most plantations or gardens, a mix of varieties provides a further safeguard because they vary in their time of flowering, with the most cold hardy tending to flower late. The fruit of those that flower late tends to ripen before some of the less cold hardy.

The worst damage occurs when spring weather has been mild, encouraging rapid growth of tender leaves and developing flowers, and then a sudden drop in temperature occurs. A gradual drop to 28°F (−2°C) is less likely to damage flowers, but if the thermometer reaches 23°F (−5°C) serious damage to all aerial parts is virtually guaranteed. Radiation frosts, which occur when temperatures drop below freezing in windless, cloudless conditions, are the most damaging. A sudden drop during a radiation frost to 28°F (−2°C) will cause leaves and young shoots to blacken and die, and there will probably be damage to fully developed flowers. Frost damage soon appears as a blackening of the young green fruit within the calyx. If the damage is not too severe then scar tissue will form, and this will result in spoilt ripe fruit with a pitted area covered by tough brown skin appearing where the damage occurred. Severe frost damage results in the abortion of the fruit.

A commercial plantation or a garden grouping of highbush blueberries, when approached in late spring and particularly on a warm, sunny day, leaves few people unmoved. The mass of dark pink, pale pink or white blooms is attractive enough, but the smell is a real bonus. Most people liken it to the pleasant, sweet intoxicating smell of the English cowslip, which comes from the nectar produced from the base of the flowers to attract pollinating insects.

Flower buds break into flower following the rapid development of the pedicels and peduncles bearing the flower cluster or corymb. Flowers at the tip of the flower clusters open first, as do those individuals or clusters near the top of the shoots. Flowers tend to hang downwards in most varieties with the female stigma protruding from the corolla at maturity. As with most other *Vaccinium* species grown for fruit, the receptive tip of the stigma is prevented from receiving most of the pollen released from the anthers of the stamens of the same flower because of a protruding collar which directs the pollen grains away from it.

Wild bees, particularly wild solitary bees, are active pollinators, successfully transferring pollen from one bush to flowers on another in most weathers and from early to late each day. They have a habit of cheating a little by puncturing a hole in the base of the corolla to reach the nectar, which avoids brushing their bodies against the pollen laden stamens. This action not only prevents pollination but makes things easy for succeeding visiting bees to make the same short cut. With approximately 65 ovules in the ovary of each flower, each requiring fertilization by one pollen grain to produce a seed, pollination is extremely important, particularly as partially fertilized flowers produce imperfect fruit.

Hives of honeybees are frequently placed in blueberry plantations to help with pollination, but blueberry flowers are not the favorite flowers of honeybees because access to the nectar is quite difficult. They are somewhat lazy too, tending to be active only in warm, dry conditions and less so in unfavorable weather and at the end of each day.

Prolonged wet or cold weather that lasts for several weeks at flowering leads to poor fertilization, smaller berries and a smaller crop. Once fertilization has successfully taken place the flower parts are no longer needed and gradually turn brown and die. The calyx, formed from the sepals, remains as a star shape at the tip of the fruit. By the time the fruit is fully ripe some varieties retain more of the calyx than others, resulting in a large calyx scar. The most desirable fruit has a small calyx scar.

Summer

As flowering progresses over a period of four to six weeks for most varieties, vegetative buds swell rapidly and leaves emerge, followed by rapid growth of the shoots. This activity follows root growth quite closely, meaning that peak activity in shoot growth benefits from a maximum uptake of water and minerals from the new mass of roots. Most of the fruit has set by midsummer and then starts to develop and swell. Temperatures tend to peak in mid- to late summer, when rainfall is often low. Root growth also slows to a minimum when temperatures reach 68°F (20°C) around this time. A pause in vegetative growth also occurs while the plant is concentrating on supplying carbohydrates and minerals for the development of fruit.

Northern highbush blueberries gradually ripen over about six to eight weeks depending on the cultivar, changing from green through red to blue or blue-black. The sugar content builds up from about 7 percent at the mature green stage to 15 percent when fully ripe (Gough 1995). Anthocyanins also increase as the color changes to blue. Warm weather with temperatures between 68° and 77°F (20 and 25°C) is ideal. An individual cluster will usually have fruit at all stages of ripening within it. Berries near the top of a bush in full sun benefit from higher temperatures and ripen a couple of days or so before those in shade lower down or deeper in the bush. Those near the top also tend to be larger, sweeter and have more flavor. Temperatures below 61°F (16°C) during ripening tend to produce less sweet berries with inferior flavor, and high rainfall or excessive irrigation during this period has a similar effect.

Fruit reaches a peak of ripeness when the whole fruit is blue or blue-black. Ripeness can be difficult to detect easily in those varieties where a ring of pink remains around the stem end of the fruit a little longer than others. "Pinkies" are not desirable in a picking basket because they don't achieve quite the same sugar content and flavor as they would have done if left on the bush a little longer, although most varieties continue to ripen at room temperature after picking.

The time to pick the fruit is when the berries are fully ripe and ready to leave their flower stalks. Removal of the fruit leaves a scar, the size of which varies according to variety. Scar size needs to be considered when choosing varieties, as does the fact that the skin near the scar of some varieties tears easily. In addition to being unsightly, large scars and torn skin make the fruit more vulnerable to shriveling and rot.

Flower buds for the following year are initiated approximately 60 to 90 days after the current year's flowering when the new shoots have reached sufficient maturity to support them. Warm weather with temperatures between 61° and 75°F (16 and 24°C) encourages the formation of flower buds.

Fall

Active vegetative growth continues until temperatures start to drop in the early fall when it slows down and finally stops and the concentration is on the maturation of the new shoots. Flower bud development continues during this time but the buds cease active growth with the onset of dormancy when temperatures drop and day length and light intensities diminish in late fall. The sap, previously responsible for transporting soluble sugars round the plant from the photosynthesizing leaves and water and minerals from the roots, is no longer flowing. The sugars are instead converted to starch for storage. Plant hormones, which are controlled by temperature and light, are responsible for these and most of the other changes that take place in the plants.

It is at this time that leaves gradually take on their fall color, with most varieties showing brilliant shades of red. (Plates 16, 17, 18) Those that grow in shade, however, do not develop their full color potential. Fall is also the time when deer tend to reappear and strip leaves, often quite tidily and in an upward sweeping motion, from young branches, usually without damaging the buds in their axils. Are they getting their dose of antioxidants to send them healthily into the rigors of winter? Abscission or leaf-fall happens naturally as temperatures drop and days shorten. That is when the hormones in their stalks dictate that the time has come to cut off the supply of water. By this time the young stems of the current year's growth of many varieties will have turned red. They will remain that way for the winter, especially if they have had the benefit of a sunny site.

Commercial Development

Cultivated northern highbush blueberries are regarded as the Rolls Royce of blueberries. They are larger and have greater eye appeal than lowbush or wild blueberries, although many would say that the latter's smaller size produces a more concentrated blueberry flavor. Whichever opinion is believed, it is undoubtedly true that the emergence of the cultivated highbush blueberry, particularly from the wilds of New Jersey, has resulted in vastly improved appreciation of blueberries in general. A huge, worldwide industry has developed.

Early Cultivation in the United States

Compared with other soft fruit, *Vaccinium corymbosum* is a relatively recent introduction to commercial cropping (it was introduced in the early twentieth century) and is still very much in its infancy as a soft-fruit crop for the home gardener. However, as with other wild *Vaccinium* species, *V. corymbosum* has been appreciated by the Native Americans for a very long time. Called "starberries" because of the star-shaped scar left on the fruit by the calyx, blueberries achieved legendary status because they saved many from winter starvation. The Indians gathered the fruit and either dried it in the sun or with smoke for later addition to winter stews or for combining with meat from wild game to make pemmican. Later, the early settlers learned to appreciate the blueberries, and those who were familiar with other vacciniums such as bilberries soon used them as they would at home—stewing them, eating them with milk or mixing them with corn or wheat flour to make cakes or bread. They also adopted the more savory dishes and, of course, pemmican. In addition to being a food source, blueberries have a long history of use in medicine. (See chapter 1.)

With fruit available in abundance from wild sources, it is perhaps not surprising that cultivation of highbush blueberries did not begin in earnest until the early part of the twentieth century. By that time the American population was rising rapidly, and demand for the wild picked fruit was high. There had been limited attempts to transplant and grow plants selected from the wild in the 1890s but these had failed, almost certainly because it was not appreciated that blueberries need poor, acidic soils to survive and thrive; early attempts were based on "giving them a good soil." Rich, well-manured, well-limed garden soil is anathema to blueberries, something that new converts to blueberry growing have a problem with to this day.

We can attribute the beginning of successful blueberry cultivation to two people, Elizabeth White and Frederick Coville. Elizabeth White's father, J. J., had been one of the leading lights in the early cranberry-growing world. Elizabeth started working on the family's cranberry farm at the age of 22. She noticed that local people picked blueberries before moving on to pick her father's cranberries and she wondered if blueberies could be added to the operation. She became increasingly interested in the areas between the cranberry fields and came to realize that blueberries, harvested in July and August, would be a useful, complementary crop to the cranberry operation.

At the same time, Coville, who was working as a botanist for the USDA, published his first paper on his work on blueberries (1910). Elizabeth read it and was inspired to write to him offering her support. They joined forces, and the combination of these two pioneers resulted in the foundation of the modern cultivated blueberry industry. Coville's scientific knowledge and ability to propagate and hybridize plants, together with Elizabeth's land, staff and financial support proved highly successful.

Elizabeth and her father had realized for a long time that there was tremendous variation among the wild blueberries growing on their land. (This may have been partly because they had the highbush blueberry, *Vaccinium corymbosum*, and *V. pensylvanicum*, a type of lowbush now thought to be a form of *V. ulignosum*, growing together, and it is now known that interspecific hybridization occurs in the wild.) They found that the local "Pineys" already knew where to find the best patches for picking. Many of the Pine Barrens inhabitants, regarded with some suspicion as being lawless and primitive by folks from outside the area, were among the last generation of skilled hunter-gatherers who had settled in the area to mine the bog iron that was used to make cannon balls at the time of the American Revolution. Some supplemented their income by picking and selling wild blueberries and then moved on to pick cranberries with the end of the blueberry season.

Elizabeth enlisted the help of Jake Sooy and Alfred Stevenson to lead groups of men to seek out the best blueberry plants within a 20 mile (32 km) radius of her home at Whitesbog. She equipped them with an aluminium gauge with a $^1/_2$ in. (1.25 cm) diameter hole in it, some labels and bottles containing formalin, presumably to preserve collected berries. She paid $2 per bush selected, and each selected bush was named after the finder. Thus, these old hunters lent their names to the beginnings of a great new industry. 'Sooy', 'Stevenson', 'Adams', 'Harding' and 'Dunphy' proved no problem, but Sam Lemon's find became 'Sam'. Rube Leek's bush proved even more difficult because it obviously couldn't be called 'Leek'. Coville called it 'Rube' but Elizabeth disapproved and named it 'Rubel'. It proved to be, in her words, "the keystone of blueberry breeding."

Coville did not confine his work to New Jersey. He had searched other states for wild blueberries before he started to work with Elizabeth and continued to do so later. The first selection, which was made in 1908, was a wild highbush blueberry from Greenfield, New Hampshire, which produced berries $^1/_2$ in. (1.25 cm) in diameter. Named 'Brooks', it has a good flavor. The second selection, made in 1909, was a lowbush blueberry from the same area, which was named 'Russell'.

In addition to making these selections, Coville solved the problem of the soil requirements of blueberries by carrying out experiments in 1908 and 1909 with blueberry plants in pots that contained a range of different soils. He not only found that blueberries grew best in poor acidic soils, but by examining the roots under a microscope, he also found out why. Blueberries do not have root hairs and so do not benefit from a greatly increased surface area of roots to aid in the absorption of water and minerals. He even discovered the presence of mycorrhizal fungi in the roots and concluded that they were beneficial, but he did not discover why this was so.

In these early days Coville did much valuable work investigating propagation techniques and culture from seed to fruiting, which proved very useful since the Whites had been singularly unsuccessful at both propagation and cultivation. Blueberries are still notoriously difficult to propagate, and even with Coville's help, success was not instant.

Elizabeth described the first efforts to propagate from bushes collected from wild populations in the ironically named *Success* magazine (1927): "Next we cut up the bushes into pieces, sometimes as many as 100 pieces per bush. These were planted under glass in carefully prepared propagating beds. But, for a long time we had very poor luck; only about 10 percent lived." She and Coville eventually selected the six varieties they considered suitable for commercial production: 'Adams', 'Dunphy', 'Grover', 'Harding', 'Rubel' and 'Sam'. These were the start of a new business, propagating and selling blueberry plants within New Jersey and later to other states. Elizabeth commented (1953) that plants or varieties grown or selected at Whitesbog were grown extensively in North Carolina, Michigan, Washington, Oregon, New England and British Columbia, with lesser acreages in New York and Connecticut. Sixty acres (24 hectares) planted at Whitesbog also proved very profitable, yielding $20,000 in 1927, and the acreage was later extended to 90 acres (36 hectares).

White's devotion to both cranberries and blueberries extended to the marketing of both. She helped organize the New Jersey Blueberry Cooperative, which came into being in 1927. She was recognized nationally as a leading horticulturist and died, a much-respected lady, aged 83. (Plate 14)

Coville's work was by no means confined to the work he did with White on blueberry selection and cultivation. While carrying out his studies he made some interesting discoveries about pollination. In 1909 and 1910 he found that highbush blueberry flowers are not very successful at self-pollination. His 1910 USDA report notes that "the flowers of *Vaccinium* in the section *Cyanococcus* have flowers that naturally hang down, with the opening to the corolla—in this case the five fused petals—being quite a narrow opening." Within this tube the pollen ripens in the pollen tubes of the stamens and is released from pores on the lower surfaces "like grain out of a grain shute" on a dry, warm, sunny day. Pollen is less ready to flow on cloudy, humid days. The tips of the stamens are shaped such that they direct the flow of pollen inwards towards the central stigma within the shelter of the corolla. This means that the sticky surface of the stigma, which is designed to catch the pollen, is held downwards and is shielded by a dry rim. This rim extends outwards, diverting the pollen away from the receptive, sticky surface. Pollen grains thus tend not to arrive at their intended destination (the waiting ovules in the ovaries), and fertilization does not occur. Coville concluded that pollination by bees, mostly bumblebees, was a significant factor in producing good yields of blueberry fruit. He theorized that the bees were attracted to the nectar being produced from the surface of the disk that lies between the base of the style and filaments and that flows freely on warm, sunny days.

Another of Coville's findings that has been of lasting benefit is his realization that interspecific hybridization occurs in the wild. From the beginning he carried out many interspecific hybridizations between species with the same chromosome number. His first cross of this kind was made in 1911 using *Vaccinium corymbosum* 'Brooks' as one parent and 'Russell', a wild lowbush selection, as the other. Three thousand hybrids resulted from subsequent crosses from their progeny. From other wild selections of *V. corymbosum* made by Coville and White came the third significant wild selection, 'Sooy', and seven others. 'Brooks' × 'Sooy' resulted in 3,000 seedlings. From these 3,000 came 'Pioneer' and 'Katherine', two of the first to be released for commercial cultivation, and 'Cabot', another interspecific cross. These three, together with the fourth wild selection, 'Rubel' (which Coville introduced at the same time as 'Cabot'), enabled him to provide the early "highbush" blueberry growers with very suitable plants. Growers were given plants that were very productive, ripened early and remained compact at no more than 18 to 48 in. (45 to 120 cm) at maturity, most of them staying at the lower end of this scale. By combining genetic material from highbush and lowbush blueberries, Coville produced the first of a series of hybrids that are now known as "half highs." Half highs are becoming increasingly popular for northern gardens, especially where space is limited, although they do not figure in most modern commercial plantations. Their genes are also found in all the successful, widely grown and modern commercial cultivars such as 'Earliblue', 'Bluecrop' and, of course, 'Coville'.

By using combinations of different species, Coville also increased the range of characteristics and genetic diversity available for future crosses. These have been invaluable in producing the modern varieties used today, but because most of the modern cultivars contain genetic material in various permutations and combinations from just the original four selections

('Brooks', 'Russell', 'Sooy' and 'Rubel'), breeders have, since the 1980s, needed to look to other species for their work.

It was many years before the commercial production of northern highbush blueberries really took off and Coville did not live to see it. He died in 1937 having originated or named 15 cultivars from 68,000 seedlings. It took many years to reach these results: his first introductions took place in 1920 with 'Cabot', 'Katherine' and 'Pioneer' all coming from seedlings that arose from crosses made in 1912 and 1913. Four more, 'Concord', 'Greenfield', 'Jersey' and 'Rancocas', were introduced in the 1920s, all from seedlings resulting from crosses made between 1913 and 1916. In the 1930s the final eight were released, namely 'Catawba', 'Dixi', 'June', 'Redskin', 'Scammell', 'Stanley', 'Wareham' and 'Weymouth'. These final selections were made from seedlings arising from crosses spanning all of Coville's hybridizing career which lasted from 1913 to 1936. He named the last 'Dixi' just before he died; it means "I am done" (Gough 1995). Few of these early cultivars are successfully cultivated today, although 'Jersey' is still grown in large quantities in Michigan.

As an employee of the USDA Coville worked as part of a team, and others, notably George Darrow and O. M. Freeman, are named as his collaborators in the 1930s and as introducers of some of their named varieties after his death. These later selections, which have much larger fruit, are the most widely planted since the main wave of planting began after the Second World War. 'Bluecrop' is the standard, and growers talk about "the 'Bluecrop'" season, meaning the peak harvest. Research continues to this day, not only in New Jersey but in all states which have developed a blueberry-growing industry. The federal USDA and state-run agricultural experimental research stations cooperate with each other, exchanging both staff and information. An example of this cooperation is the variety 'Herbert' (my favorite for flavor), which was introduced in 1952. Its production involved staff in New Jersey, Washington, D.C., and North Carolina.

Many of the early pioneers of the commercial northern highbush blueberry industry in New Jersey were immigrant families from Europe, particularly Italy. The Italians tried to grow peaches and grapes as they had done in their native country. Although they were moderately successful (the wine from New Jersey can be very good), the climate and soil were both far from ideal, and many drifted to the cities like Philadelphia for work, leaving their holdings to deteriorate. Some, such as the Galletta family, saw the potential for blueberries and became involved in the emergence of this new fruit crop and are still influential and successful today. (Plate 20)

Interest in northern highbush blueberry cultivation gradually spread north and west, especially after the Second World War. Michigan gradually overtook New Jersey as the primary producing state, mainly because of the land-use restrictions imposed by both federal and state regulations in New Jersey and the much greater scope for expansion in Michigan. North Carolina and Washington, D.C., have substantial acreages, as has British Columbia, with 6,000 acres (2,400 hectares) producing around 30 million lbs (about 13 million kg) of fruit annually. During the 1990s, Oregon also began emerging as a dynamic source of production. Worldwide cultivation of highbush blueberries increased dramatically, especially during the 1990s, and is still doing so. This growth is partly the result of greater awareness of the fruit itself, and its beneficial effects on health, now well documented, are undoubtedly another reason.

Europe

The first commercial highbush blueberry plantation in Europe was probably the 25 acres (10 hectares) planted by Bergesius in Assen in the Netherlands in 1923. Piotr Hoser of the faculty of horticulture at the Warsaw Agricultural University imported plants into Poland in 1924 but they lasted only until 1929 when they were lost to a particularly severe winter. Real progress was made by Dr. Walter Heerman in Germany. He had made contact with Coville and Elizabeth White in the United States and imported plants from them in 1929. Using these he bred a number of cultivars, some of which were cultivated for fruit production. These were named 'Blauweiss-Goldtraube', 'Blauweiss-Zukertraube', 'Heerma', 'Rekord', 'Ama' and 'Gretha'. His own plantations covered 125 acres (50 hectares) by 1951.

After the Second World War, research into blueberry cultivation in Germany was restarted, notably by Günther Liebster of Munich Technical University and Professor DeHaas of the Hanover Technical University. Most of the practical research and field trials were done in Bavaria and Lower Saxony. Liebster wrote his book *Die Kulturheidelbeeren* in 1961. The largest acreage in cultivation in Europe is in Germany, mostly in the northwest, and the more than 1,500 acres (600 hectares) produces in excess of 2,000 tons of fruit a year. About 1,000 acres (420 hectares), mostly owned by fairly small businesses, is grown north of Hanover. Yields have been as low as 2.5 tons per hectare, especially on the smaller "hobby" holdings and where farmers have been tempted to grow blueberries on traditional farms in unsuitable soil. Larger, more professional farms growing blueberries in areas not formerly used for traditional agriculture and where the soil is light and sandy may produce up to 10 tons per hectare.

Wilhelm Dierking was an early pioneer, with his first plantation established in 1962 on Luneburg Heath in northern Germany. His son, Wilhelm, and daughter-in-law, Sonja, are now leaders on the European *Vaccinium* stage. They have plantations of fruiting blueberries, blueberries under polythene protection for early cropping and even a small, dry cranberry field. Their highly successful nursery produces about 300,000 vacciniums that are sold throughout Europe and beyond. Like so many other successful businesses in the early twenty-first century, theirs is a truly international blueberry business. Working with Dr. Narandra Patel and his assistant Sydney Solomona of New Zealand's Horticultural and Food Research Institute they have been responsible for testing new New Zealand blueberry cultivars for their suitability for European climates. The Dierkings also work closely with researchers and nurseries in the United States, introducing cultivars to the European scene with potential for both commercial growers and home gardeners.

In 1949 a Methodist minister on Lulu Island, British Columbia, with family connections in England wanted to do something to add a little cheer to post-war Britain. He put an advertisement in an English horticultural trade paper, offering a gift of 100 blueberry plants to anyone in Britain who would be willing to pay the postage. My father, David Trehane (who was at that time farming 120 acres or 49 hectares of mixed fruit and vegetables), and three others accepted the offer. He had sandy acidic soil in his garden and had recently taken over 100 acres (400 hectares) of neighboring land with the same soil conditions. The plants arrived in good condition, despite being a month in transit by sea, and my father planted them. Varieties 'Rubel', 'Concord', 'Jersey' and 'Pemberton' were successfully established and they fruited the following year. The berries proved extremely attractive to the birds so the small plot was covered with netting. Over the next few years, this trial established that northern highbush blueberries would grow successfully and yield regularly in the British climate on acidic soils. In my father's case they did so with little or no irrigation.

In 1959, I graduated with a degree in horticulture from the University of Reading—and with an enthusiasm for fruit growing. I needed little persuasion to return to help establish the first commercial plantation. A note from my father that read "1,000 blueberry plants are arriving on *The Queen Mary* at Southampton docks on 8 December. How about it?" was all it took. At that time, conservation was not an issue, and virgin heathland had been prepared by the market-garden staff. The plants purchased from a New Jersey nursery included 'Jersey', 'Earliblue', 'Berkeley', 'Bluecrop', 'Blueray', 'Coville', 'Herbert' and 'Ivanhoe'. They were blackened and suffering from chemical scorch because of methyl bromide, a fumigant they had endured as part of the British Plant Health requirements. The plants survived, however, and cropped well in 1961, attracting the attention of Royal Horticultural Society members and the gardening press when exhibited in London that August. Between 1959 and 1972 our family plantations were extended to 10 acres (4 hectares) under the management of my father and younger brother, and the third generation of the Trehane family, my son, David, has more than doubled the acreage with plans to continue expanding.

Research at both the North of Scotland College of Agriculture and the trial grounds based near Oban, as well as Murray Cormack's work in the 1960s and 1970s at Dundee have resulted in efforts to establish commercial crops in Scotland. Most Scottish crops failed, partly because of climatic problems, but also because of the long wait for a commercial return on the investment required. The long wait for a return on investment during the routine care of young plantations seems to be the major reason why blueberry production has not taken off in Britain.

In Holland, where much of the soil is suitable, the industry is thriving, and this small country produces around 300 tons annually. France also has an expanding blueberry industry, mostly in small units, but a larger acreage is grown for the fresh-fruit market under the control of a German grower, Walter Dietmeier. Plantations are also expanding in Spain and Portugal. Other European countries, notably Romania, Denmark and Poland, where native *Vaccinium myrtillus* has been picked for centuries, are now replacing those with cultivated North American highbush varieties where the climate allows, the berries being grown for the export market.

Japan

Japan is not, at the time of writing, a significant blueberry-producing country. Its importance is as a major customer. Interest started when the WBANA began marketing to Japan in the 1980s. Consumption increased as the larger berries of highbush blueberries became available, and these are the ones generally favored and sought year round. The berries are used in their fresh state, but there is also a thriving industry for processed blueberries. The health benefits of blueberries are of particular interest to the Japanese.

The Southern Hemisphere

In the Southern Hemisphere highbush blueberries are becoming significant crops in Australia, New Zealand and Chile, with smaller acreages in other South and Central American countries and in South Africa. The crops in these countries ripen mainly between December and April when fresh blueberries are not available in the Northern Hemisphere. The challenge that Southern Hemisphere breeders are facing is to increase the potential of their early ripening cultivars to get more fruit onto the world markets from October to December when the availability of good fresh blueberries is low.

Australia has proved a challenge for blueberry breeders because of its tremendous range of climates. Work started in Victoria in 1969 using seed imported from the United States. (Australian Plant Health regulations are probably the strictest in the world, and live plants are rarely accepted for import.) Ridley Bell, the leading hybridizer, has managed to produce cultivars to suit most climatic conditions. He uses northern highbush cultivars for the cooler areas in most of Victoria and Tasmania, and rabbiteye or the increasingly successful hybrid southern highbush for the hotter climates of New South Wales, especially north of Sydney.

Blueberry Farms of Australia (BFA) is the largest producer of blueberries in the Southern Hemisphere, exporting to Europe and Asia, especially Japan. It is based at Corindi near Coffs Harbour in northern New South Wales. The company employs around 2,000 people, estimates that it contributes around Aus. $6 million to the local economy and was floated on the Australian stock exchange in 1995. It managed to make a success of blueberry growing despite many climatic and soil problems. Blueberry growers large and small can learn from their achievements. Summer temperatures reach between 95° and 104°F (35° to 40°C) with rainfall between 37 and 790 in. (94 cm and 20 m) falling on shallow, sandy loam soils that cover a heavy, sticky clay, which causes major problems with drainage. Ridges 1½ ft. (50 cm) high and of similar width are the solution to this problem since they allow the plants' shallow, dense root system not to drown.

Humidity tends to be high, which gives rise to a host of fungal possibilities. Winters are dry, however, with only the odd frost. About 400 to 660 hours of temperatures below 45°F (7°C) provide sufficient hours of winter chill for both rabbiteye and southern highbush varieties, but not for northern highbush varieties. Most varieties grown here are low chill, southern highbush hybrids acquired from the University of Florida, Gainesville. Others produced by Australian Ridley Bell are increasingly being grown too.

With such a warm climate and high rainfall expected during most of the growing season, BFA is able to plant rooted cuttings six to ten months old directly into the beds in their plantations. They are planted into the ridges (the ridges usually already have a black plastic mulch in place, which creates an ideal environment for young roots and prevents weeds from growing) 2 ft. (60 cm) apart in the rows, which is much closer than is conventional under normal conditions. (Plate 21) The rows are 9 ft. (3 m) apart. The young blueberry plants grow so rapidly that BFA harvests a significant crop of fruit two years later, with yields peaking after another three or four years. (Plates 22, 23) The bushes are exhausted after 12 years or so, however, and have to be replaced, whereas most blueberry growers expect their plantations to continue to grow and yield successfully for their own lifetime and beyond.

Irrigation is essential to BFA's operation, and there are reservoirs dotted over the hillsides as well as nearby tanks that contain concentrated liquid fertilizers. The mineral content of leaves is analyzed weekly and a computerized feeding program calculates the fertilizer requirements for each area. Mixing is done at the tank sites and the fertililzer chemicals appropriately diluted. The correct liquid fertilizer is then sent down the pipes to the trickle irrigation nozzles that supply each plant in all of the rows. If the soil pH rises above 5.5 it can be corrected through the same pipes. "Fertigation" is the name aptly given to the combined process of irrigation and fertilization. There is also an efficient monitoring system for pest and disease identification, and sprays are applied only as needed.

Seventy percent of the Australian blueberry crop is produced at Corindi, which is on a plateau just 330 ft. (100 m) above sea level and within sight of the Pacific Ocean, 30° south of the equator. Blueberries are harvested almost all year round here. More than 495 acres (200 hectares) are farmed, producing fruit for both the domestic fresh-fruit market and for processing. Since Australian blueberries ripen between October and March when Northern Hemisphere blueberries are dormant, an increasingly important export market is being developed, with fruit being sent to Japan, the United States and Europe.

A limited effort was made in New Zealand in the 1950s to generate interest in blueberry growing. The Waikato Basin near Hamilton on North Island has vast areas of acidic organic (peat) soils, and a few farmers in the area planted mainly North American highbush varieties and some rabbiteyes. It was not until the 1970s that blueberry cultivation really took off in New Zealand. News reached Northern Hemisphere growers that 600 acres (240 hectares) had been planted in the late 1970s, and as these plantations came into production and the volume of fruit built up, there were insufficient markets in New Zealand to buy the fruit and many small growers went out of business. This problem was solved when markets were found overseas, especially in Japan. In 2000 New Zealand shipped about 1,130 tons overseas, earning NZ $6.8 million, three times as much as in 1996. Much of the increase is the result of New Zealand growers promoting the health benefits of blueberries.

A world-renowned breeding program has been established in New Zealand, most of the developments coming after 1985. Narandra Patel supervises the program, which is based at the Ruakura Research Center, Palmerston North. Three varieties were released in 1989 under license from the HortResearch organization: 'Nui' (Maori for big), 'Puru' (meaning bright) and 'Reka' (meaning blue). They are also proving successful in Europe and the United States. Cultivars that include other *Vaccinium* species and hybrids intended for ornamental gardens as well as fruiting are being worked on.

Chile has been increasingly active in developing its blueberry industry. In the 1999 to 2000 season, highbush blueberry production reached 5,500 tons, which was an increase of 17 percent over the previous year. With ever increasing acreages coming into production, the tonnage is expected to reach 14,000 tons within a year or two. Chile claims to supply approximately 4 percent of the world market and to have exported to 26 countries, including the United States, Canada, Japan, Holland, England, Italy and Germany, mainly between December and April of both 1999 and 2000. It is interesting that all are Northern Hemisphere countries anxious to keep the supply going through their off-season.

Requirements for Cultivation

Site, soil, climate and a suitable water supply are the chief factors to consider, whether growing northern highbush blueberries for fruit production in

121

the garden or on a larger scale. An understanding of the stages of growth and the needs of the plants helps in providing the right conditions for a good crop of fruit.

Site

Planting on a slope encourages air drainage, the cold air sinking to the bottom of the slope and thus reducing the risk of frost damage to plants on the slopes, especially during the flowering period in late spring. It is generally recommended that the later blooming varieties be planted at the bottom of a slope and the earliest near the top. Keep in mind that light, sandy soils on a steep slope may be eroded if not stabilized.

Sites that are very windy during the growing season tend to have more stunted, lower-yielding plants than those which avoid these winds. On excessively windy sites where small areas are planted, it is better to use an artificial windbreak material than to plant a shelterbelt of trees because trees can provide too much shade. Their roots can also compete with the blueberries for water and nutrients. If a large area needs sheltering, then a quick-growing hedge of trees may have to be considered.

Where small areas are planted, such as in a home garden, the microclimate will tend to be more benign than in a larger area, meaning that it will probably be warmer and less windy. Such congenial conditions will encourage earlier flowering and fruiting.

Soil

Blueberry bushes, like all plants, require soil for root anchorage and for a sufficient supply of water and minerals necessary for growth and fruit formation. Both the physical and chemical characteristics of the soil are important. It took Coville's work on the growing conditions of wild blueberries in New Jersey to reveal that blueberries actually required an impoverished soil low in nutrients before plants were successfully cultivated. Northern highbush blueberries require a soil pH between pH 4.0 and 5.2, with the optimum being between pH 4.3 and 4.8. It is within this ideal range that the balance of minerals they require is available. Some commercial plantations have a natural soil pH of 5.5 or even slightly higher, and growers must make the required minerals available by using mulches and fertilizers.

A soil containing a large percentage of sand particles is good since that mix creates a well-drained, well-aerated base in which the fine fibrous roots can spread. It is even better if there is a 20 to 30 percent portion of smaller clay particles mixed with the soil because this encourages water retention in summer as well as root anchorage. Too many clay particles will create a heavy, compacted soil with poor aeration and drainage that results in a poor root system and sickly plants. Pure sand is suitable provided plenty of organic matter, usually peat (pine or fir bark is becoming more widely used), is incorporated before planting and some form of irrigation is provided to make up for the rapid loss of water in summer. Additional fertilizers become critical too.

The importance of organic matter cannot be too greatly stressed. Blueberry bushes planted on sites recently cleared of forest or heathland benefit from the residue of many generations of fallen leaves and other detritus. This organic matter not only increases soil acidity but also produces a suitable environment for soil microorganisms (mostly bacteria) to slowly rot the matter down and release a gradual supply of minerals to the blueberry roots. Sites where large quantities of brushwood have been burned are not suitable because the high levels of potash in the ash are harmful.

Naturally acidic soil that was recently used to grow vegetables or other fruit may have been limed and will probably not be successful immediately. Either let the soil remain fallow for a couple of years to allow it to return to its natural acidic state or use powdered sulfur to bring the pH down more quickly. This powder should be incorporated into the soil at least six weeks before planting and needs to be done with care as too much sulfur can lower the pH to dangerously low levels. Professional advice should be sought.

Soil that has pH 3.5 or less releases toxic minerals, and soil with an even lower pH than this may be completely destroyed. Levels between pH 5.5 and 6.5 are certainly not generally recommended, but many gardeners with this range on poor, sandy loams manage surprisingly well. All incorporate plenty of acidifying peat, leaf mold or rotted pine or fir bark in the soil before planting, or they use a similar organic mulch and acidifying fertilizers. Naturally alkaline soils with pH 7.0 or more should not be expected to grow blueberries successfully. The plants will fail to grow and will gradually turn yellow before giving up and dying. Blueberries, like cranberries and many other ericaceous plants, benefit from the presence of a mycorrhizal association.

Drainage

Highbush blueberries do not like to grow in waterlogged soils. Their fine fibrous roots need oxygen and are prone to root rot diseases such as

Phytophthora cinnamomi when it is lacking. They are actually quite tolerant of drought but yield better if kept moist and have access to plenty of water during the peak times of growth in summer. A water table ranging from 12 to 32 in. (30 to 81 cm) below the soil surface is ideal. Where the water table is consistently higher than 12 in. (30 cm) below the soil surface, soil ridges are usually constructed in which to plant the young blueberries. These ridges should be 12 to 20 in. (30 to 50 cm) high and 2 ft. (60 cm) wide.

Water

An irrigation system is part of most plantations where the water table is likely to be below the reach of the suction power (or capillary action) of the lowest roots. It is critical for blueberry growers to have access to a good supply of clean water with a low pH. Some have storage ponds or tanks where water is collected during the winter months; others have boreholes or wells, which bring water to the surface from underground sources. The really lucky growers have running streams of clear, pure water to draw from. No matter the source of the water, it is analyzed before planting begins and at regular intervals thereafter to make sure that it is suitable not only for the blueberries but also for those eating the berries, especially if overhead sprinklers are used.

Water supplied directly to the root systems by a trickle or drip system is the most common method and also the most economical, especially for young plants, since water is delivered slowly and steadily to the area where it is needed without splash and wastage. The bushes remain dry, which has its advantages both for ease of harvesting and for reducing fungal problems in humid conditions in which they are more likely to thrive. Water moves downward and, to a limited degree depending on the soil type, laterally as well.

Drip or trickle irrigation systems consist of polyethylene tubing laid alongside the plants through which water is supplied to give the volume required to maintain the health of the plants. An emitter or nozzle is placed beside each plant. The volume of water varies according to the soil type, amount of organic matter in the soil, age of the plants and so on. One line placed on one side of the plants is adequate for the first two or possibly three years, but as the plants grow, a second line is needed. This second line is laid down the rows on the other side of the plants to ensure that water reaches more of the roots' system.

Even more sophisticated systems allow nutrients to be added to the irrigation water as required, which is called fertigation. Very low doses of nitric acid may also be added to lower the pH if necessary. Regular analysis of leaf samples tells the grower exactly how much of each mineral is needed.

Climate

The reaction of highbush blueberries to climatic conditions is discussed in detail earlier in this chapter. Generally, they will grow and crop in most cool to cold temperate regions where winter temperatures include at least 700 hours at about 45°F (7°C), which provides a sufficient period of dormancy. Most varieties will be unaffected by winter temperatures of 0°F (−18°C) and even lower if there are not too many fluctuations. They are vulnerable to late spring frosts occurring after flowers have opened and growth has started.

Temperatures above 86°F (30°C) in summer may cause damage in the form of scorched leaves, especially on plants in rapid vegetative growth that are in full sun. At these temperatures roots are unable to take in water fast enough to compensate for the loss of water by transpiration from the leaves. Remember, blueberry roots do not have root hairs to give them as much surface area for absorption as most other plants. Leaves in full sun can also absorb and hold heat, so they may be 50° to 59°F (10 to 15°C) warmer than the air around them.

Soil preparation

Ideally, soil is prepared during the summer before planting, the destruction of all perennial weeds a top priority. Once the weeds are safely destroyed, the ground can be dug, ploughed or rotavated.

If the planting area is well drained and has a water table that is unlikely to saturate the root system for long periods either in winter or in summer, planting can be done after the soil has been leveled. However, where the soil is not well drained enough to remove excess water after a heavy rainfall or if the water table is high enough so that roots remain surrounded by underground water for long periods, then ridges are usually created. At the BFA plantations, where the soil is on the heavy side and monsoon-type rainfall frequent, ridges have been constructed to prevent roots from drowning. In Britain, where some plantations are on low-lying land with the water table regularly less than 12 to 16 in. (30 to 40 cm) below the soil's surface, ridges 6 to 8 in. (15 to 20 cm) high and 3$\frac{1}{3}$ ft. (1 m) across have been created.

Planting positions or rows can be marked, and if the soil is a mineral one deficient in organic matter, moist peat or finely chipped pine or fir bark may be added to a depth of 4 to 6 in. (10 to 15 cm) along the rows. This organic matter can be spread about 3 ft. (90 cm) wide and mixed in with the top 6 in. (15 cm) of soil, which will give the roots from the new plants a good environment to grow into.

In the wild, vigorous, spreading plants of northern highbush blueberries at maturity will occupy about a 7 ft. (2 m) diameter, possibly a little more, above the ground. Upright, nonspreading cultivars take up about 5 ft. (1.5 m). In commercial settings, growers ignore variations in vigor and habit in their mixed plantations. All plants are given the same spacing, and some overlapping of branches at maturity is expected. Home gardeners or small producers may wish to vary their spacing, especially if they have limited room.

The spacing of plants within rows varies between 3 and 5 ft. (90 and 150 cm). Closer spacing is used where high yields are required quickly but the plants will, in six or seven years' time, become too dense, which usually results in a drop in yield. Plants that are intended to have healthy yields for the long term are given wider spacing. A naturally fertile, organic soil will tend to induce more naturally vigorous plants, especially in good climatic conditions. A less fertile soil in similar climatic circumstances can produce equally vigorous plants if a regular fertilizer is applied as well as adequate irrigation.

The space between rows may be as little as 8 ft. (2.4 m) for hand-picked plants or as much as 12 ft. (3.7 m) for those that are machine harvested. If the latter is being planned, the cultivars are planted in blocks of two or three rows. This design allows for both the habits of bees carrying out pollination and the efficient use of harvesters. A wide headland is left to allow room for turning machinery.

Growers with a small, hand-picking business are not as restricted in their choice of cultivars and usually need about 1,000 plants per acre (2,500 per hectare). This arrangement allows for about 4 ft. (1.2 m) between plants in the rows and 10 ft. (3 m) between the rows. Many growers take pride in offering a wide range of cultivars of good flavor, to give a long picking season but do not necessarily choose varieties with a long shelf life, especially if they are selling fruit from the farm gate. The same applies to home growers.

Sourcing plants

Buying plants, including blueberry plants, from nurseries by mail order from a different part of one's own country or from other countries around the world has, with the growth of Internet shopping, become much more prevalent. While buying over the Internet has widened the choice of available plants, it has also increased the risks. It is difficult or impossible to return an unsatisfactory plant to a nursery several hundreds or even thousands of miles away. The old saying "caveat emptor" or "buyer beware" has never been more relevant. That said, there is a certain excitement about receiving a newly released cultivar from a reputable nursery with which you have established a good relationship.

Whether buying locally or from a nursery thousands of miles away, it is wise to make sure that plants to be supplied are certified as being pest and disease free. It is equally important to make sure of the varieties ordered, and if plants are being imported from another country or state, the local Agricultural and Horticultural Office should be contacted about what, if any, certification is required for importation. Additionally, any documentation that is needed from the supplier nursery, which should itself be an approved exporter, can be requested. In most countries, nurseries that export plants are inspected by plant health inspectors at least once during the course of their growing season, and each consignment is inspected just before it is shipped. Movement between countries is varied. Some importing countries have very few if any restrictions (this is the case when trading among European countries), while others such as the United States, Australia and New Zealand have many stipulations and insist on quarantined and bare-rooted plants. Bare-rooted blueberry plants intended for shipping may have most of their compost removed but usually their root systems are wrapped in polythene with a lightweight, sterilized medium such as damp peat, moss, sawdust or vermiculite included to prevent desiccation. Specialist nurseries are often accustomed to the mail-order system, where plants are sent by post or courier company, and they not only have the biggest range of cultivars on offer but also a good knowledge of their subject, which they are happy to pass on. These specialist nurseries are usually the best source for those wanting a large number of plants or a range of cultivars or for those buying interstate or from overseas.

The best time to buy plants is when they are dormant, especially if they have to travel. However, since most plants are now grown in containers, they can be bought at any time of year if being bought locally. Most commercial growers in cold climates buy in the spring shortly before they plan to plant out because they prefer to get their plants into the ground and growing quickly, as soon as the soil warms up in fact. They seldom buy in the fall as this means they have to either overwinter plants in nursery beds themselves or plant them out and risk frost "lifting," which exposes roots during severe weather.

Blueberries have a dense, fibrous root system that, in their natural habitat, spreads freely and produces active new roots in all directions. When confined in a pot or can, this system is restricted and can easily become pot bound. It may take a year or more for the roots of a pot-bound plant to escape, resulting in a plant that is not vigorous or active during or even beyond that year. The best plants to buy are those that are two to three years old, are active and strong and have not become pot bound. Plants may also be available as field-grown plants. They are lifted to order, their roots being wrapped in plastic, burlap or hessian. Provided these plants have a substantial root ball, they grow away quickly, particularly if they are planted a month or so before their aerial growth breaks dormancy.

One-year plants (they are known as plugs) or rooted cuttings are the best choice for shipping as they are less bulky and weigh less, meaning that transport costs are lower. However, they need nursing on in containers or a nursery bed, possibly under a low plastic tunnel that can later be removed in summer, to start with to maintain humidity if they have been bare rooted.

Choice of cultivars

The range of northern highbush cultivars available is such that a fruiting season can last about 12 weeks on average. The season would start with a variety such as 'Earliblue' and end with 'Elliott' or 'Nelson'.

Local conditions may influence the choice of cultivars. Some of the more "high chill" cultivars are ideally suited to the long cold winters of the more northern climates. Most of these carry a high proportion of lowbush genes and have a flexible growth habit that allows the plants to bend but not break under the weight of snow. Others will grow and yield well in areas where winters are relatively mild but still have the requisite 700 hours below 45°F (7°C). Late-flowering cultivars are obviously less risky in areas where spring comes early, but late frosts can be a problem. For home growers whose main motivation for growing blueberries is the production of fruit, flavor is very important, and personal taste will be a major consideration.

Commercial growers probably aim to sell as much fruit as possible as fresh fruit. (The other options are to freeze the fruit and sell it during the off-season or to send it for processing.) They will want a range of cultivars that span the picking season. If the fruit is headed for supermarkets, it must have a good shelf life, usually of at least five days from receipt of the consignment, so the berries should have only a small scar and not tear or split easily. Fruit sold at the farm gate or from local outlets does not need to have such a long shelf life, but appearance and flavor are all important. Bigger growers who use mechanical harvesters have to consider other factors: cultivars should ripen over a relatively short period, should need picking over only twice, should become easily detached by shaking but only when ripe, should be firm so as not to become easily squashed or bruised and should have a small scar where the stalk was attached to reduce the risk if fungal or bacterial infection.

I have listed the cultivars below in approximate order of ripening but the order may vary slightly from climate to climate and even from year to year in the same plantation. Since *Vaccinium corymbosum* is a complex species with very unclear parentage, I refer to these fruiting cultivars by their cultivar names only.

'Earliblue' ('Stanley' × 'Weymouth') was introduced in 1952. It is vigorous, hardy, open and upright but is susceptible to stem canker (*Phomopsis vaccinii*). It needs well-drained soil. The medium-large, light blue, firm fruit is borne in medium-loose clusters and is resistant to cracking. The flavor is moderate and the berry is low in acidity. Its chief merit is its early ripening.

'Bluetta' ({lowbush × 'Coville'} × 'Earliblue') is a consistently productive cultivar that was introduced in 1968. It is compact and slightly spreading, reaching 36 to 48 in. (90 to 120 cm) at maturity. 'Bluetta' is hardy, especially in its resistance to spring frosts. Loose clusters of small to medium, firm, light blue berries have a good "wild blueberry" flavor but a rather wide scar. It needs to be picked promptly as it does not hold well on the bush. It is a useful garden cultivar because of its compact, tidy habit, and it has particularly good, brilliant red fall color. (Plate 34)

'Duke' ({'Ivanhoe' × 'Earliblue'} × {['Berkeley' × 'Earliblue'] × ['Coville' × 'Atlantic']}) was introduced in 1987. It has a strong, stocky appearance and produces broad, upright, well-spaced canes. Although it ripens early it flowers late, making it good for areas prone to late spring frosts. 'Duke' requires more hours of winter chilling than most but is consistently productive, with firm, light blue, medium to large fruit that has a small scar. It ripens over a fairly short period and is a favorite for machine harvesting. The flavor is only moderate but improves to pleasantly aromatic if the fruit is left for a few days after picking. (Plate 24)

'**Spartan**' ('Earliblue' × 'US 11–93') was introduced in 1977. It has a vigorous, upright, rather open habit and reaches 5 to 6 ft. (1.5 to 1.8 m) at maturity. Hardy and late blooming, it prefers well-drained soil with plenty of organic matter. This cultivar produces large to very large firm berries with a moderate scar and needs only two pickings. The fruit has a very good, rich flavor that is sweet yet tangy. Fall color is a pleasing orange-yellow.

'**Patriot**' ({'Dixi' × a lowbush selected in Michigan} × 'Earliblue') was introduced in 1976. It has a vigorous, open, moderately upright habit. 'Patriot' is productive, very hardy and tolerant of relatively heavy wet soils with some resistance to root rot (*Phytophthora cinnamomi*). The medium blue, large to very large firm fruit is produced in rather tight clusters. It is slightly flat with a small scar and an excellent flavor. Berries must be picked carefully as they may appear ripe at first glance but may still have "red backs" and be unripe. Ripening is concentrated so it needs picking over only twice. 'Patriot' is a good variety for ornamental or fruiting use since it has a mass of brilliant white blooms in spring, attractive dark green summer foliage and brilliant orange-red fall color.

'**Northland**' ('Berkeley' × '19-H') is a spreading, productive bush to 4 ft. (1.2 m) high and wide at maturity that was introduced in 1967. Probably the most cold hardy northern highbush cultivar, it is adaptable to a wide range of soils and easy to grow. It is capable of high yields of round, firm, small to medium berries with a small firm scar. The flavor, however, is moderate.

'**Collins**' ('Stanley' × 'Weymouth'). Introduced in 1959, this upright, vigorous, hardy bush is productive but a little erratic with the odd off year. The large firm fruit is resistant to cracking and holds well on the bush when ripe. Berries have a good flavor that is low in acidity.

'**Bluejay**' ('Berkeley' × {'Pioneer' × 'Taylor'}) is a very vigorous plant introduced in 1978. It produces long, strong stems, making it an upright, slightly open bush sometimes up to 7 ft. (2 m) tall. It is hardy, blooms late and has attractive fall color. Although it is moderately productive, the firm, medium to large fruit has a small scar and lasts well on the bush without cracking or dropping quickly. Berry flavor tends to be mild but there is a pleasant tang to it. (Plate 25)

'Blueray' ({'Jersey' × 'Pioneer'} × {'Stanley' × 'June'}) is vigorous, open and upright. Introduced in 1955, it has plenty of strong canes that are produced from the base of the bush in late summer. The fruit, which grows in tight clusters, is large to very large and firm. Berries have a small to medium scar, do not crack easily and have a good flavor, especially in warm climates. The bright red fall color and winter stems are attractive ornamental features.

'Bluecrop' ({'Jersey' × 'Pioneer'} × {'Stanley' × 'June'}) is the most planted of all northern highbush blueberries. Introduced in 1941, it provides the bulk of the crop worldwide, which is reflected in commercial growers sometimes talking about "the bluecrop season." Although vigorous and upright, it is also spreading with a tendency to overproduce long, strong, single canes throughout the bush. It is hardy, drought tolerant and easy to grow. The fruit clusters are large and loose with firm, large to very large berries that are resistant to cracking. There is a tendency to pick too soon resulting in "pink backs" and stalks, which tend to stay attached, being harvested. If berries are picked when fully ripe, their flavor is good.

'Toro' ('Earliblue' × 'Ivanhoe') was introduced in 1987. A very hardy culti-var, it has been put forward as a variety complementary to 'Bluecrop'. It has a robust appearance, with strong, sturdy, well-spaced, upright growth once established. The fruit starts to ripen at the same time as that of 'Bluecrop' but its season is more concentrated so it finishes earlier. Yields are consis-tently good and the fruit's flavor is good. Large firm berries are produced in large, long clusters that may extend to 12 in. (30 cm) and have only a small scar. 'Toro', a stocky bush, is proving popular as an ornamental or fruiting blueberry because of the flower buds that open a brilliant pink and mature into pure white flowers, the young bronze growth and the deep red fall color. (Plate 26)

'Ivanhoe' ('Rancocas' × 'Carter') is a vigorous, upright plant with sturdy, well-spaced branches that was introduced in 1952. The fruit cluster is medi-um-loose with large to very large berries. Although resistant to cracking, the berries soften quickly after ripening and do not hold well on the bush, especially in hot weather. The flavor is excellent and highly aromatic with a slight tang. (Plate 27)

'Hardyblue', an old established variety in the northwest of America, it is useful because it grows in most soil types, including clay. It has a vigorous upright bush that produces vivid orange fall color and bright red stems all winter. The medium fruit is firmer than most of the other blueberries and exceptionally sweet, making it ideal for baking.

'Berkeley' ('Stanley' × {'Jersey' × 'Pioneer'}) from 1949 is vigorous and strong with widely spaced, rather brittle branches. It tends to grow too tall and "woody" unless pruned properly in the early years. Although it is hardy, inducing dormancy can be difficult and the plant frequently produces flowers in mild falls. A productive variety, the berries grow in loose clusters and are large to very large and an attractive light blue. The flesh is firm, sweet, resistant to cracking and low in acidity but it has a large scar.

'Chandler' ('Darrow' × 'M-23') was introduced in 1994 and is another vigorous, upright and well-branched selection. It has a slightly spreading habit and large leaves. Fruit yields, which continue over a long ripening season of six weeks, are consistently high in areas where winter is not too severe. It probably has the largest berry of all with excellent flavor. (Plate 28)

'Rubel' is one of the original selections from the wild made in 1912. Reintroduced in the 1990s by some nursery catalogs because of its extremely high levels of antioxidants, it is the most healthy highbush blueberry and is also excellent for baking. Tall and upright, reaching 7 ft. (2 m) at maturity, it produces a regular, heavy crop of small dark berries of intense flavor, not unlike that of "wild" blueberries. Its fall color is very bright.

'Legacy' ({'Elizabeth' × 'US75'} × {V. darrowii 'Fla. 4B' × Bluecrop}) is a 1993 cultivar with a vigorous, slightly spreading habit to 6 ft. (1.8 m) tall. It flowers a little too early for cold areas that are prone to late spring frosts, but produces very high yields of medium to large, light blue, firm berries in less demanding climates. Berries have a dry scar and an excellent flavor. In warmer areas this cultivar remains evergreen, and in colder areas the leaves turn a bright orange.

'Herbert' ('Stanley' × {'Jersey' × 'Pioneer'}) from 1952 is hardy but a little fussy about soil conditions. If grown in well-drained soil with plenty of organic matter, the bush is vigorous, open-spreading and not too tall. The large to very large, quite dark fruit tends to soften quickly after ripening and has a large scar. Its chief merit is its superb flavor. It is an excellent choice for garden use and small-scale growing, particular since its fall color is a very attractive bright red. (Plate 29)

'Bluegold' ('Bluehaven' × {'Ashworth' × 'Bluecrop'}) from 1988 is a variety that has started to attract attention because of its value as both a landscape and fruiting plant. It forms a rounded, compact, bushy plant up to just over 3⅓ ft. (1 m), with bright white flowers in spring. Heavy crops of large clusters of berries are of good size and flavor, and they are easy to pick. Its fall color is yellow with winter twigs of the same color, making it an excellent, all-round variety. (Plate 30)

'Olympia' is a variety that was introduced in 1933. A large spreading bush that produces a mass of canes, it is easy to grow with attractive bright green leaves that turn bright red in the fall. The firm, dark blue fruit is medium to large with an excellent, slightly spicy flavor. This variety can be prone to late spring frosts.

'Jersey' ('Rubel' × 'Grover') is a very vigorous, open and upright cultivar that was introduced in 1928. It grows very tall, up to 7 or 8 ft. (2 or 2.4 m) in some places. Very hardy, it is traditionally the main cultivar in Michigan, where most of the fruit goes for processing. Loose clusters of small to medium berries have a small scar, and although the fruit holds well on the bushes, it lacks flavor. 'Jersey', which is still widely available, is among the easiest to propagate and grow.

'Chandler' ('Darrow' × 'M-23'), an introduction from 1994, is an excellent variety for home growers. The fruit ripens over a long period of six weeks or more, producing high yields of very large firm berries of excellent flavor. The bush is vigorous, upright and well branched.

'Dixi' ({'Jersey' × 'Pioneer'} × 'Stanley') is a vigorous, open, spreading bush that was introduced in 1936. It is a hardy cultivar with aromatic, good-tasting fruit that is large to very large. The scar is large, however, and the fruit is prone to cracking.

'Darrow' ({'Wareham' × 'Pioneer'} × 'Bluecrop') from 1965 is a hardy, upright, vigorous bush. The very large, slightly flat fruit holds well on the bush without dropping or cracking. It has firm flesh with a small scar, and the flavor is slightly aromatic and rich with a slight tang. 'Darrow' needs regular pruning to maintain fruit size, especially in warmer areas where yields are heavier at the expense of size.

'Nelson' ({'Bluecrop' × 'G107'} × {'F72' × 'Berkeley'}) was introduced in 1965. The bush is vigorous and produces plenty of canes. The fruit is of medium size, medium quality, light blue and rather too firm for most tastes. Fall color, however, is a spectacular bright red.

'Coville' ({'Jersey' × 'Pioneer'} × 'Stanley') from 1936 is hardy, vigorous and upright. The berries are borne in loose clusters and are large with firm flesh and a small scar. They hold well on the bush without dropping or cracking. Berry flavor is good with a slight tang and an aromatic flavor that is best when fully ripe. As a late ripening cultivar, it does best in areas where the climate is warm and sunny late in the season.

'Brigitta' is a 1977 introduction from Victoria, Australia. This cultivar is upright, vigorous and highly productive. Berries are large, mid-blue and firm with a dry scar. They taste sweet and have a slight tang. They travel well and store exceptionally well, lasting up to six weeks in a refrigerator. (Plate 31)

'Elliott' ('Burlington' × ['Dixi' × {'Jersey' × 'Pioneer'}]) was introduced in 1973. A vigorous, upright bush, it is very hardy and blooms late, thus missing most spring frosts. Firm, medium fruit has a small scar and is ideal for baking. This cultivar is best suited to regions where there is plenty of sun late in the season to ripen the fruit and bring out its flavor, otherwise it remains tart and without its true taste. In the right climate it can be harvested in one or two pickings. The fall leaf color is deep red, and in winter its wood is an attractive, deep burgundy.

Cultivars from New Zealand are raised by HortResearch at the Ruakura Research Center in Hamilton and are currently available from licensed nurseries round the world. Their parentage indicates very good hardiness characteristics. The list is in order of ripening.

'Nui' ({'Ashworth' × 'Earliblue'} × 'Bluecrop') was introduced in 1989. It ripens very early, at the same time as 'Earliblue', but its yields are heavier. Large to very large fruit with good color and flavor is produced in fairly tight clusters. This cultivar has become the first choice for growing as a protected crop in cooler climates. Under glass or polythene, it can be harvested a month or more sooner than if grown without protection.

'Puru', a sister seedling of 'Nui', ripens at about the same time. Introduced in 1989, it produces very large fruit of excellent flavor in medium clusters.

'Reka' was introduced in 1989 and is the third sister seedling in the trio. Although the fruit is slightly smaller, yields are very high and of excellent flavor. A potentially very valuable commercial cultivar, 'Reka' is the perfect choice to start the season.

Among the problems faced by breeders is that the gene pool of northern highbush blueberries is relatively small and breeders are running out of permutations and combinations. More species are being introduced so that desirable characteristics such as disease resistance, compact ripening period (this would allow for mechanical harvesting), firmness of fruit, better flavor and an extended season can be enhanced.

One introduction from 1988 is 'Sierra', an interspecific hybrid that includes at least four species: *Vaccinium darrowii*, *V. ashei*, *V. constablaei* and *V. corymbosum*, which is itself probably a hybrid. 'Sierra' has an upright bush, is vigorous and productive and is likely to be hardy. It needs more chilling hours than many highbush cultivars. Fruit yield is high with firm, medium berries that have a small scar. The flavor is good, and ripening occurs with 'Bluecrop' at midseason.

Planting

The time of year for planting depends on local conditions and personal preference. In areas where winters are not likely to include severe frosts, it is best to plant in the fall as soon after leaf fall as possible while roots are still active and shortly after making final soil preparations. This way, weeds should be under control and annual weeds will not germinate or survive the winter, while some blueberry roots should start to grow and get the plants established. If winters are severe, with temperatures expected to drop below 18°F (−8°C) for sustained periods, and if the soil is expected to freeze deeply, it is better to wait until the spring thaw to both receive plants and get them into the ground. In the light, often sandy or peaty soils where blueberries are often grown, there is a danger of frost heave. Those planting in the spring may need to anticipate wet ground as well as rapid weed germination that will compete with the blueberry plant.

Before planting, plants are checked over to make sure their root systems are moist and healthy, and they are given a good soaking if necessary. If dug from open ground, any obviously broken roots should be trimmed. Pots or wrappings are removed. Pot-grown plants should not need any attention, except those that are pot bound and therefore unlikely to establish well should be rejected. Whatever the growing conditions, all the plants need to be planted into moist soil, and facilities to provide a good soaking after planting if necessary should be available.

Plants grown in the open ground should have their roots well spaced in all directions in the planting holes and they should end up being no deeper than they were when they were purchased, especially if a mulch is applied soon after planting. Once the soil has been replaced, it should be firmed in and well soaked so that water reaches the whole root system, not just the top few inches.

Pot-grown plants should have any branches bearing flower buds removed so that future energy can be concentrated on establishing both roots and shoots in the first year. Open-ground plants may need more pruning to give the plant balance since a proportion of their root systems is likely to be missing.

If planted in the fall, plants should be checked during the winter to make sure they have not been lifted by frost or washed out by excessive rain. Heavy rain can result in the "gullying" of sandy soils but grass sown between the rows stabilizes the soil. Grass does have to be mown regularly, however, and it should not intrude into the rows because it is difficult to control, especially during the fruiting season when berries are easily knocked off by mowers and weed-eaters (strimmers).

Mulching

Growers have long appreciated mulches. Fruit yields are regularly higher in mulched plantations. Organic mulches can suffocate weeds, reduce their seed germination, may increase soil acidity and provide valuable minerals as they rot. They reduce fluctuations in soil temperature both in the heat of summer and in the cold of winter. Additionally, and very importantly, organic mulches reduce the loss of moisture by evaporation in hot dry conditions. They should be placed onto moist soil to a depth of 6 in. (15 cm) in an amount that is sufficient to cover the area occupied by the root systems. Mature plants need a diameter of about 3 ft. (90 cm) of mulch around them.

Sawdust, when available, has always been the favorite mulch, whether from hardwood or softwood trees. Fine wood chips, especially those from fir or pine, are increasing in popularity, both in small commercial units and in home plots since many people have their own wood chippers and shredders and like to recycle prunings. Care needs to be taken to avoid wood infected with honey fungus (*Armillaria mellea*) because some forms of this fungus may invade a blueberry's root system and eventually kill the plant.

Soft materials such as straw and grass mowings are sometimes used but are not recommended. Straw rots down quickly and provides the wrong type of nitrogen salts for blueberries. Grass clippings, if used, must be taken from areas *not* treated with herbicide and should have had a season of rotting, as fresh grass can produce sufficient heat to steam during its decomposition, which will obviously damage roots. Fresh sawdust should be allowed to "weather" until the whole heap loses its fresh smell, which may happen in less than a year if it is turned three or four times. Wood chippings are also best if allowed to start decomposing over a year or more; if they are used before rotting starts, they are more likely to deprive the bushes of available nitrate from the soil for the bacteria to carry out their own rotting process. Blueberry plants showing chlorosis and stunted growth as a result of nitrogen deficiency may well suffer over more than one growing season because the chippings take years to decompose. Additional nitrogen fertilizer (ammonium sulfate) compensates for this.

Black plastic has been used as a mulch but there is debate about its benefits. Soil temperatures in the summer are often high and the shallow root systems therefore overheat. This in turn causes root stress and sometimes death, especially in young plants. Where it is used, growers establish trickle irrigation systems below it.

Whatever the makeup, any decomposing heap needs to be mixed at least a couple of times during the year prior to its use because this encourages even activity of the bacteria that are responsible decomposition. Any harmful salts produced in the early stages will be washed out by rain. Applying mulch is a laborious business that is too expensive for many large commercial plantations but sawdust mulch that is 6 to 8 in. (15 to 20 cm) deep will last for three or four years, gradually shrinking as it rots. It will need topping up to bring it up to its original level before the benefit of the mulch is lost.

Cultivation and Maintenance

In cultivating and maintaining highbush blueberries, the main aim in the early years is to build up the framework of young plants so that they will have a structure on which to produce fruit. Vegetative growth is therefore wanted, and this means there has to be an adequate supply of water and minerals, a good light supply, plenty of oxygen both in the ground and around the plants and no competition from weeds.

Irrigation

Although blueberries are surprisingly drought tolerant, they do need water for all their life functions. In most areas young plants will need to be irrigated because the sort of soils suitable for blueberries do dry out quickly, although some growers using organic mulch may get away without irrigation in cooler areas with high summer rainfall. It is important to remember that water is needed to dissolve solid fertilizers into a suitably dilute form and then to transport the solute into the roots. Liquid fertilizers also need to be transported into the plants.

The general recommendation is that each plant should receive about $1\frac{1}{2}$ in. (3.8 cm) of water a week. The application can be split into two if the soil is becoming dry at root level, usually defined as at about 2 in. (5 cm) below ground level. As plants get bigger, their water requirement increases. The amount they need will vary in different soils, so a knowledge of each soil type and its ability to hold water is useful. It is, of course, sensible to apply the water before the soil becomes dehydrated, making sure that the soil's water deficit is corrected by applying enough to bring the moisture level up again. A good test is to dig down to root level with your hand and see how far down the moisture level is. Dryness in the first 2 in. (5 cm) or so is not a problem, especially if the top layer is kept friable, since that reduces loss by evaporation. It also encourages roots to grow deeper into the soil in search of water, which is of long-term benefit to the plants. However, dry soil with no hint of moisture below 2 in. (5 cm) indicates that action is needed. Once wilting of plants or complete drying out of the soil occurs, it takes a great deal of water to rehydrate the soil, by which time irreparable damage may have been done to the plants.

Fertilization principles

The need to add fertilizers to encourage highbush blueberry plants to grow and provide fruit regularly is generally accepted. The reasons behind this fertilizer use as well as the type and amount to be applied is perhaps less well appreciated, however, as is the part played by organic matter in the soil.

Most people contemplating growing blueberries, especially if commercially and even if it is on a small scale, have the soil analyzed for soil pH and nutrient content before planting. They repeat this analysis every three or four years thereafter. Leaf analysis, which is used regularly by commercial growers with established plantations, reflects the actual uptake of minerals by the plants. This information may be useful for any grower, especially where blueberries are failing to thrive and advice is needed. Laboratories and advisory organizations in all countries carry out this work and also give recommendations. However, once the plants are established, the best type of "analysis" is by growers who get to know their plants and can soon tell if something is wrong. An inexpensive pH kit is probably the only necessary investment, and it needs to be used regularly as a high pH is the cause of so many chemical imbalances in blueberries.

Using fertilizers

In common with other cropping plants, blueberries need the primary elements of nitrogen (N), phosphorus (P), and potassium (K) as their regular fertilizer constituents. These elements should be added to the soil regularly, usually once a year, but twice on mineral soils where rainfall is high in the growing season. Nitrogen is by far the most important element, and nitrogen fertilizers are sometimes the only ones used on organic soils where reserves of other elements are available. The secondary elements calcium (Ca), magnesium (Mg) and sulfur (S) are needed in smaller, less regular amounts. As their name implies, the trace elements or micronutrients boron (B), copper (Cu), iron (Fe) and molybdenum (Mb) are used in very, very small amounts and are usually added only if deficiency symptoms appear. Trace element deficiencies are most effectively corrected by specific foliar sprays.

In organic soils, such as those that blueberries grow in in the wild, a constant supply of rotting leaves and other vegetation gradually forms layers over the years and decomposes very slowly. This organic matter gently supplies the minerals that the plants need at the time they need them, which is during the warm summer months when they are actively growing and producing fruit.

Fungi and bacteria digest the vegetable matter, using available nitrogen from the soil in the process to build up their own bodies. Oxygen is needed for this process, so well-drained, well-aerated soil is essential. It is only when these organisms die that nitrogen is released for the benefit of the plants, so that they in turn can create the proteins needed for growth. There is therefore a time lapse between the supply of organic matter and the supply of available minerals from it, especially where nitrogen salts are concerned. In nature this delay does not matter because everything is in balance, but if you take plants into an artificial situation, artificial measures must be used to restore that balance. This is particularly true of blueberries, which, although grown on mineral soils, are usually entirely lacking in minerals available for plant nutrition.

The need for artificial measures also applies when organic matter arrives suddenly (especially if in the form of a partially rotted mulch) instead of over a period of months and years. The organic matter needs to take in nitrogen before it can give it up. The other elements required for growth are also supplied through their release during the rotting process. Unlike nitrogen salts, these elements are more persistent in the soil and less easily lost through leaching.

I deliberately refrain from suggesting the amounts of fertilizer to use as that depends on so many variables. Getting local advice is best. The main fertilizer requirement is for nitrogen, the need for which is difficult to assess as it is so quickly used or leached from the soil, especially in free-draining soils with a high sand content. Most growers simply get to know their plants and feed them accordingly. As a very general guide, mature plants may need 100 lbs (45 kg) of nitrogen fertilizer per acre, assuming there are 1,000 plants per acre. Plants less than four years old will need half that amount. A leaf analysis should be sought if symptoms of any mineral deficiency are seen, especially since the results are usually accompanied by advice.

Nitrogen (N). This element is essential for the manufacture of protein, for plant growth, for building up the structure of the plant and for flower-bud formation. It needs to be used sensibly though, as excess nitrogen can result in too much soft vegetative growth, a lack of flowers and fruit that fails to ripen. Soft growth late in the summer can lead to frost damage since the shoots fail to mature before winter. Bark splitting is also likely.

Nitrogen is available in ammonia (NH_4) and nitrate (NO_3) form and is appreciated best by blueberries in its ammonium form. Ammonium sulfate or urea is the most acceptable salt for blueberries. Both are very soluble and quickly absorbed by blueberry plants, their presence being evident in the greening leaves within two to three weeks after application. Ammonium sulfate also has a particularly acidifying effect on the soil and should be used on soils with a pH above 5.0. If used too regularly or too heavily on naturally acidic soils that are being watered by a naturally acidic water supply, the pH is likely to drop too low. Urea is less acidifying and is useful where the pH is below 4.5. Urea is sometimes used as a foliar feed, especially to correct nitrogen deficiency, but care should be taken with timing as it can scorch both leaves and fruit, especially when temperatures are high in summer. Urea also evaporates at high temperatures so an evening application on a dull day is recommended. Since most of the liquid reaches the plant in the form of run off from the foliage into the soil, liquid feeding is preferable if possible. Excess minerals should be washed off by overhead irrigation to avoid leaf or fruit scorch.

Nitrate salts are sometimes used because they are readily available for purchase and are commonly used on farms for grass and arable crops and in garden stores for vegetable growing and general garden use. In whatever form they are used, if they are the only source of nitrogen, the result on blueberries is likely to be poor growth and reduced yields. Many proprietary garden fertilizers include both ammonium and nitrate nitrogen and are much more acceptable.

A symptom of nitrogen deficiency is pale yellow coloration, especially on older leaves that may become red and drop off early. If not corrected, growth becomes stunted and fruit yields are poor.

Phosphorus (P). This element is used in the manufacture of proteins so it is needed to build up the plant, including encouraging good root formation. It is also used in the day-to-day activities such as transferring the energy needed for sugar manufacture in the leaves during the summer months.

Phosphorus is usually supplied as superphosphate in fertilizers. This element is insoluble in water and is broken down by a complex process in the soil before being made available to the plant. It is a slow process that leaves relatively immobile chemicals in the soil, which explains why phosphorus remains available long after the more mobile and rapidly available nitrates and potassium salts have been used up or washed away.

Phosphorus deficiency is not a common deficiency in blueberries, as it is so persistent in both soil and plants. Symptoms include pale leaves with a purple tinge at the tips, with lower leaves becoming dark purple.

Potassium (K). This very interactive and mobile element is involved with several other elements in many of the day-to-day functions of the plant. The use of potassium by a heavy crop of berries may exceed the uptake and deficiency symptoms seen in the leaves for a few weeks. The symptoms then disappear once the crop has been picked. Potassium is usually supplied as potassium sulfate, which is water soluble and has a neutral affect on the soil. When potassium is in short supply, it is quickly transported to the areas of greatest demand, namely to the young leaves and shoots. Thus, the older leaves are the first to become deficient. Brown spotting followed by color-less older leaves with red margins appear as first symptoms, followed by yellowing between the veins on young ones. The death of the growing point of young shoots produced in late summer, especially on plants carrying a heavy crop, may be another symptom.

Magnesium (Mg). This element is vital in the making of chlorophyll, the transfer of energy during sugar manufacture and the production of healthy flowers. Usually supplied as magnesium sulfate (Epsom salts) or as potassium magnesium sulfate. On soils where the pH is below 4.0, magnesium limestone or dolomitic lime is used to help raise the pH.

Symptoms of magnesium deficiency generally appear late in the summer just before or during harvest. Red coloring of the outer parts of older leaves on the lower branches happens first, with green remaining around the veins. The resulting characteristic "Christmas tree" effect generally identifies a magnesium deficiency. Leaves may have brown spots and yellowing, or they may become red and then brown later.

The trace elements iron, boron, copper, manganese and zinc are all necessary, in very small amounts, for the growth of healthy blueberry plants. Leaf analysis will show if any are deficient and recommendations for correction may be made. It is not a good idea to apply these elements unless deficiencies are actually shown because some, especially boron, can be toxic to plants if given in excess. Others such as iron, manganese or copper, if applied to the soil (especially where the pH is high) simply become "locked up" and unavailable. These micronutrients are usually supplied as foliar sprays under expert guidance.

For gardeners and small-scale commercial growers, the easiest means of applying fertilizer is to buy a compound, granular fertilizer that is formulated for plants that prefer acidic soils (the ericaceous plants) and scatter it over the ground. These are usually proprietary products that are available in most horticultural and gardening supply stores. Granules should be spread evenly under the canopy of the plants where the roots also extend. They should not be placed too close to the stems or in concentrated lumps because this can cause root damage. Rain will usually dissolve the minerals and wash them down, but if conditions become too dry, as they usually do in summer, some form of irrigation should be used.

The amount of fertilizer used will depend on the soil, whether an organic mulch has been used, the size of the plants and the size of the crop they are supporting. Splitting the application into two doses is advised, since this gives the required boosts in the form of a fresh supply of nitrogen that cater to the two spurts of active growth. Vigorous plants growing in mineral soils that are low in organic matter will also benefit from the potassium and phosphorous contained in general fertilizers, but bear in mind that these elements are retained longer in the soil than nitrogen and an excess can cause problems. One application just before the buds break in spring and another in midsummer is often recommended. Where there is high rainfall and excessive leaching, fertilization may be split into three doses.

Since the fertilizer requirements of blueberries are relatively low and the roots are easily damaged by strong chemical solutions, most advisers advocate not using additional fertilizer in the first spring after planting young blueberries, although a small dose in midsummer is advised. Many recommend that no fertilizer be applied at all in the first year if the soil is naturally fertile or if a slow-release fertilizer has been used in the nursery compost and has not been fully released. As a very rough guide, squeeze a polymer-coated pellet, and if more than a small drop of liquid comes out, there is probably sufficient left to last for a few months of growth.

Most newly planted young plants probably benefit, however, from a very light dressing of fertilizer in midsummer and another a month later, especially on mineral soils or those plantations using an incompletely rotted organic mulch. By midsummer new roots should have emerged from the root ball and the plants should be in active growth. Application needs to be done when the soil is adequately moist to allow the fertilizer to dissolve and be absorbed in sufficiently diluted form to benefit the plants. Dry conditions can result in concentrated chemicals being in the soil, which can cause root scorch because of plasmolysis, the reverse of osmosis, in which water moves out of the root cells and into the soil. If plasmolysis is suspected, the excess chemicals should be flushed out of the soil with plenty of water.

As the plants grow they will of course use more nutrients and need more fertilizer. The amount required depends on several factors, and growers soon learn the needs of their plants by observing leaf color and general vigor. Sandy soils with no mulch will quickly allow fertilizer to leach away, whereas soils containing more clay particles will hold both water and nutrients for a longer time. Recently mulched soils need more nitrogen fertilizer to fill the needs of the bacteria that rot them down.

Many proprietary fertilizers are on the market for both commercial and home growers, including some for use on plantations producing organic fruit. Cottonseed meal, which provides a good, safe base and a supply of balanced fertilizer, is available in the United States but generally not in Europe. Mineral fertilizers formulated for other ericaceous plants like camellias, azaleas and rhododendrons are recommended, especially for home growers who can buy them at any European garden store. Ericaceous plants prefer gentle, gradual fertilization, and many fertilizers designed for them are based on organic materials that are gradually released over eight to ten weeks. Those derived from seaweed seem to be ideal for blueberries but tend to be low in nitrogen.

In dealing with soils that need acidifying (that is, where the pH is over 5.2), a fertilizer mix with a ratio of 14–8–8 that contains ammonium sulfate and diammonium phosphate for nitrogen is a good mix for most soils in this category. If the soil is already acidic (below pH 5.0), use urea to provide the nitrogen in an 18–10–10 mix.

Slow-release fertilizer granules designed for top-dressing are being used increasingly since they are easy to apply: just one application a year at bud break in spring is needed. They are designed to release their minerals gradually over the warm growing season, with none being wastefully released during the cold months of dormancy. An analysis of 14–13–13 is fine for most areas. Extra nitrogen may be needed, however, especially in areas of high rainfall where minerals are quickly leached out and on organically mulched plantations.

Liquid feeding is a practical alternative for those who have drip lines or low-spray nozzles for irrigation. It is used extensively in areas where rainfall is low during the growing season and on big commercial enterprises where regular leaf analysis is done to monitor the needs of the plants. Liquid feeding is a much more accurate method of applying minerals because the liquids can be mixed to the correct proportions and to safe dilutions in containers situated in the irrigation supply line. Many home gardeners have drip lines for watering their plants, and adapters are available for incorporating liquid fertilizer supplies too. There are also adapters that can be fitted to handheld water hoses. Acidifying fertilizers are available, as are those that provide more neutral fertilization.

Weed control

Weed control, especially during the first two years when the plants are young, is very important. Most small plantations that fail to succeed are those that do not undertake such measures. Young highbush blueberry plants are quickly swamped by competition from more vigorous weeds that take water and nutrients and also exclude light and air. Vigilance during these first few months of spring and summer in those first few years will prevent a capital investment—and much preparatory work—from turning into a liability. It is easier to destroy small weeds than large ones.

Whatever the size of the plantation, an area approximately 5 ft. (1.5 m) wide around the plants (the area within which the roots are expected to spread) should be maintained weed-free. Black plastic or organic mulch helps accomplish this. In between the rows, the ground can either be kept weed-free using herbicides or a sward that is established and kept mown to prevent seed from forming.

It is best to hand weed within the rows of recently planted small areas for the first year as damage from hoes and herbicides is more likely with young plants that have root systems concentrated in small areas near the soil's surface. Hand weeding is not generally economic in larger areas, and growers use either mechanical hoes or herbicide sprays or granules. Controlling weeds with herbicides is by far the most economical method, but only those listed for use on blueberries should be used. Great changes are taking place in how these chemicals are used, so seek advice from the local agricultural or horticultural advisory body before purchasing or using any.

Broad spectrum contact herbicides that act quickly by being absorbed through the leaves of green plants and that are deactivated very rapidly in the soil are excellent, especially when applied to actively growing weeds. They should not be allowed to contact any green part of blueberry plants, however, especially young ones. Hooded spray-heads are useful to prevent risk of chemicals landing on the blueberry bushes. Pre-emergent herbicides that kill germinating seeds of weeds are also available, as are those specifically designed for grasses and sedges or broad-leafed weeds. All herbicides must of course be used with care and with due regard for soil and weather conditions.

Pruning

The importance of pruning highbush blueberries should not be underestimated if steady yields of accessible, good-sized berries are to be maintained year after year for the 50-plus years of the life of the bushes. Light pruning may be needed when plants are young but will increase as they mature.

The timing of pruning can affect the timing of flowering in the following spring. In some of the colder areas that are subject to late spring frosts, it is sometimes desirable to encourage late flowering. Early pruning immediately after harvest results in a delay of up to a week in flowering the following year. It also encourages a flush of late growth if fall temperatures remain high. Pruning as early as this is not desirable where fall temperatures continue to be warm enough to encourage growth and where frosts are expected during the winter since all or most of this late growth will be killed. Flower-bud formation may also be adversely affected. In the main highbush blueberry growing areas of the Northern Hemisphere, it is traditional to prune after Christmas once plants are fully dormant. Pruning can continue until just before growth starts in March.

Assuming that newly set plants are two to three years old and of good quality (meaning they are strong, with three or more strong branches and healthy root systems), they should need only to have any spindly twigs removed and shoots bearing flower buds cut back at planting time. This encourages plants to concentrate on building themselves up instead of putting energy into fruit in their first growing season.

During the first growing season after planting out, much of the growth activity occurs underground as the roots reach out and establish good anchorage and an efficient system with which to absorb water and nutrients. Growth above ground will probably be limited to short branches and some flower-bud initiation. Pruning can be limited to removing most of the flower-bearing twigs and tidying up any low or spindly wood. Just a few flower buds may be left on the strongest plants—a reward for two years' work is deserved!

After the second growing season, more strong branches should be growing well and some may be about 2 to 3 ft. (60 to 90 cm) high. Although some flower buds may remain, those plants that have set too many flower buds at the expense of vegetative growth should have most if not all these buds removed. Poor, twiggy growth should also be cut back. Any flower buds at the tips of tall growth that is likely to bend to ground level or even break with the weight of berries should also be removed.

After their third growing season, plants should have a good framework and start to produce more berries. The plants will continue to develop over the next few years, gradually being allowed to yield more fruit. They must be pruned for the rest of their life, however, if growth is to be encouraged. As they mature they form a substantial crown from which the canes develop. (Plate 32) Highbush blueberry bushes are not considered mature and fully yielding until they are eight to ten years old.

All plants have a natural tendency to achieve a balance between root systems and the canopy of branches above ground, and blueberries are no exception. Balance is achieved in nature when the ultimate natural size of the plant has been achieved for its particular species or cultivar and situation. It will continue to fruit and grow, but the fruit tends to become small as the plant gets increasingly woody and "senile." Many highbush blueberry bushes grow taller and taller with berries far above head level. Branches crowd together, and the competition for light means that canes become spindly and produce poor fruit or none at all. An ideal environment develops for pests and diseases to flourish. In cultivation we demand healthier bushes with accessible, bigger, better fruit. Pruning is the answer; it stimulates the vegetative growth, which forms the framework that carries future crops. It keeps the bush "juvenile" and active, and transport systems within it remain efficient.

Pruning should be done consistently every year with the aim of encouraging steady regular fresh growth and consistent annual yields. The policy when pruning is to encourage enough growth in the current year to produce next year's crop while leaving enough of last year's wood to produce this year's crop. It should maintain the balance between roots and shoots. Regular harsh pruning disturbs this balance because over the years the root system decreases in proportion to the amount of canopy removed.

Pruning removes dead or spindly wood as well as branches that have done their job and produced a crop but have no more vigor left for future cropping. It also leaves space for new growth to develop. The general recommendation is that a mature bush should have six to ten strong, healthy canes that vary in age from one to six years old. One-year-old canes bear the biggest fruit in clusters near their tips, while those older than that will bear lateral branches that are expected to carry the bulk of the crop.

Varieties have slightly different growth habits so some adjustment in pruning technique is necessary when moving from one to another. In those varieties that tend to overyield and produce masses of small berries ('Jersey' is one such variety), fairly severe pruning reduces the number of branches and leaves fewer, stronger ones that will bear bigger berries. In those cultivars that tend to produce an excess of canes such as 'Bluecrop', some thinning of new canes should be done. Most growers aim for a framework of up to ten canes per bush.

Old branches that have become thick and woody to the base also need to be removed. These tend to develop on varieties such as 'Berkeley', which produces a relatively small number of thick young canes that are usually left too long because they, in turn, produce more such canes from higher up the plant. It is sometimes difficult to make the decision to cut these back as they often produce the biggest and best berries, but cutting the tallest back will encourage branching from lower down. Cultivars such as 'Earliblue' tend to produce leggy plants that also become too tall for berry pickers to reach. These leggy cultivars need to be cut back hard enough so that vigorous canes will probably develop behind the cut. Twiggy varieties that have become too dense and bushy also need their branches thinned by cutting them to the base.

Low branches or those that may bend low with the weight of fruit should also be cut back, as should those that intrude too much into the space between rows. Likewise, any canes that have developed low down in the bush, especially in its center, late in the previous season and that are still green and soft will not mature before the onset of cold weather and so should be pruned. They usually die at their tips during the winter and fungal infections creep in, not only here but also on the immature bark of the stems. Any canes growing from the ground away from the main bush (these are known as suckers) will also need to be removed; they can sometimes be pulled out with a sharp tug, but should otherwise be cut back to base with secateurs.

The main branches of neglected blueberry plants that are an inch or more in diameter can either be sawn off in stages over two to four years (one would start with the biggest and oldest branches), or the whole plant can be felled with a chainsaw. Gradual rejuvenation keeps the plant cropping and encourages big berries, but it is a skilled job to maintain the balance between encouragement of new growth and the maintenance of productive branches. Complete felling means accepting no crop for one year and very little in year two; however, it does result in a completely juvenile "new" bush that should yield better fruit and be more manageable in the future.

The stumps start to produce buds from the bare wood, and these buds quickly grow into shoots during the first summer. They usually develop into a mass of canes that may need thinning to remove the weaker ones and leave a spaced framework of strong branches. This is especially true in prolific varieties such as 'Bluecrop'. In the second summer there should be some large fruit at the tips of these shoots, provided there has been no frost or fungal damage during the winter. Lateral branching should develop from vegetative buds behind the fruiting area, and these branches may be expected to provide a good crop of quality berries in the third summer after felling.

In varieties that are not prolific cane producers and that tend to produce canes from older branches, it is good policy to pinch out some of the growing tips once they have four or five maturing leaves behind them, typically during the second growing season. This means compromising the first crop of berries, but it is worth it in the long term. From then on it is a case of keeping the bushes cropping using the same management system as is used with younger bushes.

Pests and diseases

The most troublesome pests for anyone growing blueberries are fruit-eating birds, followed by mammals such as deer and rabbits that may damage bark and eat foliage, especially young shoots or fruit. Other mammals that are native to a particular country may also compete with us for the berries. Among the most damaging but also amusing pests in Britain is the European badger (*Meles meles*). There is nothing more annoying than watching a family of these heavy-bodied mammals feeding at dusk, pulling laden branches down, snapping them as they do so, and feasting on the fruit. Their piglike grunts of satisfaction and communication and the joyful antics of the young do, however, bring a smile to your face. Those living in bear country might not be quite so amused by the competition.

Most mammal predators can be excluded from blueberry plantations that are surrounded by a strong, wire-netting structure. It needs to be at least 8 ft. (2.4 m) high to keep deer out. Rabbits and badgers may attempt to burrow under the wire netting. Surprisingly, most rabbits (but not badgers) are deterred if the base of the netting is laid on the soil surface and extended for about 12 in. (30 cm) and then covered with soil sods. The sods soon grow grass and become anchored by the roots. Burying the netting 9 to 12 in. (23 to 30 cm) is effective too, but the acidic nature of typical blueberry soil destroys the lower parts of it in three to five years. Electric fencing may have to be used to deter the most persevering animals during the summer, the charges coming at certain intervals and especially at night. Whatever type of wire structure is used, it will need regular checking. Expect also to have to make repairs—these animals have good taste and are very persistent!

Voles and mice can be a problem in some areas of the United States. Many gnaw the bark of blueberry bushes, damaging the conducting vessels responsible for transporting water up to the canopy of the plants, and their burrows can interfere with roots. They seek the protection of long grass, so clean cultivation and regularly mown grass helps control them. In extreme cases growers may have to resort to poisoned bait that is approved for the purpose.

Birds are serious pests in small plantations or in gardens in urban areas where bird feeders and nesting sites proliferate. They usually wait until the berries are just beginning to color and then swoop in and remove them before they have a chance to ripen. Unprotected garden plants may lose 100 percent of their berries, and the average loss in unprotected commercial plantations is accepted as being, on average, about 20 percent, with the higher losses in semi-urban situations.

Most of the damage is done by a wide variety of berry-eating birds. The smaller ones such as the finches peck the fruit, moving from berry to berry leaving damaged but not devoured fruit behind them. Larger birds like pigeons, starlings and crows not only eat whole berries but also break the young growth that bears the following year's flower buds as they land and take off. The only effective measure is bird netting. In small home or commercial plantations, a support system is constructed, usually using the mammal predator netting as the mainframe. Strong, lightweight nylon netting can then be used to cover the area. Most growers devise a system that enables them to roll back each block of netting for the winter to prevent snow from settling on it. Using equipment supplied by the netting manufacturers, they then roll it out again and link each block to the next.

Large commercial enterprises have to rely on other methods. Helium-filled balloons variously shaped to look like birds of prey are designed to swoop down as the wind blows; these are sometimes effective but are very attractive to human predators in semi-urban areas who cannot resist shooting at them. Gas-controlled imitation cannons that make loud, gunlike explosions are quite good, but may annoy the human population and must certainly be turned off at night. Electronically controlled transmitters that emit the calls of predatory birds or the distress calls of the bird species that are invading the plantations can also be effective, but such instruments may interfere with local radio and television reception.

It is sometimes permissible to shoot some bird pests, such as pigeons and crows. A few clusters of feathers from a dead pigeon scattered around the plantation can be an effective follow-up. The old farmers' method of suspending a dead bird here and there, however, is not popular with pickers or customers.

Highbush blueberry plants are largely trouble free in home plots and in countries where there is no long tradition of blueberry growing or a concentration of commercial plantations. We have never had to use fungicides or insecticides on our 40-year-old plantations in Dorset, England, although we have had low levels of insect and fungal attacks, which we have monitored carefully. These attacks have either been controlled naturally without our involvement or have remained at sufficiently low levels of activity to be tolerable. Blueberries lend themselves to organic cultivation (where no pesticide has been used) in such situations.

Pests and diseases are more likely to be a problem in the United States, particularly in the East Coast states and in Oregon and Washington in the West where there are many acres of cultivated blueberries. Nearby wild blueberry populations can also sometimes act as reservoirs for pests and diseases, some of which are also common to other members of *Vaccinium*, such as cranberries.

As with cranberries, IPM is encouraged in dealing with highbush blueberries' pests and diseases. Weed control is important as it reduces the habitats where pests can shelter or pupate and hibernate. It is useful too, especially in plantations being managed on organic principles, to observe surrounding habitats and, if possible, to control the pests being harbored there. It is essential to regularly prune and remove and burn all debris, and to remove all unwanted fruit from the bushes. Beneficial insects such as ladybirds often hibernate in the angles of branches during the winter. They are effective natural predators on pests like aphids, which may damage young shoots and leave sticky honeydew on which mold fungi grow or they may transmit viruses to uninfected plants.

When a pest or a disease has been identified, the grower has to decide whether or not to spray. The cost of spraying has to be balanced against the threat of the pest or disease to the crop's commercial value. Where significant damage is likely to occur to any part of the plants, or if a potentially serious long-term problem has been identified, then there is no choice but to get the sprayer out. Some chemicals are suitable for organic plantations, and local advisory bodies are the best source of information about which chemical is both suitable and permissible.

Choosing when to apply pesticides is just as important as choosing the type to use, and local advice is again highly recommended. The value of both hive bees and wild bees must be considered because they are so important for pollination. Systemic sprays (those that are taken in and circulated within a plant) should be avoided close to and during flowering. Contact insecticide sprays should be applied when hives are not in the plantations and wild bees are not working, meaning that application should take place very early or very late in the day and during cool weather. Powders should be avoided because they can be picked up by bees and taken to the hive or nest, where they can kill the whole colony.

Spray operators in both a garden setting or commercial unit should read and follow instructions carefully, wear protective gear and make sure that all surplus chemical is washed out and disposed of safely without damaging water courses. Most countries offer training courses for all categories of operator; in Britain they are compulsory for commercial enterprises.

Most commercial growers walk their plantations at least once a week during the summer, from bud burst through harvest. They follow the three principles of observation, identification and action. Many have strategically placed sticky traps, which attract and catch insects and help with the identification and scale of any attack.

There are only about 20 pests that may at some time be a problem in blueberry cultivation, of which only five or six are of sufficient importance to warrant a regular spraying program in commercial plantations.

Wasps are a common problem everywhere, especially to human pickers during the harvest, as are ants. Fire ants may also build colonies under blueberry plants, creating tunnels that cause roots to dry out. Wood ants build tall mounds sometimes among the blueberry plants to shelter their colonies and have a nasty bite if frightened. Many ants, however, act as natural predators for insect pests. Fruit buds may occasionally be affected by a variety of cutworms, spanworms or the cranberry weevil, which may damage developing flowers. One insecticide spray applied before blooming should control these three pests.

The pests I list are generally more problematic for commercial growers but they could also be a problem in one area but not in another, nearby area.

Blueberry bud mites (*Aceria vaccinii*) overwinter beneath bud scales and dormant flowers, and as these start to develop in spring, they move to the next generation of flower buds as they form. Eggs are laid beneath the outer scales of these buds and the mites feed on the tissues beneath them, destroying the buds so they fail to open and flower in the following spring. Infected bud parts are discolored with a rough red appearance. Control is by using a higher than normal pressure spray of a suitable acaricide or insecticide after harvest.

Blueberry maggot (*Rhagoletis mendax*) is the larva of a fly. It is a significant pest especially since recently hatched larvae feeding within the berries are not easily detected. Berries that become soft and mushy and collapse after picking should be closely checked.

The adult fly looks much like a small housefly but with white bands across its pointed abdomen and with black banded wings. The female lays a single egg under the skin of a berry as it begins to turn blue. Each female can lay up to 100 eggs, thus destroying at least 100 berries. Dead flies can sometimes be seen with their ovipositors still stuck inside the fruit. Larvae hatch after seven days and feed on the pulp of the fruit, the skin of which gradually turns pale and fails to develop. Larvae fall to the ground after about 21 days and burrow into the mulch or leaf litter, where they pupate and sometimes remain for up to three years.

Since this pest is also endemic among other *Vaccinium*, growers should observe both wild and cultivated plants closely. Where it is already a known pest, yellow sticky traps baited with ammonium acetate or protein hydrolysates (there are trade names for these) are used. In commercial plantations, about three traps per acre are set among the bushes to act as monitors, and spraying is carried out when three adults per trap per week are caught. If infestations are not too heavy, growers using organic methods set more traps and expect to catch a high enough proportion of the insects to prevent significant loss of fruit.

The choice of insecticide is very important because larvae may be feeding over virtually the whole of the ripening period and because fruit will be harvested at least twice during this time. The insecticide needs to be "residual" or absorbed by the berry if it is to be absorbed by the feeding larvae but it must also be of very short duration so that the fruit should be free of chemical at harvest. Growers harvest all the ripe fruit just before each spray application. They may have to repeat the spray every seven to ten days, preferably using a tractor-mounted machine, since the spray reaches fruit clusters low down in the bushes more effectively. Aerial spraying is used over some of the biggest plantations, especially when ground conditions are unsuitable for tractors.

Blueberry stem borers (*Oberia* spp.) are found especially in plantations and gardens that are near rhododendron and laurel populations, as well as in wild and cultivated blueberry areas in the eastern states of the United States. The first obvious sign of damage is the wilting of young shoots about 4 in. (10 cm) or longer in midsummer. A double ring of puncture holes below the wilted area indicates the area where adult females have laid their eggs. Pale brown beetles with long antennae may be seen, but their larvae, which are active and feed within the stem, actually cause the damage. Removal of the shoot several inches below the wilted portion should halt the life cycle and prevent the larvae migrating down the stems. If they are not halted, larvae can continue feeding until they reach the base of the stems, overwinter and then attack more stems in a second summer before pupating in their third spring and emerging as adults that summer.

Where infestations have become established, other signs to look out for are blobs of frass emerging from holes in the stems and little piles of frass at the base of plants. Canes are eventually killed. The only way to control these stem borers is to remove all infected canes as soon as possible, including host plants in surrounding areas. Spraying is not practical.

Cherry fruitworm (*Grapholita packardi*) is a serious pest in all major blueberry-producing areas. The adult moths are dark gray with brown bands on their wings and can be seen at dusk. The females start to lay their small white eggs on the undersides of the young leaves during the flowering period. More may be laid on the green fruit. The eggs hatch into black-headed white larvae after about a week, and these then enter the fruit through the calyx. The larvae gradually darken from white through pink to red and feed on the pulp within the fruit, reaching about $1/4$ in. (5 mm) in length. The shriveled berries fall to the ground while the larvae move on to their next target. Each larva may devour several berries within a cluster during its 21 days of feeding. They then leave the fruit and seal their exit holes with silk plugs, which may hold a second berry within the plug. They pupate and overwinter in debris below the bushes or under the bark of older branches or stubs.

Removing all debris, pruning older branches and getting rid of old rotted stumps (known as "boot pruning") undoubtedly helps. Small infestations can be controlled if affected fruit clusters are removed by hand, but if plants are regularly affected, an insecticide spray should be applied as soon as pollination is complete and flowers drop, then repeated two weeks later.

Cranberry fruitworm (*Mineola vaccinii*). The fruitworm's female moths lay their eggs inside the calyx rim on the outside of young green fruit, particularly of early and midseason ripening varieties. After about seven days the eggs hatch and tiny green larvae migrate to the stem end of the fruit where they enter and eat the pulp of the berries, often forming a web that enmeshes several berries together. Affected berries turn prematurely blue and are smaller than healthy fruit. After about three weeks the larvae emerge from the fruit or their webs, leaving a plug or trail of excreta or frass. They fall to the ground, pupate and overwinter in trash or in mulch. This pest should be controlled the same way the cherry fruitworm is.

Weevils such as the black vine borer (*Brachyrhynus sulchatus*), black vine weevil (*Otiorhynchus sulcatus*), rough strawberry root weevil (*O. rugosotriatus*) and others can inflict considerable damage, especially to young plants. They are not specific to blueberries. Nursery plants in containers are especially vulnerable. Larvae cause the significant damage by girdling the bark at the base of stems, cutting off the supply of water from the soil and eating young roots.

Black vine weevils are a major pest in nurseries, gardens and strawberry plantations throughout the world and are among the most difficult to control. Chewed leaves, especially if a circular cut is made, indicate adult feeding. Adults, which are brown with small spots on their backs, are visible during the day in summer almost anywhere, even climbing up windows, but they tend to rest under debris until nightfall, which is when they start to feed. They can run quite fast but feign death if disturbed.

The best way to prevent this pest is to inspect the root systems of newly purchased plants, looking especially for the white grubs with brown heads in the deepest area of the root ball. Drenching containers with one of the specially prepared nematode drenches, which are widely available, is also effective when temperatures are between 50° and 77°F (10 and 25°C). Chemical drenches are also appropriate. The best controllers of pests in the ground are pheasants and other birds that eat ground grubs. Otherwise, a soil fumigant on soil that is known to be infested works well. Professional advice should be sought if an infestation of black vine weevil is suspected.

Scale insects, notably putnam scale (*Aspidiotus ancylus*) in older neglected plantations, generally suck sap from the foliage, leaving honeydew on leaves and fruit on which sooty mold fungus then grows. This makes fruit inedible and reduces the efficiency of the leaves. Scale insects are controlled by regular pruning to remove old woody growth. Severe infestations can be controlled by using "superior oil" or "white oil," which is sprayed on the plants during the dormant season and smothers the insects.

Sharp-nosed leafhoppers (*Scaphytopius magdalensis*) do not do significant damage themselves but may carry the pathogen responsible for blueberry stunt disease. The adults are brown-gray, about $1/4$ in. (5 mm) long and wedge shaped. They lay their eggs on leaves shortly after appearing in mid-summer. The nymphs have a white hourglass-shaped mark on their backs. A spring application of an insecticide might be sufficient to control this insect, but a repeat spray late in the summer may be needed in warmer areas.

A number of fungal and bacterial diseases cause damage and loss of crop, but as with pests, they are much more of a problem in established commercial plantations or in areas where wild populations of blueberries or other compatible host plants are growing. They are much less likely to occur where weeds are controlled, where plants are well cultivated with space for good air circulation and where sufficient fertilizer is provided to maintain plant vigor but not overfertilized to produce overlush growth. Low-level irrigation by seep hose or trickle is better at keeping fungal and bacterial diseases to a minimum than overhead systems.

Gray mold (*Botrytis cinerea*) is such a universal disease infecting many plants around the world that it hardly needs describing. It is most damaging in areas where spring and summer tend to be cold and damp, especially in maritime or mountainous regions. Plants that have been grown too soft by overuse of fertilizer and water and those watered by overhead irrigation are most vulnerable. It affects young shoots and leaves, flowers and fruit.

The fungus overwinters on infected twigs, especially on prunings left on the ground or in leaf litter. Tough black bodies or sclerotia form. They germinate in wet conditions in spring, releasing spores that are carried onto vulnerable tissues by the wind. Shoot tips, especially those that are frost damaged, developing flowers and soft, young leaves are all vulnerable, as are tight clusters of fruit or fruit developing among dense foliage. The infection can spread fast throughout young tissues, especially in wet weather. Newly infected parts become brown, black and then gray as the mycelium spreads.

Control is by prevention first in the form of good cultural techniques. Spraying with an approved fungicide initially during the blooming period is often necessary in susceptible areas.

Mummyberry (*Monilinia vaccinii-corymbosi*) is probably the most widespread disease affecting blueberry crops in almost all countries. It may reduce yields by up to 10 percent in severe infestations of some main commercial areas. It is often confused with frost damage or early-stage botrytis and, like so many fungal diseases, is worst in cool, wet weather during bud break and flowering.

The life cycle of this fungus begins when infected berries or twigs are left on the ground or bush from the previous season. Infected berries overwinter on the soil surface or just a fraction below it as sclerotia. When conditions are favorable (meaning when temperatures reach 15°C or more and there is 30 to 40 percent moisture in the air around them), the sclerotia produce small, cup-shaped bodies that release spores into the air. Emerging shoots or flowers quickly shrivel and blacken if these spores land on them. The fungus continues to develop on the dead tissues, and about two to three weeks later produces a mass of spores. The spores are carried by the wind and pollinating bees to the opening flowers and are responsible for the main damage to the plant. The ovaries are infected making the developing seeds abort, and the flesh inside the berries is replaced by fungal mycelium. Lastly, the berries turn pink (they fail to develop to the next, blue stage) and fall to the ground, where they mummify and overwinter as sclerotia. Even if they do not get the right conditions for germination, they can survive on or near the surface of the soil for several years.

Prevention starts with good hygiene around the bushes but control is usually carried out by burying the sclerotia. Burying involves cultivating the soil around the bushes in late winter or early spring so that as many sclerotia as possible are an inch or more below the soil surface. A mulch applied at this time is also effective, at least for the current year. Fungicide sprays can also be used at both bud break and flowering.

Twig blight (*Phomopsis vaccinii*) is another fungus that is spread by infected twigs left on the bush or the ground from the previous season. Spores are released in spring from bud break to petal drop. Twig blight is particularly damaging to shoot tips weakened by frost or mechanical equipment because the fungus spreads rapidly down the stem, destroying the best flower buds up to 4 in. (10 cm) or so behind the terminal buds. It can also affect the whole plant, including the fruit, in severe cases. 'Blueray' and 'Earliblue' are more susceptible than most varieties. Control is achieved through good hygiene or the use of a fungicide from the time buds swell to full bloom.

Stem blight (*Botryosphaeria dothidea*) is a disease that is of particular danger to young plants, both in the nursery and in one- to two-year-old plantations, where plants are not yet growing strongly. Since the fungus can enter through cuts, it is best to leave susceptible plants unpruned until they are stronger. The sudden death of an isolated stem is often the first sign of stem blight. Examination of other stems may reveal browning of just one side of the stem, with chlorosis or reddening of leaves that do not fall. Infected stems, sliced vertically, have brown discoloration of the woody tissues within them. Controlling this disease requires cutting out infected stems to well below the infected tissue. Vigorous plants that are not soft are less susceptible to infection.

Phytophthora root rot (*Phytophthora cinnamomi*) is a worldwide fungus that thrives in waterlogged soils with low oxygen levels, both in containers and in the open ground. It is a particular problem in areas such as Florida and in New South Wales, where heavy rainfalls combined with high soil temperatures are experienced. It is also found in plants grown under glass or polythene tunnels. Once established in the soil it is difficult to eradicate, so prevention is the answer.

The following symptoms, if seen in poorly drained areas, often indicate phytophthora: a general lack of vigor, chlorosis of leaves and defoliation and premature reddening of the leaves. Wilting, especially early in the day, is another symptom of damaged roots, followed by the plant's complete collapse. Improved drainage is the only long-term solution, which may be achieved by planting bushes on ridges. Managed irrigation to prevent over-watering is also important. Fungicide drenches that are used before the infection gets too established are especially useful for plants grown in containers.

Fruit rots are caused by a variety of fungi, some of which are common to many plants all over the world and can cause severe losses to commercial blueberry growers, especially on early ripening varieties. In 1994, Germany recorded a 37 percent loss of fruit on 'Bluetta' and 42 percent on 'Earliblue'.

Anthracnose fruit rot (*Glomerella cingulata*) is probably the most common and the most damaging to fruit. Small brown circles or irregular-shaped lesions may appear on leaves. In wet weather these may spread rapidly causing defoliation and destruction of shoots, affecting all aerial parts of the plant including flowers and fruit. The infection does not show any symptoms on the fruit or develop in the fruit clusters until they ripen. They then decay quickly, by which time it is too late to treat. The overwintering phase of these fungi is on twigs left on the bush or on the ground, which release spores during wet weather in the spring. Efficient pruning and removal and burning of all infected wood is an effective control measure. Fungicides may be used every seven to ten days from flowering onwards.

Some diseases are caused by viruses rather than fungi or bacteria. These can be especially damaging in commercial plantations because they weaken and slowly kill plants, reducing yields. Berries from infected plants are often poor in color and size. Since most viruses are transmitted by insect vectors, controlling those vectors is very important. It is wise to remove and burn all infected plants, although this is usually not a complete solution because of the long time between infection and the appearance of symptoms; infected plants are likely to be left behind. I recommend that growers buy plants that are certified as virus free when they are establishing new plantations. The modern method of micropropagating blueberries has proved beneficial because virus diseases can be removed from the plant material in the laboratory.

Red ringspot is a serious disease, particularly in New Jersey, that is caused by a virus. It affects both stems and leaves and can cause a 25 percent loss of crop since it leaves the berries pockmarked, sometimes blotchy, and poor tasting. Red spots, rings and oak-leafed patterns appear in the summer on the upper surfaces of the leaves, especially the older ones, and on stems of older plants. When the stems are affected they fail to develop leaves. The spots, which are $\frac{1}{8}$ to $\frac{1}{4}$ in. (3 to 5 mm) in diameter, usually have a green center. Sometimes confused with powdery mildew, this disease causes spots on both sides of the leaves. It is thought but not known for sure that mealybugs transport red ringspot virus. The best way to prevent this disease is to obtain disease-free plants in the first place, particularly since controlling it requires removing and burning diseased bushes. The variety 'Bluetta' sometimes shows similar red spotting on its leaves but no virus is detected. It is thought to be a genetic disorder.

Blueberry shoestring disease is the most widespread virus of northern highbush blueberries, especially in Michigan and New Jersey, where it has caused severe losses. It may take four years from initial infection for symptoms to appear.

Signs of this disease include elongated red streaks on the side of young stems that is exposed to the sun and long narrow leaves with wavy edges and red coloring along the midribs and veins. Unusual red streaks on flower petals followed by prematurely colored, red-purple berries that never turn blue are other signs. Yields drop steadily over the years.

This virus is spread by the sap-sucking blueberry aphid, *Illinoia pepperi*, a crawling insect that moves from bush to bush along intermingling branches, moving down rows rather than from row to row. Disease-free plants should be purchased, and any infected plants, including wild plants found nearby, must be burned. Aphids should be controlled by spraying.

Stunt disease is caused by a mycoplasma, which is similar to a virus. It is known to be transmitted from diseased blueberry plants by the blunt-nosed leafhopper and other hoppers that may also be found on raspberries, blackberries and cherries.

Symptoms develop from midsummer with leaves developing yellow along their edges and between the veins. These areas then turn prematurely bright red. Infected plants tend to become unnaturally dense, bushy and very much smaller than healthy ones. Infected leaves are smaller than healthy leaves and twisted. The few berries, which are small, hard and unpleasant tasting, cling to the bushes. The best way to control stunt disease is to order plants from a reputable nursery, preferably plants that have been certified as being free of this disease. To keep this disease under control, first kill any leafhoppers on or near the infected plant, then dig up and burn infected plants. This is the best way to halt the cycle of infection.

The Highbush Blueberry Harvest

Harvesting begins when sufficient fruit of each variety is judged to have reached its optimum size, sugar content and flavor to warrant the effort. In commercial plantations, there is the additional consideration of the cost of picking. This means waiting until sufficient fruit has been blue all over for three or four days. If this policy is followed, the biggest yields of quality fruit will be available. However, if fruit is left too long and becomes overripe (meaning it is dark and soft), it deteriorates very rapidly after picking and is extremely prone to squashing and damage. It also develops an unpleasant taste. It is best to pick fruit when it is dry because wet fruit rots more quickly.

Most varieties will need picking four times during a four- to six-week harvesting season. Some ripen in a more concentrated period, and those varieties that are ideal for mechanical harvesting will only need two picks. The first pick will usually yield the biggest berries. Berries that are picked while they still have a slight pink tinge will continue to ripen after picking but are likely to be less sweet and flavorsome.

The supply of water to the roots up to and during the 10- to 12-week harvest period has critical effects. Ripe blueberry fruit can contain 80 to 85 percent water and it needs a steady supply to encourage steady swelling. A sudden rush of water, either from rain or irrigation, can cause considerable damage. Where skins have stopped growing and are no longer elastic, a sudden expansion of the flesh of the berries will result in split fruit. Some varieties, such as 'Collins' and 'Berkeley', are more prone to splitting than others. Fruit that lacks water is small, dry and of poor flavor, and it sometimes has shriveled skins. Whether split or small and dry, the result is poor quality fruit that cannot be marketed successfully except possibly for use in processing. Excessive watering can sometimes cause no harm, especially when irrigation systems are used more or less continuously in hot weather on free-draining soils. The problem is not soil saturation but a distinct lack of flavor in the fruit.

The very large plantations, which are often in rural areas remote from a large, available labor force, are usually but not always mechanically harvested, especially if the fruit is destined for processing rather than the fresh-fruit market. The increasingly high wages required by pickers also makes machine harvesting an attractive alternative. It is quite an awesome sight to see one man atop one of these giant machines that straddles the rows and shakes the fruit into collecting trays. One operator on one machine plus one person on the ground keeping an eye on the quality being picked and removing filled trays can harvest about 1.5 acres (0.6 hectare) an hour. In other words, one machine, skillfully operated, can replace 100 hand pickers. Modern harvesters are refined to the extent that, provided the operator is an expert, relatively little damage is done to the fruit or the bushes, but it is obviously less thorough and more damaging than well-trained hand pickers. The fruit needs thorough sorting in the pack house as some unripe and damaged berries, as well as debris, is collected.

Pack houses vary greatly. Some have basic conveyors that carry the fruit under a blast of air that removes leaves and other debris, including some of the small and green berries, leaving the heavier fruit to continue moving along. Workers remove the remaining unripe, damaged or small fruit by hand, leaving the sound, sizeable berries to fall gently into hoppers or trays at the end of the line. More sophisticated sorting and packing lines use optical systems to detect fruit density.

Many growers prefer the method of hand picking because there is little wastage and better control. Well-trained and well-supervised pickers in a commercial operation pick each bush thoroughly while also starting the process of quality control, which continues into the pack house. In most hand-picking operations, hygiene is tightly monitored. High-quality, regularly maintained portable toilets and hand-washing facilities have to be provided adjacent to but not in the fields, with pickers instructed to wash hands after mealtimes or visits to the toilet. No smoking or eating is allowed in the plantations, and there must be no pets. Most pickers are paid on the basis of the weight picked so it is tempting to pick any old rubbish very quickly and hide it under a layer of good fruit. Such "chancers" are soon found out and are then supervised more closely. Fruit that is considered well picked will be undamaged, unsplit, have no tears at the stem end and be unbruised. It should preferably have retained its bloom, which is important to growers selling their fruit on the fresh-fruit market or to home growers who value the aesthetic pleasure of picking unblemished fruit. The best technique for picking a blueberry by hand is to cup the fingers and the hand below the fruit, then roll the individual berries with a single downward push of the thumb into the palm of the hand.

If pickers have their picking basket (or bucket or box) strapped to a carrier supported by a belt round their waist, both hands are then free to do the picking. On some farms, fruit may be picked straight into the containers in which it will go to market. This has the advantage of minimum handling of the fruit but it requires skilled and conscientious picking to make sure that no unripe fruit, stalks or other trash is included. Others, especially those who have large, mature bushes, prefer to put the fruit into larger boxes that will be sent to the pack house for final grading and packing since it is virtually impossible to avoid leaves and other debris from falling among the fruit. The fruit then undergoes final sorting in the pack house, where it is transferred into small plastic boxes that will then be weighed, usually lidded and labeled before being chilled and sent to market.

Cooling the fruit is important, whatever the scale of the operation, because fruit that is left in the sun will deteriorate rapidly. Fruit that is chilled as soon as possible after picking will not only have a longer shelf life but will better retain its flavor too. The reason is that the berries, like all living things, respire more rapidly when hot, using their own sugars in the process and generating more heat. Bacteria responsible for decay are also more active at higher temperatures. Commercial growers ensure that newly picked fruit is kept as cool as possible. Fruit in plantations is put in the shade and collected and taken to the pack-house chiller regularly, which removes the field heat before the fruit is packed for its final destination. Packers working in the pack house will often work in hats and warm clothing under their regulation overalls because many pack houses operate at around 41°F (5°C). The low temperatures are maintained throughout the fruit's transportation to the retail shops where the fruit finally reaches the customers. This is known as a "chill chain."

Markets

In producing countries, highbush blueberries that are sold in most supermarkets and in many smaller retail shops have reached them via marketing agents or wholesale markets. Smaller growers prefer to sell their fruit more directly to the public if possible; some even have their own farm shops or roadside stalls. Many smaller growers also find that farmers' or growers' markets are an excellent way to sell their fruit directly to the public. Here they have the chance to answer questions and to encourage customers to taste and compare different varieties. In other words, they provide a good opportunity to encourage interest in and enthusiasm for the fruit. Many people taste their first blueberries this way.

Self-pick or pick-your-own (known as "PYO" in Britain) blueberry farms are usually located near highly populated areas or in tourist regions. They often have a variety of fruit that can be picked in addition to blueberries. Customers are usually sent to help themselves to fruit from specific rows and are encouraged to pick thoroughly. This avoids the problem of too much "grazing" or picking just the best berries, leaving those later customers with the poorer fruit.

In many areas, including those in Europe where there is a concentration of blueberry farms, blueberry festivals where the public car tour the plantations, enjoy processions, attend fun fairs and festivals and so on are quite common. The public is also given the chance to try different dishes based on blueberries. Since ancient times, the harvest has been a time of celebration.

Storage and Processing

Until the 1980s, thousands of tons of blueberries were canned, but this method of storage is now less popular. Jars of fruit are sometimes available in small quantities, with the fruit being kept in a light syrup. Blueberries also store well as dried fruit in an airtight container.

Highbush blueberries freeze extremely well, as was demonstrated by how the Indians used them. Those that are grown and picked at home or at self-picked areas are usually stored unwashed. If they go into the freezer dry they can be put straight into polythene bags with no need to spread them on trays first. Some people prefer to wash fruit, in which case it needs to have moisture removed before putting into the freezer. This is typically done by spreading the berries out on a tray lined with absorbent kitchen paper and then freezing the dryish berries on trays before bagging them up for more permanent storage. Fruit that is commercially grown is quick frozen individually in 13 or 26 lb packs (6 or 12 kg) packs in boxes lined with polythene. Frozen fruit that is kept frozen at −0.4°F (−18°C) will last for years.

Storing fresh fruit in a controlled atmosphere will prolong the fresh-fruit season by up to six weeks. It is based on the introduction of carbon dioxide gas to chilled fruit kept just above freezing point. Since this gas is produced naturally during respiration, an increased concentration of carbon dioxide surrounding the chilled berries will suppress respiration and slow down the natural progress of the organisms responsible for decay.

Dried blueberries are popular with bakers and confectioners. The technique of sun drying the berries is the classic method used by Native

Americans. Nowadays the fruit is freeze-dried, a method that is quick and efficient, and that also preserves flavor very well. At home the fresh berries can be spread out on a baking tray lined with greaseproof paper and left for 24 hours in the oven set to its lowest temperature. Once cold they can be packed in sealed jars and will keep for a year or more. They provide a pleasant and healthy alternative to sweets or candy.

The uses for blueberries are almost unlimited. Fresh fruit is delicious eaten raw, especially with a dash of sugar, a light sprinkle of lemon juice and plenty of cream. Blueberry pies and muffins are legendary, but the simple stewed fruit, again with a dash of lemon juice and a sprinkling of sugar, chilled and accompanied by cream or ice cream, takes a lot of beating. Blueberries are surprisingly good in savory dishes, including casseroles (especially those made with chicken and pork), and are also wonderful in many salads.

Chapter 5
Rabbiteye, Southern Highbush, Half-high Blueberries and "Huckleberries"

Rabbiteye, southern highbush and half-high blueberries may be of lesser importance in terms of their contribution to the total tonnage of blueberry fruit produced worldwide, but they each have their place. Rabbiteyes provide crops of valued fruit in warm climates where northern highbush blueberries have failed to thrive. The introduction of southern highbush since the 1970s has added a new option to growers of vacciniums and extended the growing season in warmer areas. Some of these modern hybrids have also become popular with home gardeners in a wide range of climates because of their ornamental attributes. The term "half high" refers only to the habit of some blueberry varieties that have been selected out and grouped together under this name in response to the demand of home gardeners for less vigorous blueberry plants that are more suited to small containers or small gardens. Most older varieties originated in cold climates, where they adapted to the climate, and are able to bend under protective coverings of snow.

Rabbiteye Blueberries

Botany and Geographic Range

Rabbiteye blueberries were formerly classified under *Vaccinium corymbosum*, then *V. corymbosum* var. *ashei*. They are currently allocated full specific status as *V. ashei*.

To all but the most knowledgeable, picked rabbiteye blueberry fruit looks identical to northern highbush blueberry fruit. There are differences, however, especially in the habits and in the chilling requirements. Rabbiteyes, which require only 400 to 500 chilling hours per winter with temperatures below 45°F (7°C) to maintain dormancy, are grown in the warmer climates where northern highbush, with their requirement for more chilling hours during their dormant season do not crop.

Rabbiteye blueberries were apparently so named because it was noticed that the calyx (the blossom end of the fruit) looks like a rabbit's eye when it starts to ripen. The pink spot, which first forms as the berry begins to ripen, has been likened to the pink eye of a rabbit. Fruit is small to medium in size and very similar to the northern highbush blueberry. They are native to the warm southeastern states of the United States from central Florida to eastern North Carolina and northern Arkansas, west to eastern Texas and southern Arkansas.

Plants in wild populations are erect, spreading shrubs that frequently reach 10 ft. (3 m) or more in moist, well-drained soil in the upland regions of these areas. They are relatively deep rooted. They have further adapted to their native climate, where summers can be very hot and dry, by having leaves that retain water more efficiently than those of the northern highbush.

History of cultivation

Selections were made from the wild as long ago as 1887. Moses A. Sapp, a logging contractor, made a selection from the wild in northwestern Florida about five years later. He planted them out in rows and they continued to yield fruit for picking for over 35 years. Other growers followed his example, and by 1930 there were about 2,000 acres (800 hectares) of rabbiteye blueberries in cultivation in Florida, all derived from the wild selections. Most were unnamed, and it has been estimated that there were over 50 of them. These varied in their habit, fruit characteristics and ripening season, and some were obviously better than others.

In 1926 the University of Georgia began research on the best of the wild selections at its Coastal Plain Experiment Station at Tifton in Georgia. Five plants from 12 selections were planted out. Other growers such as J. T. Bush, a railroad engineer, H. H. Hapgood, a parson, and Moses Sapp's son W. B. Sapp named what they regarded at the time as their best selections from the wild.

As had happened with their relatives further north, a breeding program was initiated to select the best characteristics from the wild selections and to use these to produce even better cultivars. Most of the earlier cultivars are being superceded by superior cultivars from more recent breeding programs, but it is interesting to look at the origins of modern breeding and to appreciate the scale of work and the lengthy time spans involved.

A cooperative breeding program was put together in 1939 involving E. B. Morrow of the North Carolina Agricultural Experiment Station, O. J. Woodard of the University of Georgia and Darrow of the USDA in Beltsville, Maryland. In 1949 'Callaway' and 'Coastal' were released from this program and 'Homebell' in 1955. The state of Georgia, with Dr. W. Thomas Brightwell in charge, started work in 1944. In 1945, 25 acres (10 hectares) of land was acquired to form a new Research Station near Alapaha. Seedlings from a previous cross between the named wild selections 'Ethel' and 'Clara' were planted in 1948. 'Tifblue', until the 1980s the most popular rabbiteye blueberry in the world, was selected and named in 1955. 'Woodard' was released in 1960.

Thousands of seedlings were selected for evaluation in the next few years and three were named and released from the cooperative program in 1969, namely 'Briteblue', 'Delite' and 'Southland'. 'Bluebelle' was selected by Brightwell in 1951 but was finally released for cultivation in 1974. Darrow released 'Garden Blue' and 'Menditoo' in North Carolina in 1958.

Brightwell, who was probably the most influential breeder of rabbiteye blueberries, spent 30 years working on them. He retired in 1974 and the cultivar, 'Brightwell', which he had selected in 1963, was released and named after him in 1983. 'Baldwin', popular with pick-your-own farms, joined the other cultivars in 1985, the year of the University of Georgia's bicentennial. It was named after the first president of the University.

Cultivation and Maintenance

Rabbiteye blueberries enjoy the same soil conditions as other cultivated blueberries, thriving in acidic soils with pH 4.5 to 5.5, ideally a loam or sand. A mineral, sandy soil enriched with acidifying organic matter such as peat or rotted leaf litter is good. Rabbiteyes also need good drainage because root rot will result if the water table is such that roots remain saturated and starved of oxygen for too long. Roots of many rabbiteye varieties may penetrate down to nearly 3 ft. (90 cm) which is a factor to consider. In areas where drainage is poor (and particularly where high rainfall is expected), it is essential to create ridges or mounds. In extreme cases these may be up to 3 ft. (90 cm) high, but more usually they are 12 to 18 in. (30 to 45 cm) high.

Young rabbiteye blueberry plants, being shallow rooted, need irrigation, so a source of nonalkaline water should be available especially during the first two to three years after planting. Sand filters are usually used to clean pond water. Good air drainage is also beneficial, as moving air reduces the risk of damage from late spring frosts. In addition, good air circulation discourages fungal diseases from developing since they prefer humid conditions.

A black plastic or organic mulch is beneficial for rabbiteyes too. Mature rabbiteye blueberries, being naturally deeper rooting than northern highbush blueberries, are more tolerant of drought. However, to get a good crop of plump fruit as well as good growth and flower-bud formation for the following year's crop, many growers use irrigation throughout the growing season. This practice also reduces the risk of split fruit, which occurs if plants suffer a period of drought followed by heavy rainfall. Trickle irrigation is often used on young plants. If plenty of clean water is available, especially if overhead frost protection is required, then a system of overhead sprinklers will suit older plants

Rabbiteye blueberries are particularly liable to frost damage because their chilling requirements are low. They are therefore very prone to break dormancy during warm spells in late winter, only to be caught by a spell of cold weather and hard frosts before spring really arrives. Growers use a variety of frost-protection methods based on encouraging movement of air by using wind machines or even helicopters and on providing a protective coating of ice over the developing flowers or fruit using a sprinkler system.

Varieties

Rabbiteye blueberries are not efficient at self-pollination, so a mixture of varieties is planted to encourage cross-pollination. In the United States, the start of harvesting of rabbiteye blueberries grown in the warm southern states precedes the northern highbush season of the more northern states. Picking of the earliest ripening cultivars starts in late May. Late-season cultivars, such as 'Baldwin', however, extend the season into September, well past the peak northern highbush season. In New Zealand, where the climate experiences are less extreme, rabbiteye and highbush blueberries are often grown together. In Britain, highbush blueberries are picked before rabbiteye bushes.

The earliest fresh fruit traditionally receives high prices, so cultivars with an early ripening are especially valued by growers. Cultivars that have the lowest chilling requirement are not grown in areas where spring frosts are normally expected. High-chill cultivars are favored in these areas since they remain dormant for a longer period. Since mechanical harvesting is common on commercial plantations, those cultivars that have robust qualities both in bush habit and in fruit characteristics are grown. Large firm fruit with a good color, dry scar at the stem end and good flavor are all valued characteristics for the fresh-fruit market. Those varieties that ripen over a short period and have the above characteristics are also suitable for mechanical harvesting. Those that ripen over a longer period are more favored for home growing and pick-your-own operations.

I describe the chilling requirements for each variety in terms of the number of hours required below 45°F (7°C) during the winter months if good flower-bud development is to be achieved. In the southern states of the United States where late frosts are not expected, those varieties with low chilling requirements and a tendency to produce a heavy crop of flowers, pollinated by a compatible variety, are favored. Those with a higher chilling requirement generally fail to crop successfully in these warmer areas. Varieties are listed in order of ripening, and again, because of the unclear parentage of rabbiteyes, I use their cultivar names only.

'Climax' ('Callaway' × 'Ethel'). Introduced in 1974 in Georgia, these plants are upright and spreading, with canes arising from a relatively small crown. Only enough stems are produced to renew the crowns. It is not self-pollinating. Fruit ripens over a short period, and 80 percent may be harvested at one time. The medium blue berries are of medium size, have a small stem scar, are firm and of good, slightly aromatic flavor. 'Climax' can be mechanically harvested, and it is also a good variety for home gardeners in warm climate areas because of its superior fall colors.

'Brightwell' ('Tifblue' × 'Menditoo') was introduced in Georgia in 1981 and named after the noted breeder, Brightwell. Plants are vigorous, upright, with good but not excessive cane production. It produces good crops consistently and the berries are medium sized with small scars. They are firm, light blue and of good flavor. 'Brightwell' is popular in most areas where rabbiteye blueberries are grown.

'Premier' ('Tifblue' × 'Homebell') was introduced in 1978 in North Carolina. It is vigorous and spreading with young branches that tend to have difficulty supporting heavy fruit loads, especially if they are pruned in winter. Summer pruning encourages more robust cane growth. The soil requirements of this cultivar are less critical than most blueberries, and it will tolerate a higher pH. Although the flowers are often misshapen, they are more self-fertile than most. Pollination, however, is better when it is planted with other varieties. The chilling requirement is 450 to 550 hours. The berries, produced over a short period, are large with a small stem scar, firm and with a good, slightly aromatic flavor. 'Premier' has spectacular fall foliage.

'Beckyblue'. Released from Gainesville, Florida, in 1978, this is a vigorous, tall, spreading bush. It is not self-fertile and is selective in the varieties that will pollinate it. ('Climax' is a good choice to plant with it as a pollinator.) 'Beckyblue' has low chilling requirement, about 300 to 400 hours, and it is an early-season plant. Round, medium fruit is firm with a small dry scar. Its color and flavor are both good.

'Chaucer'. Introduced in 1985 from Gainesville, Florida, this vigorous, spreading bush has upright canes. It flowers prolifically and sets heavy crops with cross-pollination from other varieties. A low chilling requirement of 350 to 400 hours makes it suitable for warmer winter climates. The fruit is produced over a long period, is light blue, of medium size, with good flavor. However, it tears easily when detached from its stem. It is an excellent garden or pick-your-own variety.

'Tifblue' ('Ethel' × 'Clara') was introduced from Tifton, Georgia, in 1955 and is a mid- to late-season selection. The most widely planted rabbiteye blueberry in the world, it is the standard against which all rabbiteyes are measured. The bush is a typical rabbiteye type, meaning it is vigorous and upright with good production of new suckers or canes replacing the old. The chilling requirement is 550 to 650 hours. The light blue, firm fruit is medium to large with a dry stem scar and good flavor. Full flavor develops several days after apparent ripening and the berries hold well on the bush after this. They are prone to splitting after heavy rain or on wet soils.

'Briteblue' ('Ethel' × 'Callaway') was introduced from Georgia in 1969. A mid- to late-season cultivar, it is slow growing in the early years and becomes moderately vigorous and spreading as it ages, producing only enough canes for renewal. It requires only moderate pruning, and its chilling requirement is 500 to 600 hours. Flower buds develop late and generally avoid late spring frost damage. The berries, which grow in large clusters, are large, firm, with a small dry scar and a waxy bloom. They have a tendency to remain red at the stem end and taste very sour until the whole fruit is blue, after which they will remain a long time on the bush without deteriorating.

'Centurion'. Introduced in North Carolina in 1978, this is a late-season cultivar that ripens one to two weeks after 'Tifblue'. The bush is vigorous, narrowly upright, with limited production of suckers. It is prone to fall over on windy sites. About 550 to 650 chilling hours are required. Moderately self-fertile flowers are produced late, and they still benefit from being planted with another variety for improved pollination. The moderately firm fruit is medium sized, dark blue and of a good, aromatic flavor. This is a good variety for home or pick-your-own use.

'Baldwin'. Introduced in 1985 in Georgia, it is a vigorous, upright plant that is very productive and consistent. Chilling requirement is 450 to 500 hours. Its chief merit is its long ripening period of over six to seven weeks, which makes it very suitable for home and pick-your-own use. The firm, dark blue berries are of medium size with dry stem scars and a sweet flavor.

Management
The management of rabbiteye blueberries is much the same as for other highbush blueberries, with the need for weed control being important especially in the early years. Fertilizer requirements are similar, and growers use a fertilizer with a high, ammonium-form nitrogen content. Ammonium sulfate, which is acidifying, is suitable for soils with pH 5.2 or above, and urea, which is nonacidifying, is suitable for soils with pH 5.0 or less. Overdosing should be avoided because root scorch is likely to occur, especially if water is lacking in dry weather. Irrigation requirements vary according to soil, climatic and other conditions, but the basic principles are the same as those for highbush blueberries.

Pruning
The objective in pruning rabbiteye blueberries is the same as with highbush blueberries: to keep the bushes growing with an annual production of young canes that bear healthy laterals on which a decent crop of good-sized berries will be produced the following year. Pruning rabbiteyes is slightly

different, however, as they are grown in warmer climates that have longer growing seasons than highbush blueberries, and growth tends to be rapid and very vigorous. Bushes tend to grow too tall and must have their height controlled. Some varieties can grow up to 16 ft. (5 m), and many reach 9 or 10 ft. (3 m) if left to their own devises. This is obviously undesirable—few people wish to use a stepladder to reach their fruit. Many varieties also produce suckers from the roots so growth can extend well beyond the plant canopy. Those that extend this far should be removed at ground level.

Many growers recommend cutting back young plants by 50 percent before planting because this encourages a good framework of growth in the following year. No pruning should be needed in the year after. After that year of no pruning, dead, damaged, weak or low growth should always be removed. As the plants develop they will start to produce very tall vigorous canes that are often several feet in length. The top third of growth should be cut back to encourage branching, which will mean that fruit develops lower down. If the top third is not pruned, these branches will carry fruit near their tips, making them top-heavy and drooping and leaving nothing lower down.

Old woody stems produce small fruit that does not ripen well, so the plants need constant rejuvenation. Any large, woody, unproductive canes should be removed to ground level each year. If plants have got out of control and reach unmanageable heights, they need more drastic treatment.

One system of pruning is to implement a three-year cycle, often referred to as "hedging," which involves cutting back about one third of the older canes to about 3 ft. (90 cm) each year. Another system involves cutting out 50 percent of the canes every two years. The most extreme method is to cut the whole plant back in one year. New canes will grow from the area behind the cuts, and they may then need cutting back by about one third to encourage further branching. This results in a system of branches that should fruit in each following year. It also lets light into the center of the bushes, and this encourages ripening.

In the hotter climates where rabbiteye blueberries are grown, the growing season is long enough for summer pruning (which usually occurs immediately after harvest) to be effective because the young growth this stimulates has time to mature and produce flower buds before dormancy. Winter pruning is favored by many because research has shown that even though there is a loss of crop in the year following, the amount of growth that takes place in that year more than makes up for it in terms of crop yield the year after that.

Pests and diseases

There are relatively few pests and diseases that affect rabbiteye blueberries; they seem to be more resistant than northern highbush blueberries. This resistance, combined with good hygiene around the plants, means that few growers have a spray program. However, growers should keep a lookout for botrytis, mummyberry, twig and stem blight, which I describe in detail in chapter 4. There are incidences of attack by most of the insects and mites that affect highbush blueberries, some of which could become major problems in the future but which do not at the time of writing need routine spray programs. The biggest insect problem seems to be when colonies of red fire ants (*Solenopsis invicta*) build their nests in or near plantations. They are a considerable nuisance to pickers, and when they build nests among the plants, their tunnels disturb root systems and cause bushes to become desiccated.

Birds, deer, rabbits and other mammals can all wreak havoc on rabbiteyes, and they need to be controlled if they compete for the crop or damage the bushes.

Southern Highbush Blueberries

"Southern highbush blueberry" is a somewhat vague term that covers some exciting late twentieth-century hybrids that may contain genetic material from two, three and sometimes four *Vaccinium* species. Most of the work in producing them has been done in Florida and Georgia and in countries in the Southern Hemisphere, particularly Australia. The main objective was to produce improved highbush blueberry cultivars that would do well in these areas. Their characteristics come mainly from the northern highbush species *V. corymbosum*, in particular earliness and high-quality fruit. Low chilling attributes are taken from rabbiteye (*V. ashei*) and *V. darrowii* is native to the southern states. *Vaccinium darrowii* also provides heat and drought resistance, and because it is an evergreen species, it contributes genetic material that makes many southern highbush varieties either evergreen or wintergreen (meaning the leaves remain all winter but are shed in the spring) depending on the climate.

Genetic incompatibility prevents direct hybridization between *Vaccinium ashei* (6*n*) and *V. corymbosum* (4*n*). Other species such as *V. angustifolium* (2*n*), the lowbush blueberry, were crossed with rabbiteye to produce fertile progeny (4*n*), which can then be crossed with other 4*n* species such as *V. corymbosum* varieties. This hybridization produced the first commercially released varieties, 'Flordablue' and 'Sharpblue'. More have followed, and they all fruit very early and have low winter-chilling requirements. This combination makes them ideal for the southern United States, much of California and places around the world with a similar climate. The quality of fruit from the best of these varieties is excellent, and they are tolerant of heat and dry conditions. Some are noted for their tolerance of a wide range of soil conditions, including much heavier soils than are tolerated by most blueberries, making them ideal for gardeners with such soils in warm climates. Another feature is that a number are surprisingly cold hardy so they are suitable for some upland areas where the number of hours of winter chill is low but where temperatures drop to levels that were damaging to less hardy varieties. Most of these hybrids are successful in Germany and other parts of central Europe too.

Although initially bred for commercial purposes, it is evident that southern highbush blueberries are of great value to the home gardener, both for their fruiting value and as ornamental plants. The bronze young growth and gray-green or blue-green mature leaves and attractive flowers of most varieties are definite bonuses, while those varieties that lose some or all their leaves display a pleasing range of fall colors and red stems that were inherited from their northern highbush parents.

Growers have found that some varieties are successful in gardens from San Diego to Seattle, which is some range. In addition, in many areas, especially those with warm climates where temperatures rarely drop below freezing such as in coastal California and the "gold coast" region of New South Wales, Australia, southern highbush varieties are true evergreens and never become fully dormant. Even in slightly colder regions, varieties such as 'Sunshine Blue' may be termed "wintergreen," seldom losing their leaves during the winter but shedding them as young growth starts in spring, which adds to their ornamental appeal. The combination of blue and gray-green leaves on red stems is most attractive. Garden-planted specimens may, however, look a little messy for a week or two in spring when they shed the older leaves. Once growth starts, they produce attractive, pale bronze young leaves throughout the summer and flowers that vary from pale to deep pink.

1 Bilberries (*Vaccinium myrtillus*) grow in large colonies on upland moors in Derbyshire, England.

2 Harvesting cranberries using water-reel harvesters in New Jersey.

3 The lingonberry 'Erntedank' was found growing on wild heathland in Germany.
Photo by Art Dome.

4 The lingonberry 'Koralle' is the most widely planted lingonberry to date.
Photo by Barry Starling.

5 The lingonberry 'Red Pearl' on the left is more versatile and suitable for the garden than 'Koralle', another lingonberry.

6 The lingonberry 'Sanna' carries heavy crops of top quality berries.

7 Wild, lowbush blueberries (*Vaccinium angustifolium*) may be harvested using hand rakes in August into September in Maine.

8 (right) Some mechanical blueberry harvesters are taller than a man and straddle the rows.
Here, Gary Pavlis of the USDA stands inside one such machine.

9 The brilliant red colors of wild American lowbush blueberry plants are dazzling.

9a On Blue Hill in Maine, the fall colors are spectacular until the leaves fall as winter sets in.

10 Bilberries fruit in August on the moors near Sheffield, England.

11 (right) *Vaccinium myrtillus* on the left is smaller in every way than *V. corymbosum*, including the size of its fruit.

12 The pistils of *Vaccinium myrtillus* protrude from flowers as they age and fruit starts to swell.
Photo by Art Dome.

14 (below) A North American highbush blueberry, 'Elizabeth', named after blueberry pioneer, Elizabeth White, has small pure white flowers, which open with the new growth.

13 The swollen flower buds of the northern highbush blueberry are found near the tips of shoots, with the narrower vegetative buds below.

15 In spring, blueberry plantations burst into flower and give off a sweet smell. Many varieties come into flower before the leaves open.

16 In autumn northern highbush blueberry plantations become a sea of red.

17 Rain glistens on cobwebs amongst the green, yellow and reds of the autumn leaves of northern highbush blueberries.

19 Close-up of the fall leaves of northern highbush blueberries.

18 (left) The fall leaves of *Vaccinium corymbosum* in silhouette against a sunny sky.

20 Outdoor propagation benches at the Atlantic Blueberry Farm in New Jersey.

21 One-year-old southern highbush blueberry plants on high ridges at Corindi in Australia.

22 A year later, these are two-year-old blueberry plants on Corindi's high ridges.

23 Two years later (the plants are now four years old), the Corindi plantation is mature in the hot climate of Australia's gold coast.

24 A North American highbush blueberry, 'Duke' is a heavy cropping early variety.

25 A North American highbush blueberry, 'Bluejay' has firm fruit of moderate size, which holds well on the bush.

26 A North American highbush blueberry, 'Toro' has some of the largest fruit, carried on exceptionally long corymbs.

27 A North American highbush blueberry, 'Ivanhoe' sets its fruit at the top of the corymb.

28 A North American highbush blueberry, 'Chandler' is excellent for home growing, with good flavored fruit ripening over six weeks or more.

30 A North American highbush blueberry, 'Bluegold' is aptly named as it is a wonderful dual purpose, heavy cropping variety, also excellent as a landscape plant.

32 (right) Old, woody canes have been removed and the bush, a year later, has strong, young canes.

29 A North American highbush blueberry, 'Herbert' has attractive pink tinged buds that open to white bell-like flowers.

31 It is possible to store fruit from the North American highbush blueberry 'Brigitta' for almost two months in a refrigerator.

33 Half-high blueberry plants are much more compact than highbush blueberries.

34 'Bluetta' is regarded as being a half high but is sometimes grown in highbush plantations.

36 A mixture of *Vaccinium* species in a large tub creates an unusual display that is also very pleasing, especially in the fall (Dierkings, Germany).

35 (left) Highbush blueberries are good container subjects, especially when in flower.

37 *Vaccinium acrobracteatum* from New Guinea has most attractive young, bronze-red leaves.

38 *Vaccinium arboreum* is the only vaccinium with genuinely inedible berries, but its white flowers are very attractive.

39 *Vaccinium arctostaphylos* flowers precede brilliant red autumn color.
Photo by Barry Starling.

40 *Vaccinium* 'Branklyn' is possibly a form of *V. sikkimense* with beautiful pink flowers.
Photo by Barry Starling.

41 *Vaccinium chaetothrix* is native to New Guinea but is hardy outdoors in rock gardens in southern England. *Photo by Barry Starling.*

43 (below) The crowded, pendulous clusters of pink-tinged blooms of *Vaccinium cylindraceum* are probably its most attractive feature.
Photo by Barry Starling.

42 *Vaccinium coriaceum* comes from Borneo and is tender with bright red young growth.

44 (right) The blue-black berries of *Vaccinium cylindraceum* that follow the flowers have an attractive bloom.

45 *Vaccinium cylindraceum* 'Tom Thumb' is an exciting interspecific hybrid bred by Barry Starling. *Photo by Barry Starling.*

46 The cascade bilberry (*Vaccinium deliciosum*) forms dense mats that make good ground cover. *Photo by Barry Starling.*

47 *Vaccinium fragile* is a beautiful low-growing evergreen with masses of tiny flowers that are pink or pink tinged with white in spring.
Photo by Barry Starling.

48 The berries of *Vaccinium fragile* go from red to black, with each plant often having an attractive mixture of shades.
Photo by Barry Starling.

49 *Vaccinium glauco-album* has a mass of pink-tinged, silvery white bracts among the pale pink flowers. *Photo by Barry Starling.*

50 The long narrow leaves of *Vaccinium griffithianum* turn bright red in autumn. *Photo by Barry Starling.*

52 *Vaccinium macrocarpon* 'Hamilton' is a dwarf cranberry grown mainly for its attractive flowers and foliage. *Photo by Barry Starling.*

51 (left) *Vaccinium japonicum* thrives in some shade. *Photo by Barry Starling.*

53 *Vaccinium nummularia* has glossy evergreen leaves that show off the mass of rosy pink flowers to perfection. *Photo by Barry Starling.*

54 In full sun, the leaves of *Vaccinium nummularia* take on a purplish tinge.
Photo by Barry Starling.

55 The flowers of *Vaccinium ovalifolium* appear in late spring before the leaves.
Photo by Barry Starling.

56 *Vaccinium ovatum* is widely grown in gardens. This form from St. Andrews, Scotland, is dwarf in habit and very hardy.
Photo by Barry Starling.

57 *Vaccinium retusum* is a good species for the rock garden and has highly attractive flowers and fruit. *Photo by Art Dome.*

58 The pink or white flowers of *Vaccinium sikkimense* are an attractive feature of this compact, evergreen shrub. *Photo by Art Dome.*

60 *Vaccinium vitis-idaea* colonizes dry hillsides in Sweden. *Photo by Barry Starling.*

59 (left) The flowers of *Vaccinium uliginosum* are quite pleasing. *Photo by Barry Starling.*

61 With its glossy red berries, *Vaccinium vitis-idaea* is well suited to rock gardens. *Photo by Barry Starling.*

62 *Vaccinium vitis-idaea* 'Minus' is very variable and may have pure white flowers.
Photo by Barry Starling.

63 Bright pink flowers are also possible with plants of *Vaccinium vitis-idaea* 'Minus'. *Photo by Barry Starling.*

65 *Vaccinium* 'Prince Charming' was introduced by Barry Starling in 2002. It is an interspecific hybrid between *V. arctostaphylos* and *V. cylindraceum*.
Photo by Barry Starling.

64 *Vaccinium vitis-idaea* 'Minus' grows slowly and is a dwarf form of the species. *Photo by Barry Starling.*

Varieties

The first of these hybrid southern highbush blueberries, 'Flordablue' and 'Sharpblue', were introduced from the University of Florida at Gainesville in 1975, the result of selection from an extensive breeding program carried out by R. H. Sharpe and his team in the 1960s. The breeding program continues, with new releases being introduced to this day. Arlen Draper of the USDA, working with colleagues from Arkansas, North Carolina, Georgia and Mississippi, has used wild species extensively both to introduce desirable characteristics into low-chill varieties suitable for warm climates and to act as movers of genes from *Vaccinium ashei*. Some southern highbush hybrids may carry as many as six species in their breeding. Since the species come from a diverse range of habitats, many of these hybrids are more tolerant of a wider range of soil types than other blueberries. They will grow successfully in mineral soils with a higher pH and with a denser soil structure.

The varieties I list vary somewhat in the characteristics described depending on the climate and conditions in which they are growing. They are listed in approximate order of ripening, but this is very approximate because ripening depends on the climate in which they are grown.

'O'Neal'. Originated in North Carolina, this variety was introduced in 1987. Its genes are mainly from *Vaccinium corymbosum*, but it also contains some from *V. angustifolium, V. ashei* and *V. darrowii*. Bushes are vigorous and rather spreading, and although they are tolerant of a wide variety of soil conditions, they perform best under pH 5.0. The leaves are an attractive gray-green and stems have a red tinge, making them bushes that are appreciated as ornamental plants. 'O'Neal' is self-fertile and blooms over a long period. It produces good crops of large to very large, light blue berries that are firm with a small scar, and ripening is fairly concentrated. The flavor is excellent and the fruit does not deteriorate on the bushes in hot weather. Only 400 chilling hours below 45°F (7°C) are required during dormancy.

'Sharpblue'. Originated by R. H. Sharpe at Gainesville, Florida, and introduced in 1975, it contains genes from *Vaccinium ashei, V. corymbosum* and *V. darrowii*. This spreading, vigorous bush produces many canes and tolerates a wide variety of soils. It is not self-fertile. Tasty berries are borne in tight clusters and are medium to large, reasonably firm, with a moderate scar. 'Sharpblue' has a very low chilling requirement. Although one of the very first southern highbush to be introduced 'Sharpblue' is still popular, especially in areas where winters are mild and almost no chilling occurs such as northern New South Wales, Australia. Where it fruits all year round with two main harvest periods, one in fall and the other in spring.

'Misty'. Released from Gainesville, Florida, in 1990, 'Misty' is proving popular in many warm areas, where hot summers and mild winters are experienced. It needs only 150 chilling hours. It is highly ornamental with bright blue-green leaves, bright pink flowers and light blue fruit. The fruit has a good flavor and grows on an upright bush, and winter pruning encourages larger fruit. 'Misty' is evergreen in mild winters but loses its leaves in cold areas. It takes time to produce new leaves, meaning that the stems are vulnerable to stem blight. Flowers may precede the leaves in this situation. It is not self-fertile so needs other cultivars for pollination. Its tendency to produce masses of flowers makes it valuable for ornamental use.

'Southmoon'. A high yielding, midseason variety from Florida that was originally released in 1995. It ripens about ten days after 'Sharpblue'. The berries are attractive, large and of excellent flavor. It thrives in lighter soils.

'Jubilee'. A midseason variety from Mississippi that was released in 1994, it has a compact, vigorous and upright bush and is particularly adaptable, tolerating heavier soils, hot summers and sudden winter cold. It has very attractive orange-yellow fall foliage. 'Jubilee' should be planted with other varieties as it is not self-fertile. The berries are medium sized, form in large clusters and are produced near the outer parts of the bush, making picking easy. About 500 chilling hours are required.

'Sunshine Blue'. This is probably the best variety for garden cultivation in a wide variety of climates. It is highly ornamental and is proving very successful in climates as diverse as San Diego in California to northern Germany and in soils from light acidic sands to moderately heavy loams of pH 6.0 to 6.5. It is easy to grow, bushy and compact, reaching about 3 ft. (90 cm) tall and 3 ft. (90 cm) wide, which makes this variety ideal for small gardens or containers. Bushes retain their older, blue-green leaves during the winter (except in colder climates) and lose them when new growth is imminent and flower buds are coloring. Pale bronze young growth and attractive red young stems follow. Flower buds are red with purple calyces, and these are followed by bright pink, self-pollinating flowers that fade to white. Prolific crops of medium berries with an excellent flavor are produced over a long period from midseason. About 150 chilling hours are required.

'Reveille'. Introduced from North Carolina in 1990, 'Reveille' has a substantial amount of northern highbush in its makeup and requires 600 to 800 chilling hours. An upright, vigorous variety that is adaptable to most climates and soils, it is easy to grow. A late midseason plant, it produces a mass of bright pink flowers in spring. It has particularly firm, almost crunchy, light blue berries of medium size. They have an excellent flavor.

'Ozarkblue'. Released in 1996 by the University of Arkansas, this variety has a large percentage of northern highbush in its makeup so it is quite cold hardy. It also does well in areas with hot summers, provided they have 800 chilling hours. The fruit is large, light blue, firm and of good flavor. With a habit and fruiting quality and time similar to the popular northern highbush 'Bluecrop', 'Ozarkblue' is a good replacement in climates where the summers are too hot for 'Bluecrop'.

Half-high Blueberries

"Half-high blueberry" is a somewhat loose term given to a group of blueberries that do not exceed about 3 ft. (90 cm) at maturity, but most have the bushy, woody habit of highbush cultivars. They are generally hybrids produced from *Vaccinium corymbosum* (highbush) × *V. angustifolium* (lowbush). (Plate 33) They could be described as "dwarf highbush" blueberries, a happy medium between the two species.

Half-high blueberries are particularly cold hardy, having inherited the ability of their lowbush blueberry parent to survive the harsh winters of northeast America and Canada. They are most suitable for garden or small-scale commercial cultivation in cold areas. One of their advantages is that they have inherited medium-sized, more easily picked fruit from the highbush blueberry while retaining the ability to rest undamaged under thick blankets of snow, which comes from their lowbush parentage. Their fall color is often a particularly spectacular red and long lasting. Half-high blueberries are excellent, dual-purpose ornamental and culinary plants, provided the birds are kept at bay during the fruiting season. Even if the birds do get to them first, their ornamental assets are valuable enough to make them worth growing. Since the term half high came into general use as a group classification only late in the twentieth century, and since the demand for half-high blueberries is localized and more concentrated in cold areas, it may take a little searching to obtain plants of some of the cultivars listed outside these cold climate areas.

Varieties

I list the following half-high blueberries in approximate order of ripening. Both 'Bluetta' and 'Northland' are included here (as well as in chapter 4 on northern highbush blueberries) because their compact habit means they are sometimes sold as half highs.

'Bluetta'. Introduced in 1968 in New Brunswick, New Jersey, 'Bluetta' combines a lowbush parent with the early fruiting highbush 'Earliblue'. The bush is compact, spreading and productive and it has brilliant red fall color. The medium-sized fruit is produced early, just after 'Earliblue', light blue and of good flavor. (Plate 34)

'Greenfield' is an old (1913) variety from the famous Whitesbog, New Jersey, trials of Coville. The bush grows to no more than 2 to 3 ft. (60 to 90 cm) and produces small, sweet, dark blue berries. Its advantage is that it ripens very early.

'Sunrise'. Introduced in 1988, it only just qualifies as a half-high blueberry as in some more favorable situations it will reach over $3^1/_2$ ft. (1 m) in height. It ripens at the same time as 'Bluetta' but grows a little larger. It has moderate, erratic yields of medium-sized, firm, mid-blue fruit of good flavor.

'Chippewa'. Released in 1996 from the University of Minnesota, 'Chippewa' is based on a series of lowbush and highbush crosses. It is upright, with large, firm, sweet, light blue berries that ripen in midseason. Yields may reach 7 lbs (3 kg) at maturity. It is moderately self-fertile but produces best if planted with another variety to act as a pollinator.

'Friendship'. This fairly upright plant reaches 4 ft. (1.2 m) in favorable conditions. It has medium-sized fruit with a pronounced, intense flavor derived from its lowbush genes. It is among the best blueberries for its antioxidant properties.

'Northcountry' was introduced in 1986. It has a slightly open habit, reaching only 3 ft. (90 cm) in height at maturity. White flowers with a slight pink flush are produced in great abundance in spring and are followed by medium-sized, powder blue fruit early in the fruiting season that has a pronounced lowbush flavor. Its fall colors are spectacularly red.

'Northblue'. A very low-growing variety, it was introduced in 1983 by the University of Minnesota. It grows quite quickly but reaches no more than 20 to 30 in. (50 to 75 cm). With dark, glossy green leaves it is an attractive plant. It produces large, sweet, well-flavored berries.

'Northland'. Introduced in 1967 by Michigan State University, this variety is often marketed as half high but it grows to about 4 ft. (1.2 m). It is of a spreading, quite dense habit with ground-hugging branches that need to be removed to avoid fruit trailing on the ground. It is ideal where snowfall is expected as the branches are "whippy" and bend easily. Berries are medium in size with firm flesh and moderate flavor.

'Northsky'. Introduced in 1983 from the University of Minnesota, 'Northsky' is truly dwarf, growing to no more than 20 in. (50 cm) high and 2 to 3 ft. (60 to 90 cm) wide. It is particularly hardy, able to survive −45°F (−43°C). The small- to medium-sized berries are a very attractive light blue with an exceptionally good bloom and a good flavor that is similar to the wild lowbush blueberries. With its dense foliage of glossy green leaves in summer and brilliant red color in the fall, this variety is particularly suitable for planting in small gardens, in groups in larger gardens or in containers. It is self-fertile.

'Redskin'. Bred by Coville, it dates back to 1932 when it was introduced from Whitesbog. With white berries flushed red on the sunny side, it is really a curiosity of more ornamental value than a plant to grow for its fruit.

'Tophat', introduced in 1977 from Michigan State University as a highbush and lowbush cross, it has been and continues to be widely marketed as a tub plant for home growing. Dwarf in habit, it forms a dense, round bush no more than 2 ft. (60 cm) in height and diameter. The berries are small to medium in size, firm and bright blue. It is frequently offered in nonspecialist mail-order catalogs. It is a very temperamental plant, either performing well or not at all. 'Tophat' tends to lose its leaves in patches and, with that, its ornamental attractiveness. It seems to be susceptible to phytophthora root rot or similar root disease. Its fall color is a brilliant red provided plants are kept in full sun.

"Huckleberries"

I use quotation marks around "huckleberries" deliberately because there is no universally acceptable berry that fits this word; it does not even cover a defined genus or any particular species within a genus. The word seems to have become a widely used general term that covers a number of types of round or oval berries harvested from shrubby bushes growing in the wild. The Oxford English dictionary describes huckleberries as "any low-growing North American shrub of the genus *Gaylussacia*" and as "the blue or black soft fruit of this plant." It adds the caution, however, "probably an alteration of the hurtleberry or whortleberry."

Vander Kloet puts huckleberries firmly under Vaccinieae, the same tribe as blueberries but under the genus *Gaylussacia*. They are often found growing in colonies in moist acidic soils in northeastern states, often in association with wild blueberries. The berries of these *Gaylussacia* huckleberries are darker, less fleshy and contain up to ten large seeds each. They do not have the characteristic five-pointed calyx scar of the blueberry. Despite their large seeds, these fruits are sought after by those who regard the flavor as superior. Some even prefer them to wild blueberries and can be quite fanatical in their support of these fruits, making annual pilgrimages to a favored spot and rejecting the wild blueberries.

Between 40 and 50 species of *Gaylussacia* are native to North and South America.

The most common is *G. baccata*, which is known as the black huckleberry. It is a small deciduous shrub up to 3½ ft. (1 m), with small, urn-shaped, dull red flowers in short racemes. Round, edible, glossy black fruit follows.

Gaylussacia frondosa or blue huckleberry is commonly called a tangleberry or dangleberry because of the long arching stems.

The most commonly picked species is *Vaccinium membranaceum.* Sometimes called mountain huckleberry, big huckleberry, black huckleberry or blue huckleberry, it is harvested from the wild in the Cascades and Rocky Mountains and other cold, upland areas of the United States. It prefers moist conditions, while a form with the synonym *V. globulare* thrives in dry conditions in Montana. There the form is known as the blue or globe huckleberry, and its harvest is sufficiently important for a system of burning to rejuvenate old patches of these wild huckleberries to be in place. This system probably accounts for the biennial cropping of the berries.

Both the species and the form are difficult to cultivate in ordinary gardens as they seem to need the very specific climatic conditions of those that occur in their natural habitats at 3,000 to 7,000 ft. (900 to 2,100 m). They prefer well-drained slopes, often under scattered trees, where they clamber over fallen timber. With their rhizomatous root system these plants spread to form patches, and their habit and the quality of the fruit varies greatly from patch to patch. The variation is usually the result of the varying microclimates as well as the variable seed from different parent plants. Late spring frosts can cause flowers to abort and crops to fail where cold air accumulates in frost pockets on the mountains. Local people get to know which are the best areas to pick and can be quite possessive about their favorite patches.

Vaccinium caespitosum is sometimes called the dwarf huckleberry. This very hardy species is found from Alaska to Newfoundland in all sorts of sites from those on the mountains to those at sea level. The Indians of British Columbia harvested the fruit in large quantities. In Alberta, *V. myrtilloides*, the velvet-leafed huckleberry, has been harvested by local people, while a form of *V. uliginosum* (known as *V. occidentale*) is called the Western huckleberry and is sometimes harvested in subalpine wet meadows on the Idaho-Montana border.

Vaccinium ovatum is known as evergreen huckleberry or shot huckleberry, and I have enjoyed huckleberry jam made from fruit that grows on plants in the coastal strip of Oregon. There it is harvested from the wild on a semicommercial scale. This species is more important in the garden, where it is appreciated for its ornamental value with some home gardeners picking the fruit for home use. Then there is the red huckleberry, *V. parvifolium*, with its glossy red berries that look like and have a similar flavor to cranberries.

The term "huckleberry" is not confined to *Vaccinium* and *Gaylussacia*. On the Pacific coast from Vancouver to northern California, the false azalea (*Menziesia ferruginea*) is found in coniferous woodlands. It is known as the fool's huckleberry or false huckleberry, not so much because of its fruit, which is small, dark purple and dry, but rather because its general appearance is very similar to that of plants belonging to *Vaccinium*. Its urn-shaped, pale pink flowers are especially similar. The false azalea also has brilliant fall color and is often found in association with *Vaccinium* species such as *V. ovatum* and *V. parvifolium*. Thank goodness for Linnaeus, who gave us the benefit of universal Latin names!

Propagation

All cultivars and species of the highbush blueberries, be they the northern highbush, rabbiteyes, hybrids such as the southern highbush or half highs, are propagated by cuttings unless they are being bred for a new variety, in which case seed is used. However, when bulking up new, rare or difficult to root cultivars, the modern technique is to use tissue culture (known as micropropagation), which is usually carried out by professional companies with the necessary technical know-how and facilities.

Micropropagation is increasingly used because this method can produce plants of guaranteed health and even of vigor since growth is originated in a laboratory. Mother plants are first "cleaned up" by ensuring they are free of all pests and diseases. Samples are taken and examined under powerful microscopes, and if signs of a virus are detected, any tissues to be used for propagation are treated such that all harmful organisms are removed before they can be passed on to the resulting plantlets. Clean mother plants are then brought into active growth. Small, actively growing shoot tips are removed and placed under sterile conditions on specially formulated cultures in flasks. These cultures then produce small offshoots that are multiplied in further cultures until the required number of offshoots have been produced. Offshoots are cut from the multiplication cultures and weaned. Each plantlet is potted into sterile compost with a very small amount of nutrient and grown as an independent plant that is gradually hardened off before being grown on in normal nursery conditions. It may take twelve to eighteen months to produce a plant suitable for planting out or potting on into 1 gallon (4 liter) containers. Some of the more experienced nurseries take less time.

Most traditional propagation nurseries use hardwood cuttings, but many nurseries use softwood as well. They do so to get a maximum number of plants in a year, which is a kind of insurance policy for those varieties that are more difficult to root as hardwood cuttings.

Highbush blueberry cuttings are not among the easiest of shrub cuttings to root, whether soft or hardwood is used. Anything between a 50 and 90 percent success rate can be achieved, depending on the condition of the cutting material, the skill of the propagator, rooting conditions and the variety being propagated. Bottom heat from specially manufactured electric heating cables in the compost is used extensively in colder climates to aid rooting.

It is possible to select cutting material from fruit-producing plantations but this reduces the following season's crop. Most growers and propagating nurseries, in trying to obtain a source of strong, healthy, disease-free propagating material set aside special areas where selected plants of the varieties they use can be grown under close supervision. These stock plants must be true to name, free from pests and diseases (including viruses) and well away from potential sources of infection. Bushes in stock beds are cut to about 12 in. (30 cm) above ground level each winter during the dormant period as a way of stimulating growth from the crown during the following growing season. They are fed a high nitrogen fertilizer as soon as growth starts in spring and are given another, more balanced fertilizer in midsummer. The objective is to produce plenty of strong canes, which will be fully mature before winter frosts damage the shoots.

Glasshouses or polythene tunnels are used as overhead protection for cuttings in most commercial nurseries, but on New Jersey's plantations, raised, outdoor propagating frames with mist spray facilities are the norm. Propagating beds are usually raised off the ground, especially if cuttings are to be put directly into a rooting medium on the bench and not into cells or trays. Raised beds make life easier for the nursery staff and it improves drainage, air circulation and disease control.

Propagating beds, frames or boxes may be supplied with some form of bottom heat in the form of individual cables or mats with cables inside them. Temperatures from 63° to 70°F (17 to 21°C) are advantageous, especially in areas where spring comes late and summers are uncertain, and rooting percentages are definitely improved. No shade is necessary except in areas of very strong light intensity where mist is used, but if polythene is used over the beds to maintain a moist atmosphere, it is essential to provide some shade because the cuttings are easily scorched by bright sunlight and high temperatures if under unshaded polythene. Many nurseries have propagating houses that make use of fog, a method that prevents droplets from accumulating on the leaves but keeps humidity high.

The rooting medium of 50 percent peat to 50 percent sand or perlite is commonly used, but some varieties root better with a higher percentage of peat. If cuttings are around 4 in. (10 cm) long, 2 in. (5 cm) of which will be inserted in the rooting medium, the rooting medium needs to be 4 in. (10 cm) deep to prevent the cutting from touching the bottom of the propagating bench. It should be soaked thoroughly before the cuttings are planted so that it is evenly wet throughout but should not be firmed.

Hardwood Cuttings

The science behind hardwood cuttings may explain the sequence of events that takes place inside them when they are struck and rooted. Deciduous shrubs such as highbush blueberries lay down stores of carbohydrate in the form of insoluble starch in the living tissues just under their bark. This storage process takes place before the leaves lose their green coloring in fall when temperatures drop and the stores remain inactive during dormancy. When temperatures rise again, these reserves are gradually released as a result of temperature-sensitive hormone activity; they are turned into soluble (and therefore mobile) carbohydrates or sugars that can then be transported in the sap. The sugars are used as the source of energy to start green shoot and leaf growth. Once green leaves appear, the plant is again able to manufacture its own carbohydrates by photosynthesis. Later, with the help of relevant plant hormones, it makes proteins and other substances to carry out its life functions, including the building of new tissues, which results in the growth of roots.

Hardwood cuttings are basically pieces of stem with dormant buds and no leaves. They should be made from wood that is firm and with very few or preferably no flower buds. Unripe wood is unsuitable as it is usually frost damaged and has a soft center with a squashed appearance. Cuttings are usually taken in early spring just before bud growth starts and after their required chilling period of dormancy. The ideal time to take cuttings is when the worst of the winter is over but the stems are still dormant. Lengths of about 12 to 20 in. (30 to 50 cm) of young shoots from the previous year's growth are cut from the parent plants. If it is more convenient, they may be taken earlier and stored in clean, damp moss (the moss must not be wet) in plastic bags and kept at 5° to 12°F (−11° to −15°C) for up to two to three months if necessary. The ideal storage period, however, is two to three weeks.

Cuttings are then prepared from these lengths of young shoots. The ideal cuttings are about 4 in. (10 cm) long with the diameter of a pencil. Thinner cuttings root more quickly but do not make strong plants, and thicker cuttings take longer to root or may fail altogether. Shorter lengths may not have sufficient food reserves to carry the cutting through to successful rooting and so are more vulnerable to extremes in their surroundings.

Cuts should be made with a very sharp knife or with secateurs because bruising that results from blunt cutting tools inhibits rooting. Some of the largest plantations make cuttings in bulk and they use a chainsaw or other very sharp cutting device with a thin blade to avoid bruising. Traditionally, where bulk cuttings were not the norm, the upper cut was made directly above the top bud with the lower cut slanting below the lowest bud. In varieties that are difficult to root, a ½ to ¾ in. (1.25 to 2 cm) slice of bark was removed from opposite sides of the base to expose a maximum number of the critical cells (the cambium cells) from which the roots will develop. Such precision is not possible in a commercial propagating unit, so the stems are cut to a length that depends on the presence of suitable beds. The only criteria are that the shoots are healthy, of the right diameter and with very few, if any, flower buds.

For a few days after preparation, cuttings are often stored upright with their bases in damp sphagnum moss or moist sand in bundles of 50 at 7° to 12°F (−11° to −14°C). They may be dipped into a weak fungicide solution to prevent fungal infection, especially on the cut surfaces. Hormone rooting liquid or powder suitable for hardwood cuttings is usually used to encourage rooting.

Prepared cuttings are then inserted in the moistened rooting medium so that just a couple of inches appear above the compost. They are planted about 2 in. (5 cm) apart each way in the beds. Their bases should never touch the bottom of the propagating box or bench, especially if heating cables are used. If it has not been possible to allow a depth of 4 in. (10 cm) of compost, then cuttings should be inserted diagonally with no more than 30 percent of the cutting exposed. Cuttings are then firmed in by pressing the rooting medium with fingers or by watering. Management of the propagating box or bench includes making sure that the rooting medium is kept moist but not waterlogged, that the air surrounding the cuttings is humid enough to prevent wilting, that there is enough shade to prevent scorching and that there is a monitoring of pests and diseases.

Within three to four weeks buds will begin to show growth and shoots soon develop from them. It is tempting to think that you have an independent plant but this is not so for another three to four weeks (or three to four months without heat). The cuttings have used their stored energy to produce shoots and need to pause for a while so that their newly grown shoots can produce sufficient food by photosynthesis for the growth of roots and the next new shoots. When signs of new growth appear then rooting has occurred. With luck and good management, 90 percent of the cuttings should root, but many have to settle for a 50 to 60 percent success rate.

The time between initial shoot growth and rooting is critical in management terms as this is the time when a shortage of water, excessively high or low temperatures above or below the cutting, strong sun or wind or any fungal infection can wreak havoc. All fallen leaf litter and dead cuttings should be promptly removed, and fungicide soil drenches may be necessary if there are signs of infection.

Softwood Cuttings

Propagation is regarded as being more difficult using softwood cuttings but a few varieties seem to root more easily this way. They do, however, require a mist or fogging system (the latter is better) because they are taken at a time of year when temperatures tend to be high and transpiration rapid. In cooler climates where rooting-medium temperatures drop below 63° to 68°F (17° to 20°C), thermostatically-controlled soil heating is used to maintain the compost at this temperature. It is especially important to heat soil in this way when overhead cooling is done with mist because water droplets frequently drop into the compost, which tends to lower the compost temperature.

The best time to take softwood cuttings is in midsummer when the parent plants are in active growth. It is best to use shoots from the first flush of spring growth before they set flower buds. Cuttings should be about 5 to 8 in. (12.5 to 20 cm) long with the lower leaves removed. Only two or three leaves remain at the top, and a clean cut is made at the base below a leaf node. If the shoot is very soft, the top should be removed. Some propagators use hormone liquid or powder, but others do not believe they are of any great benefit on softwood cuttings.

The rooting medium should be the same as for hardwood cuttings and the softwood cuttings need to be inserted to a depth of about 2 in. (5 cm). Their bases must be kept well above the bottom of the rooting medium if soil heating is used, and two or three leaves should remain above the soil. Mist or fog need to be controlled in such a way that the humidity is high enough to prevent wilting but not too high that the cuttings and rooting medium become saturated. Shade is necessary if weather conditions become hot and sunny enough to scorch the leaves. Fungicide sprays may be needed to control botrytis and other diseases that are common at this stage.

Softwood cuttings should root in four to nine weeks and then should gradually be given more ventilation before being weaned into a less humid environment with good air circulation. They will need shade until the sun's strength diminishes in late summer or early fall.

Potting Up

Most professional growers pot up the rooted plants as soon as possible and keep them under protection as a way to get some late summer growth and produce plants with a good system of three or four strong shoots before winter sets in. Home growers may prefer to keep their plants in their propagating trays or benches until the following spring. However, it is best to remove plants from open benches or boxes before their root systems get too large and intertwined with those of neighboring plants. It is surprising how extensive the root system of a young blueberry plant is—and how easy it is to accidentally remove it from its cutting when potting them up for the first time. Some growers use trays of long, narrow "root-trainers" for rooting their cuttings in because such containers avoid the problem of accidental root removal.

The choice of compost for potting varies but does incorporate some peat. Some growers use pure ground peat with added nutrients, while others use a mixture of peat and bark. A good commercial mix is 80 percent fir bark, 10 percent peat and 10 percent pumice with a slow-release fertilizer to provide nutrients.

Young highbush blueberry plants, especially those rooted from softwood cuttings, need the protection of a glasshouse or polythene tunnel for their first winter in all but the mildest climates. Growing-house ventilation should be gradually increased, and shading should be reduced so that the plants are hardened off before winter sets in. Some form of emergency heating may be kept on hand in case of damaging cold winter weather.

Rooted cuttings can be planted out in the spring of the following year after the danger of hard frost has past, but most growers in cooler climates pot their blueberries up into 1-gallon containers (2- or 3-liter pots in Europe) and grow them on outside for another year before planting them in the field. Others set them out in nursery beds in clean ground. The rooted cuttings usually have the tips of their young growth pruned back during the summer (some nurseries do this up to four times) to encourage branching and to make a more dense, compact plant.

Part IV

Vacciniums as Garden Plants

Vacciniums that are grown primarily for their fruit—cranberries, lingonberries and blueberries—have been enjoying a huge surge in popularity since the mid-1990s as people discover their health benefits and also how to use them in the kitchen. Gardeners have, however, been a little frightened of growing them in the belief that they are difficult because of their need for acidic soil conditions. Perhaps the pundits, in reacting to the "old" days when their attempts failed because they simply didn't know what the plants' requirements were, thus killing them with kindness in the form of too much animal manure for example, have been a little overzealous in stressing the needs of vacciniums. Whatever the reason, many more people all over the world are growing and enjoying the fruit of these plants from their own gardens. But what about their ornamental value? Why has it taken so long for this to be appreciated? Maybe the beauty and versatility of these wonderful shrubs are being discovered because more and more people who are growing them for their fruit are finding out about their additional ornamental value and so are extolling their virtues. Perhaps, too, more and more people are prepared to go to a little extra trouble to provide the right conditions for plants that give so much.

Interest in vacciniums is getting to the next stage with the discovery that although there are many more *Vaccinium* species that may not provide delicious fruit, there are those that instead provide great value in ornamental terms. With many species providing glowing colors in their young growth, highly attractive flowers and fruit as well as gorgeous fall color, there is a host of vacciniums to choose from for a number of different locations in the garden. All are worth seeking out.

Chapter 6

Vacciniums Grown Mainly for Fruit

Blueberries

Vaccinium species have been collected and introduced into cultivation since the latter part of the eighteenth century. Kew Gardens in London seems to have received most of them (they may be seen in the herbarium), but a number of collections appeared in some of the great English gardens, especially those where their owners supported the plant hunters of the early and mid-twentieth century. J. C. Williams of Caerhays Castle in Cornwall and Lionel de Rothschild of Exbury in Hampshire, for example, received some of the Chinese and Himalayan species through the work of Ernest Wilson, George Forrest and also the French plant hunter Father Jean Marie Delavay.

However, some limited spread of cultivation, especially of *Vaccinium corymbosum*, goes back to the turn of the twentieth century. Bean (1951) lists 37 species in volume 3 of his classic text; admittedly, some have been integrated to become "forms" of others. The famous American horticulturist Liberty Hyde Bailey, writing about the North American highbush blueberry, in the late 1800s, said "The plant is beautiful when in flower, the fruit is attractive and of the best quality and the bright scarlet and crimson effects in late fall, rivaling the sumach in brilliancy, are unsurpassed. As an ornamental plant the species deserves a place in every garden."

The problem was that it was not fully explained that highbush blueberries in particular needed nonalkaline soil with plenty of slowly decomposing organic matter rather than well-manured plots or alkaline soil. Some gardeners fed them generously on standard fish, blood and bone fertilizers, or they mulched the plants with plenty of partly rotted farmyard manure so that the roots suffered chemical root scorch and died. Consequently, the plants were thought impossible to cultivate and best left to the wild.

It was at about this time that Elizabeth White and Coville started their collaboration. Coville was the first to really research the needs of highbush blueberries. His research was aimed at commercial blueberry production, and the emphasis remained firmly fixed on commercial fruit production until 100 years later at the turn of the twenty-first century. With both the health benefits and the ornamental values of highbush blueberries coming to the fore, gardeners are flocking to their nurseries and garden centers to buy plants. The hybrid varieties known as half highs are particularly popular because they are compact and therefore suitable for small gardens or containers. In each year since 2000, there has not been a single blueberry plant available in nurseries and garden centers in Europe by the end of the spring-planting season. Our own company, like all the other British nurseries and garden centers, was forced to look to nurseries in Europe, but without success. It is now our policy to order plants one or two years in advance!

Many people are still entirely focused on fruit production, their visions being of shelves full of blueberry jam and freezers entirely stocked within a few years. And many do achieve this vision. I know of one gentleman whose only garden is on a rooftop in the center of London. With the 12 blueberry plants he has in tubs for 20 years, he fills his own freezer, gives masses away to friends and even supplies the local corner shop. His plants needed to be replaced only in 2002, but that is after having been potted up again and again until they ended up in 24 in. (50 cm) pots for seven or eight years.

At the other end of the spectrum is another gardener who has blueberries scattered among the roses in his 2½ acre (1 hectare) garden, purely for ornamental effect. They provide flowers and scent in spring before his roses flower, and bright red leaves followed by red stems after the roses have finished flowering. Their summer leaves provide a neutral background to fill the border during the main rose-flowering season in high summer. He cuts the blueberry bushes to ground level when they get too tall, which results in fresh young growth that starts all over again. This garden is friendly to wildlife, and its owner likes to see flocks of blackbirds, thrushes and finches devouring the berries. The soil is far from ideal (it is pH 6.0), but with plenty of rotting pine chippings applied as annual mulch, he can provide a more acidic soil environment in the area around his blueberry plants, which are thriving. The roses also benefit since they do not need artificial rose fertilizer. One reason for this grower's unexpected success may be his entirely fortuitous access to free pine chippings and pine needles. It is, after all, among the pine forests of eastern New Jersey that one of the largest concentrations of wild highbush blueberries is found, and the soil mycorrhiza that blueberries enjoy occurs in well-rotted pine detritus.

Cranberries and Lingonberries

Gardeners regard *Vaccinium macrocarpon* as the cranberry for gardens with plenty of space and suitable soil conditions, particularly if the climate is not too severe or where some form of protection can be provided during harsh winter conditions or late spring frosts. Cranberries can provide an attractive, dense, ornamental ground cover or can extend over and cover the margins of garden ponds where unsightly black liners are used. The effect is rather striking, especially when their trailing green branches are loaded with attractive, glossy red berries. Birds are not attracted to cranberry fruit to nearly the same degree as blueberries and so cranberries may often be seen adding color to the bushes through the winter months if it is cold enough to prevent rotting bacteria from doing their work. The overall reddish appearance of the leaves in winter is also quite attractive.

It is surprising how well cranberries do in the shrub border once they are given suitable conditions to get them established. They make excellent ground cover among rhododendrons and azaleas. Similarly, if the light intensity is sufficient, they will do well in the front of a border in a lightly wooded garden where the soil is acidic because of the high organic content from decomposing leaves that release humic acid. Cranberry plants can also look good trailing over a wall or bank and even cascading over the rim of troughs and hanging baskets. However, their naturally vigorous, spreading habit with roots that form at nodes as they go means that in the most artificial environments, their life span is a relatively short four or five years. Where space is limited, a relatively compact grower such as 'Franklin' is worth considering. 'Early Black', because of its reliability and ornamental value, is an automatic choice for less confined areas.

For those wishing to make a collection or grow enough plants to have berries to store as well as use fresh, it is probably worth considering having a special area set aside for cranberry cultivation, especially if soil conditions are not ideal. They are ideal plants to cover the ground of a berry bed, which I describe later in this chapter. In areas where the ground freezes solid as temperatures drop below freezing for several days and nights and where cold winds cause desiccation if there is no snow cover, it is worth giving cranberry plants some overhead protection to reduce potential damage to the fruit buds. Horticultural fleece may provide effective insulation and can be used again if a late spring frost is threatening to damage young growth.

Lingonberries (*Vaccinium vitis-idaea*) are another story altogether because they are naturally more compact and slow growing in habit; they are altogether more controllable. This makes them unrivaled as plants for small gardens or even for those with no garden at all. Their compact size, glossy evergreen properties, two annual flowerings in milder areas (and therefore fruiting periods) and brilliantly glossy fruit earn them a place in tubs and troughs and even in window boxes since they do fairly well in exposed situations.

The lingonberry has a richer, more "rounded" flavor and many regard it as the gourmet cranberry. It is also the species to provide cultivars in gardens in colder areas, and there is nothing to beat it where there is limited space. The pretty flowers and glossy berries provide an unusual feature for much of the summer and fall, as do the permanently glossy, dark green leaves.

Requirements for Cultivation

Given that *Vaccinium* species and cultivars can provide both fruit and ornamental value, most people end up compromising when faced with the dilemma of which aspect to choose, especially when it comes to providing sites in the garden. Compromise is especially prevalent when blueberries are part of the scheme. Some opt for putting those plants that are being grown to provide fruit in the protected environment of a specially constructed wire fruit cage (one that is bird-proof) with the other soft fruit, either directly in the soil if it is suitable or in containers. They then accept that any ornamental features such as the scented flowers and the bright fall color of the foliage may not be fully appreciated. This method means that birds and large predators are prevented from eating the berries and that a full crop of fruit goes into the kitchen.

Others put higher value on the ornamental aspect and therefore grow their plants in shrub borders, berry beds or containers. They simply cover the plants with netting that keeps the birds out during the fruiting season. Those who like to encourage birds and other wild animals to their gardens forgo the fruit and leave their plants unnetted.

Soil

Vacciniums grown in gardens require much the same conditions as those grown commercially. Soils with a high percentage of dense clay particles and a high pH are not considered suitable for the cultivation of vacciniums. Soils based on truly alkaline conditions such as chalk are also definitely out. Alkaline soils with pH 7.0 or more, such as the loams of former farms where corn or vegetables have been grown and including those that have been recently limed, are also not suitable. Similarly, garden soils where vegetables have been a priority or that have been limed in recent years do not suit vacciniums. The plants are not able to absorb the necessary minerals for growth and they fail to thrive. It is better to use containers or make a raised ericaceous bed that contains a suitably acidic compost.

Clay soils are often acidic but have such small, densely packed particles that not only form an impenetrable barrier for the fine fibrous roots of vacciniums to penetrate but also tend to become easily waterlogged and starved of oxygen, which kills the roots. It is possible to make acidic clay soil suitable for ericaceous plants. Some gardeners incorporate a lime-free sharp sand or coarse grit into such soils, often mixed with peat or a combination of both finely and coarsely chopped bark. The idea is to separate the clay particles by forming crumbs, thus allowing better drainage and air circulation, which is an altogether healthier environment for roots. Each blueberry shrub should have an area of about $3^1/2$ ft. (1 m) square and at least a spade's depth that is treated with sand, peat or chopped bark, preferably at least six months before planting to allow time for its incorporation. Simply putting organic matter in a planting hole is not acceptable since this tends to form a sump in wet weather where water accumulates and drowns the roots.

Irrigation

Some form of irrigation will be necessary in most climates. It is essential to keep the area around the roots moist during the growing season otherwise growth and flower-bud formation will be poor. It is also difficult to rehydrate a peaty soil. In areas of high summer rainfall where additional water needs are relatively infrequent (such as in many parts of northern Europe), it does not matter if the water supply is alkaline. However, where frequent watering is needed over a long period, it should come from a neutral or acidic supply. Collected rainwater is ideal.

Planting

Once the necessary site and soil conditions have been sorted out, the chosen blueberry, cranberry or other vaccinium can be planted. Many growers plant in the spring to allow a full growing season to get the plants established, ensuring that the plants are never allowed to dry out. This means that the root systems should be well established before the following winter. Fall planting while the soil is still warm may be preferred in areas where heavy frosts—and therefore considerable frost heave—are not expected. It is surprising how quickly roots will establish in these warm, fall soil conditions, especially if a mulch is applied to damp soil after planting.

Most suppliers provide container-grown, two- or three-year-old plants. Some specialist nurseries provide "open-ground" plants or larger "specimen plants." When ordering from another country, plant health regulations may require a phytosanitary certificate from the nursery owner. Plants are usually sent bare rooted but they typically have plenty of peat attached because peat is regarded as being a "soiless" medium; it is also impossible to remove all the peat from the densely packed fibrous roots.

Plants should be put into their planting hole, whether in the garden, berry bed, trough or pot, so that after being firmed in they are no deeper in the soil than they were in their original pots. They should be well watered in, and a mulch to a depth of about 2½ in. (6.4 cm) should be applied to the damp soil to reduce weed growth and water evaporation. Well-rotted, finely chopped bark, peat or sawdust should be used. For the small, low-growing alpine species, a thin layer of fine chippings of granite or noncalcareous sand or similar material should be used instead of an organic mulch.

Berry Beds

Berry beds provide a most attractive ornamental feature in any garden, large or small, and can be inexpensive and easy to construct. A more permanent, high-quality structure can make a big difference to an otherwise unremarkable garden. Raised beds filled with suitable compost provide the special conditions needed for all ericaceous berry plants, enabling gardeners who do not have the naturally acidic, free-draining soil needed for these plants to widen their horizons and to enjoy both their edible fruits and the year-round ornamental interest. Most people, especially those with small gardens or yards, find that the combination of culinary delight, year-round ornamental interest and a supply of local wildlife that eats the fruit means that berry beds add a whole new dimension to gardening.

Berry beds can be of any size or shape and be designed to the scale of the garden and the owners' taste. Different materials can act as soil-retaining edging. They can be filled with a selection of blueberries, cranberries, lingonberries and indeed some of the purely ornamental vacciniums. The height of the bed depends partly on the taste of the owner and how windy the site is. It is worth bearing in mind, however, that highbush blueberries can grow to 5 to 6 ft. (1.5 1.8 m) or more and will need at least 2½ ft. (80 cm) of rooting medium to provide sufficient anchorage so that they do not blow over. The size of the bed depends on the number and type of plants chosen. I offer the slight warning that it is better to allow space for adding more plants because vacciniums can become addictive and new varieties are always coming along.

A bed with a surface area of about 7 sq. ft. (2 sq. m) should accommodate two of the more compact North American highbush blueberries, one southern highbush and one or two half highs. At least 6 cranberries and 12 lingonberries can be added to cover the ground. A flat stone placed here and there will mean not trampling on the cranberries when harvesting the blueberries. Incidentally, the delicious alpine strawberry (it is not a vaccinium) adds further interest well into the fall and grows well in similar conditions.

Siting and construction

The *Vaccinium* species grown for their fruiting or ornamental value all tend to give of their best when sited either in full sun or just a little shade. This ensures ripening of the fruit, especially in the case of late-ripening species or varieties, and provides the best conditions for the most vivid fall color. Also, as many vacciniums tend to have growth spurts in very late summer and often well into fall, such a siting gives the best chance for the tips of this growth to ripen before winter sets in.

Brick or noncalcareous stone fitted with drainage holes about 6 in. (15 cm) above ground level make good retaining walls for a permanent feature. Wood may be less permanent, but if chemically treated well in advance of planting, will give years of use. When growing edible vacciniums, I recommend ensuring that the preservative used does not contain arsenic as many do. This is obviously not as important if a good polythene liner is used. Log rolls that consist of sawn lengths of treated wood about 2 ft. (60 cm) long linked by strong, flexible wire are widely available and are quick and easy to use, particularly if wavy edges to the beds are required because they can be bent to any shape. Strong, vertical supporting posts will be needed for retaining walls made of wood or other similar material.

Heavy-duty polythene (or any other lining material suitable for ponds) is useful if the bed is to be constructed in a garden with an alkaline soil of pH 7.0 or higher. Liners such as these reduce the risk of alkaline water seeping into the beds. However, they may cause problems in areas of high rainfall so it is worth making sure that drainage from the sides of the berry bed also penetrates the polythene. The soil needs to provide good drainage, especially in winter, but a degree of water retention in dry conditions, especially during the summer growing season, is desirable. It also needs to provide acid conditions (the ideal is pH 4.5 to 5.0) so that ericaceous plants can take up nutrients.

Proprietary ericaceous composts that provide low pH and plenty of organic matter are widely available. Traditionally, they consist of moss peat with added nutrients. These composts do become compacted however, especially if used in beds where it is necessary to walk to keep weeds under control, scatter fertilizer, harvest fruit and so on. An additional consideration is the rising concern about what is regarded in many quarters as excessive use of unsustainable natural resources such as peat.

Many peat substitutes are now available in garden stores. I would still recommend using some peat, no matter how small the amount, because it contains the beneficial soil mycorrhiza. The most suitable for many vacciniums are those that mirror as nearly as possible the conditions in which the plants grow in the wild, namely pine- or fir-based products. Chipped coniferous bark combined with chopped pine needles makes a good base, provided that it has been composted for at least a year, preferably two, after which the composted bark will be brown. The test is whether there is the smell of resin since the slightly musty smell of decaying wood should be there instead. Leaf litter collected from beneath deciduous trees and composted for six months to a year also seems to be useful, especially if mixed with peat or chipped pine bark. A mixture of 80 percent fir bark, 10 percent peat and 10 percent pumice, perlite or lime-free horticultural grit is a good base. As a result of conservation efforts, it is illegal to go into the forest and take home bags of pine litter or leaf mold, but some forest enterprises sell composted pine litter or chipped bark. These products are often available, conveniently bagged, from garden stores.

If the garden soil is pH 6.0 or less it is possible to incorporate some or all of the soil excavated out of the site during construction, especially if irrigation water is to be rainwater or water from a neutral or slightly acidic source. Nonalkaline sand (sand this is not extracted from a marine source) is very useful and can act as a cover to reduce weed germination. Commercial cranberry growers have found it especially useful for low-growing vacciniums such as cranberries that spread by sending out runners which root from their nodes.

If the available water supply is alkaline or high in mineral salts, some form of rainwater storage is needed, especially in climates that experience low rainfall in summer. Where a high number of ericaceous plants in the garden justifies the expense, acid-dosing systems that inject acid into alkaline water supplies to bring the pH down to the required level can also be used.

I have outlined below the steps to take in constructing a berry bed.

1. Mark the outline of the site to be constructed. The shape can be square, rectangular, circular, semicircular or any other shape that fits in with the existing or planned design of the site. A basic bed to suit most situations is 6 ft. × 6 ft. (1.8 m × 1.8 m) and about $3^{1}/_{3}$ ft. (1 m) deep.

2. Dig out up to 12 in. (30 cm) of the soil within the marked-off area. Retain the soil and mix it later with organic ingredients if its pH is 6.0 or less. Remove the soil if the pH is above 6.0. If building a retaining wall of stone or brick, lay foundations and build the wall, leaving drainage holes as I discussed. If using log rolls, split poles, wooden boarding or planks of wood or other material, you will need to incorporate vertical supporting posts.

3. Mix the materials that will form the compost and fill the bed very near to the top of the retaining wall, bearing in mind that organic matter will shrink as it decays.

4. Plant up the bed and water it thoroughly.

5. It is a good idea to plan for when the fruit appears. When the blueberries begin to show the slightest color, they must be protected from birds and berry-eating mammals. Either purchase or build temporary fruit cages that allow access for picking and remove them once the crop is harvested.

The choice of which vaccinium to plant in a berry bed can encompass the whole species. It need not be confined to just blueberries, cranberries and lingonberries. Many of the less well-known ornamentals are well worth considering, especially if they can be sited so that their various features are enjoyed all year. Perhaps they can be planted in a separate bed that has no bird protection so that birds and other wildlife can enjoy some of the berries.

Those who favor an alpine bed or border can plant several of the species that originate in similar situations among rocks and scree that can be tastefully arranged over the bed. Evergreen, wintergreen and deciduous species have habits small enough for this arrangement, and a suitable selection can provide interest year round. A mulch of noncalcareous fine gravel or coarse grit sprinkled over the top of the compost after planting is beneficial for these small plants with shallow root systems because it helps reduce evaporation and possible dehydration in hot weather. It also discourages weeds and rotting of the lower leaves, especially in those evergreen species that derive from dry, well-drained habitats in the wild.

Pots, Tubs and Troughs

Most vacciniums will thrive in containers for years, so if there is no room in a garden for a berry bed or if growers wish to have portable or semiportable vacciniums, they will not be disappointed. Indeed, some of the smaller species are better kept under the controlled conditions of a container, and when growing the more tender species it is often more practical to keep them in a container under glass. Large clay, plastic or wooden pots and tubs are used as the final containers for larger species, including highbush blueberries.

Many highbush blueberries, both the northern and the more recently introduced southern blueberries, as well as those half highs grown in cool climates make ideal container plants because they give great value as ornamental features: attractive and tasty fruit in summer, brilliant color in fall, red young stems in winter and scented flowers in spring. (Plates 35, 36) All these features make the extra effort of container growing well worth the trouble.

It is tempting to buy a small plant and put it straight into a large container. This temptation should be resisted, however, as the volume of compost in relation to the plant's size and its suction ability is too great to create water movement and air circulation through the soil. Stagnant, sour soil results, which causes root death. It is better to gradually pot up into larger and larger containers as the years pass, eventually reaching a pot or tub that is about 2 ft. (60 cm) in diameter, particularly for highbush blueberries and some of the more vigorous ornamentals. The main problem with using pots or tubs is that in summer the roots of plants fill the container and their demand for water exceeds the supply, especially as many people are away from their homes for summer vacations. Insufficient water during the summer can result in a lack of flowers and fruit the following year. The reason why most container-grown blueberry plants fail to flower and fruit, and the cause of almost all summer or fall death, is the lack of water during the peak growing and fruit-bud formation season.

Cranberries need similar conditions to blueberries, but an ideal container for them will have a larger surface area to allow them room to spread their runners and support plenty of fruit-bearing uprights. An old cattle trough makes an interesting if artificial cranberry container. Lingonberries can be grown even in window boxes since they spread laterally relatively slowly.

Where there is a shortage of garden space, a halved, wooden beer barrel makes an ideal home for a collection of different *Vaccinium* species. It does not matter that they really need much more space as individuals; they make a very interesting and unusual display, especially in the fall when they exhibit a whole range of leaf colors from red through vermilion to orange to gold. Individual species do warrant container space, however, so try *V. japonicum* or *V. griffithianum* in a shady spot.

Chapter 7

Vacciniums Grown Mainly for Ornamental Value

The genus *Vaccinium* is certainly a source of fascinating and enduringly ornamental plants suitable for a wide variety of situations in gardens, from the shrub border to an alpine trough or bed. Even those that are grown primarily for their fruit will do well in containers. (See chapter 6) There are more than 450 species, widely distributed over diverse climatic regions, from arctic through temperate to tropical, and includes species that appear on relatively isolated islands such as the Azores, Madeira and now three fairly recently discovered species on Madagascar. Most vacciniums, other than highbush blueberries, cranberries or lingonberries, in cultivation for their ornamental value are straight species or named clones selected from species, and as interest in them grows, more are emerging as a result of active hybridization.

Species provide plants ranging in size from more than 20 ft. (6 m) to those that grow to no more than 2½ in. (6.4 cm). There are sprawling species that can cover old tree stumps or range over other host plants, large, tidy bushes, small mounded bushes and plants that spread horizontally and act as ground cover. Some are ideal for rock gardens or for growing in pans in an alpine bed. Some are suited to general cultivation in shrub borders and are not as fussy in their soil requirements as has been previously thought, while others are adapted to dry conditions or to moist, boglike conditions. Some like to be in full sun, particularly those species that are grown for their fall color. Others, being found in woodland in their native habitats, need some shade.

Many of the species in cultivation in temperate climates are of North American and European origin; plants that are associated with acidic soils resulting from glacial deposition, sometimes in moist situations and at others in dry well drained sites. They are often associated with coniferous trees or birch scrub. There are also some interesting species from mainland Asia, from countries in the Himalayan region, and from Japan, Korea and China.

Some of the most technically interesting vacciniums come from areas with soil formed by volcanic activity especially from Southeast Asia; from Japan, Taiwan, Borneo, Indonesia, New Guinea for example. Included in this category are many that are associated with recent volcanic activity, in soils with a high sulfur content and even in climates that still contain high sulfur dioxide levels. Some are early colonizers, and need the poorest of acidic soils in cultivation. They are great survivors and even individual species can adapt to varying soil and climatic conditions. *Vaccinium varingiaefolium* is an example of a species found on the mountains of Java, Indonesia at altitudes above 5,900 to 6,650 ft. (1,800 to 2,000 m). If conditions are favorable, in subalpine forests, it can reach 20 ft. (6 m) or more but forms a shrub of considerably less height in the poor, dry soils on open, exposed sites. Researchers from two Indonesian universities found that plants near the rim of volcanic craters, where ambient concentrations of sulfur dioxide were relatively high, were small but had extra thick leaves, and were still capable of fruiting. Those even 30 ft. (9 m) away from the rim had measurably thinner leaves and were larger.

Those species growing in countries such as New Guinea and the Philippines, which have a largely tropical rain forest climate, are generally found at high altitude, between 3,300 and 9,800 ft. (1,000 and 3,000 m) where the climate is cooler and the tree canopy sparse or absent. This makes them suitable for cultivation in gardens in temperate climates. Those that do grow in the rainforest tend to be epiphytic, growing in rotting leaf litter in the angles between trunks and branches of trees. Here they get their water and mineral requirements from the decaying humus and are elevated to be in a better position to receive sufficient light and to attract insects for pollination.

Most frequently, however, these vacciniums that are found at high altitudes are terrestrial, with species that have become accustomed to dry, exposed conditions often colonizing newly disturbed ground as pioneers. They may be found colonizing the margins of newly cut forests, newly constructed roads and other "hostile" sites. Some thrive on boggy sites or among rocks or growing on tussocks in grassland. There are deciduous plants, semi-evergreens and true evergreens. There are moisture loving vacciniums and those that are more accustomed to dry conditions. Some prefer to be planted in full sun, others prefer marginal or woodland sites.

Most species produce edible berries, but they don't compete with those grown for their fruit, and of those which are classed as inedible some are regarded as being edible in certain forms or in some habitats. There are very few that are actually poisonous. Most produce berries that are too small or too seedy to be attractive to us but provide excellent food for birds and other wildlife. Birds tend to leave many of these berries until they have been on the plants for some weeks or even months allowing us to enjoy their beauty first.

Vaccinium floribundum, in some montane habitats in South America, is host to a couple of mite species that are spread from plant to plant in the nasal passages of certain hummingbirds! The mites apparently evolved within the flowers of the plants.

Although blueberries and cranberries are the most well known vacciniums because of their fruit, many are actually highly ornamental too. The scented flowers, bright fall color and red winter stems of most highbush blueberry cultivars are compensation for the time it takes for bushes to reach their full fruiting potential.

The varied species that come under the heading "blueberries," such as *Vaccinium angustifolium*, *V. ovalifolium* and *V. uliginosum* vary in their use as a source of edible berries but almost all have good fall color and other assets for use in the garden, including ground cover and as providers of food for birds and other wildlife.

For those with limited space or who may prefer to grow vacciniums in containers there are more half-high hybrid blueberries emerging in nurseries. Mostly interspecific hybrids between *Vaccinium corymbosum* and *V. angustifolium*, they certainly have a place as compact fruiting or ornamental shrubs especially in cold climate areas.

The newer hybrid southern highbush blueberry plants are set to provide a whole new dimension for home gardeners. Although bred to give high quality fruit in climates that are not able to provide sufficient chill hours for northern highbush cultivars, two further aspects have emerged. One is the fact that many are much hardier than first appreciated and are doing well in cool but not particularly cold gardens in both the United States and in northern Europe, where temperatures do not sink below 23°F (−5°C) for more than a few days in winter. The other aspect is the highly ornamental nature of the plants of some of the cultivars. Who can resist the lovely gray green leaves of 'Sunshine Blue'; leaves that are wintergreen, staying on the bushes all winter but are pushed off by emerging young growth in spring. The purple calyces of large clusters of attractive creamy pink flowers are a pleasant surprise too. Then there is the bronzy red young growth, which seems to keep its color for most of the summer. All this on plants that are compact in habit. Many other species and cultivars are gradually becoming more appreciated and available from the nursery trade.

The evergreens usually have bright glossy leaves and many have bright red or bronze young growth. Most of the deciduous species produce superb fall color. The flowers of others are the main attraction. Who can resist the mass of pink and white blooms produced by *Vaccinium fragile*? Or the pendent clusters of different shades of red and pink blooms emerging from the bright red flower buds of *V. cylindraceum*, often accompanied by red tinted young growth? The dwarf form of this species, 'Tom Thumb' is particularly compact and suitable for small gardens.

Apart from named selections from the wild there is some hybridizing taking place. Barry Starling's new *Vaccinium cylindraceum* × *V. arctostaphylos* 'Prince Charming' is superb, as is his 'Cinderella', a *V. ovatum* × *V. floribundum* cultivar.

Those who grow *Acer palmatum* 'Senkaki' or one of the other "snake bark" maples in their garden because of the ornamental bark may want to try *Vaccinium oldhamii* too.

Growing Tender Species

If growing in warm temperate, subtropical or tropical climates or in colder areas where a reasonably substantial frost free glasshouse is available the lovely leaves and attractive flowers and fruit of some of the tropical species like *Vaccinium acrobracteatum* and *V. auriculifolium* are worth trying.

Neotropical vacciniums

Those New World countries that lie between the Tropic of Cancer (latitude 23.5°N of the Equator) and the Tropic of Capricorn (22.5°S) are hosts to a fascinating and, as yet, not fully classified flora, including possibly about 40 species of *Vaccinium*.

They have proved to be quite a challenge as many different names have been given to colonies of plants in diverse locations over the years. There has been considerable discussion among botanists over their nomenclature. In some cases several of those "species" or "varieties" of species, which have now been more closely studied have been found to have identical characteristics or extremely small variations and have now been lumped together as a single species, with the other "species" names allocated as synonyms.

The work carried out since the 1970s by James Luteyn and his team at the Institute of Systematic Botany at the New York Botanical Garden is regarded as the most authoritative and is the source of the information I provide here.

Vaccinium plants in the neotropical region are found mostly at higher altitudes in countries ranging from Mexico to northern Argentina, and on some of the Caribbean islands, especially Costa Rica, and Cuba. They occupy cool, moist upland forest habitats between 4,900 and 9,800 ft. (1,500 and 3,000 m) and many colonize recent rock slides or recently constructed roadsides, where they get plenty of light. Savannah shrubberies, where dappled shade is normal, are also habitats. They are not found in heavily shaded sites such as in the tropical rainforests or in arid situations in the lee of mountains.

Those neotropical species pollinated by hummingbirds tend to have bright, tubular flowers in pendent clusters, may have colored bracts, and the flowers lack scent. Most are of purely botanical interest, and some, such as *Vaccinium distichum* and *V. elvirae*, are rare and on the endangered list. A few are in cultivation or deserve to be, notably *V. consanguineum*, *V. crenatum*, and *V. floribundum*; the two species *V. berberidifolium* and *V. reticulatum*, which in Hawaii have the collective name 'Ohelo'; and the native *Vaccinium* species on the islands of Madeira and the Azores and three species on Madagascar. Some of the so-called tropical and neotropical species are much hardier than expected, probably because they were originally collected at higher, colder altitudes in otherwise tropical countries.

With such a varied genus, there is a place for *Vaccinium* plants in almost any garden.

Propagation

Vaccinium can be divided roughly into three groups when it comes to propagation: those that are successfully propagated by seed; those that are best propagated by removing rooted stolons or rhizomes or by dividing plants; and those that are best reproduced by taking cuttings and rooting them in a cold frame or with some bottom heat in a glasshouse or polythene tunnel.

Seed
Although it takes a little longer to produce a plant from seed than from vegetative methods, sowing seed is widely used for species propagation. The exception is when a known clone or form is propagated or when it is known

that two genetically compatible species or forms that are being grown close to each other may hybridize naturally, so producing seed that is not the same as either parent.

The first school of thought says that seeds should be gathered as soon as they are ripe and sown straight away, flesh and all, just as they would be in nature; the theory being that the flesh contains chemicals that help to preserve the seeds within the fruit in a moist condition and that the rotting of the flesh helps to soften the seed coats which helps germination. Those who argue against this say that harmful rotting agents thrive on the rotting flesh and then move on to the seeds and either rot them or their emerging roots and shoots in spring.

In nature of course the berries are often eaten by birds or small mammals, which disperse them, digesting the soft flesh of the fruit, leaving the seeds to pass out in their feces. This happens in late summer or fall, so the seeds reach the soil wrapped in a convenient amount of fertilizer. By the time spring arrives and germination takes place the feces will have lost its concentrated substance and become suitably mellowed and spread into a wider area. Perfect for the nutrition of young seedlings.

The second school of thought, which is widely accepted when growing seeds in artificial surroundings, is that it is better to remove all flesh and skin to avoid harmful rotting agents. Whatever the method it is important to avoid the seeds drying out at any stage as dried out seed may stay dormant for two years or more or fail to germinate at all.

Berry seeds need a period of rest (dormancy) before germinating and start the process of dormancy as soon they are harvested. Different species have different requirements for the duration of rest and temperatures required to keep them dormant. Those native to warmer areas, where winter soil temperatures are not likely to be much below freezing, require little if any dormancy while those from cold climate regions need more chilling before they will break dormancy and germinate. (A few days in a freezer will usually trick the hormones, which trigger the changes, into stimulating the seeds to germinate.)

Berries are harvested as soon as they are ripe and the flesh removed by gently washing it and picking out the clean seeds when they have separated from the flesh and skins. If harvested late in a mild fall germination of some warm climate species may sometimes have started within the fruit. Some gardeners remove any deformed or small seed and select the biggest and best seeds; others leave this selection to the pricking out stage.

Seed may be sown immediately in a 50:50 moist peat and sand compost in seed trays or in pots and covered very thinly, then put into a mouse or bird-free cold frame for the winter. It is a good idea to protect from frost, especially in the British climate as seeds often achieve their chilling requirements early in winter and may germinate prematurely during a warm spell before winter is over.

Most cold climate vacciniums, which fruit in late summer or in the fall, and experience regular cold weather, below 45°F (7°C), will not germinate until warm weather arrives in spring. Some may take longer. It is not unknown for seeds to suddenly germinate a year or more after sowing.

Cleaned seeds may be stored until sowing in the spring. They can be kept in a clean, lidded, air tight container, to keep mold fungi out, on moist absorbent paper, in a refrigerator or similarly cool place at about 5°F (−15°C), imitating the sort of winter temperatures they would experience in the wild. They can then be sown as above, in late winter in a heated propagator if an early start and a longer growing season are required or in spring in a cold frame. Some experienced growers favor sowing in unheated conditions, in an open, unheated frame, as this, although slower, gives better germination. Fungal infections are also less likely.

Once the young seedlings start to grow away, after about six weeks, when they should have two true leaves, they, like all young seedlings, need to be pricked out into individual small cells or pots, in ericaceous compost. They should not be fed immediately but should be very lightly fed with a suitable (ericaceous), general-purpose fertilizer after another couple of weeks once they have become established. Slow-release fertilizer pellets, especially manufactured for small plants, are however incorporated into the compost in a commercial nursery as they do not release their fertilizer immediately, and once they do so they release it very gradually as the plants' requirements increase. Some brands of slow-release fertilizer may release too much fertilizer too soon and scorch young roots, so only brands especially formulated for propagation and small plants in the relevant climate should be used.

The young seedlings need to be kept moist and protected from strong sun and wind for the summer, during which they should be given increasing ventilation in the frames. By the fall they should be strong young plants capable of overwintering in well-ventilated cold frames with protection only in severe weather. The species that grow in arid, alpine conditions suffer from excessive wetness so protection from prolonged rainfall in winter is beneficial. In the following spring many species will be ready for planting out, while others need another year with some protection from strong summer sun or severe winter weather.

Suckers, stolons or runners

This is simply the removal of lateral extensions from plants, which have already formed roots. It is the simplest and cheapest method for naturally spreading plants like cranberries, lingonberries and ground cover species such as *Vaccinium caespitosum*, *V. crassifolium* and *V. deliciosum*. It is easy to slice off a rooted section of plant and either transplant it to another garden space or pot it up and send it elsewhere.

Some of the larger shrubs like *Vaccinium glauco-album* also send out suckers that can be sliced off and transplanted or potted up, but they may be slow to establish and may need longer than expected in a nursery frame to produce a good root system.

Cuttings

(The propagation of blueberries, cranberries and lingonberries is fully described under "Propagation" in their own chapters.)

This is a widely used method for propagating ornamental vacciniums, especially the evergreen species as most of them root readily as semihardwood or even hardwood cuttings. Although late summer is the most usual time for taking cuttings, when the current year's growth has become firm but not yet woody, most evergreens, especially those with small leaves, seem to root at any time of year except when in full lush growth in high summer.

The deciduous species can be more difficult and the timing of propagation more critical. For best results they need to be propagated as semihardwood, rather than hardwood, cuttings, preferably taken as soon as they are firm enough in summer, and certainly well before leaf fall. Some will root in trays or pots in cold frames, taking anything from 6 to 16 weeks to root. Others need bottom heat and mist or heavily shaded plastic covers over them to maintain near 100 percent humidity. A 50:50 percent peat or sand mix is the traditional rooting medium, with perlite or similar product being used as a full or part alternative to sand.

There is some disagreement over the use of hormone rooting agents. Hormone liquid or powders are not always used for the easier evergreens but are very useful for the more difficult deciduous and semi-evergreen species.

Timing of propagation varies but the general philosophy is to take cuttings as early as possible in summer, as soon as the "wood" is ready, to allow sufficient time for the cuttings to root while plant hormones are still active within the plant. It also means that the resultant small plants can overwinter in cold frames, albeit covered with some form of insulation in those short sharp frost periods sometimes experienced, without needing heated protection from frost except in the more severe winter climates.

The basic technique is to remove short lateral shoots when their growing tips are firm enough to remain firm without flopping as soon as their cut stems are put into a moist rooting medium. Terminal cuttings, which include the growing tip of the shoot, are normally used. The length of the shoots depends on the species. *Vaccinium chaetothrix* will only yield shoots about 1/2 in. (1.25 cm) long, while more vigorous species like the shrubby *V. glauco-album* or spreading *V. nummularia* have much longer side shoots that have to be shortened to 2 to 4 in. (5 to 10 cm) to make cuttings. At least four potential growth buds should be included. Some propagators favor taking cuttings with a "heel" (small piece of parent stem torn off when removing the side shoot), especially for more difficult subjects, but most do not feel this is necessary.

Lower leaves should be removed so that none will be inserted in the rooting compost, and the lower cut done with a very sharp knife with a thin blade to avoid bruising. Cuttings are then inserted with 30 to 40 percent of their lower length in the rooting medium, set about 1 to 2 in. (2.5 to 5 cm) apart depending on size, and firmed in by watering. One hundred percent humidity should be maintained by using mist or by keeping the cuttings in a propagating box or pot covered with clear or white shading plastic supported over but not in contact with the cuttings. No shading is needed when using mist, otherwise some form of shade is needed to prevent excessive transpiration and scorching. The rooting medium should be kept moist but not too wet as this excludes oxygen, which is vital for root development.

If a propagator with bottom heat is used great care needs to be taken to not only avoid cuttings coming into contact with the hot cables but also to make sure that the compost at the base of containers or the propagating bed, nearest the heating cables, does not dry out or become overheated. Daily checking of the soil thermometer and a good thermostat is essential.

Cuttings should root within three to six weeks in the easier species, but 12 to 16 weeks should be allowed for the more difficult ones. Some take even longer and may not root until the following spring or summer. When ready, with the majority having a strong, well branched root system, they should be gradually hardened off by lifting the glass or polythene covers little by little until, after about a week or ten days they can be removed completely.

If rooted in late summer or early fall they are best left in their containers until they start to grow in the following spring, when they are potted up into small pots in ericaceous compost, preventing wilting if in lush growth by using some temporary covering and shading to reduce transpiration if necessary.

Chapter 8
Descriptive List of Species and Hybrids

Species

Vaccinium acrobracteatum. A very attractive, large-leafed species suitable for outdoor cultivation in frost-free gardens but requiring some protection elsewhere as it is not fully hardy. It forms a small tree or large shrub, which may vary from being erect to having pendulous branches. It is often epiphytic in its native habitat, but when terrestrial grows in poor sandy soil.

The reddish stems and young, large, ovate, brilliant bronze-red leaves are a highly ornamental feature. It flowers in midwinter under glass in Britain, producing panicles of round greenish fruit. This species is native to New Guinea and surrounding islands.

Semihardwood cuttings can be taken almost all year round. (Plate 37)

Vaccinium alaskaense, the Alaska blueberry, is a very hardy species found along the coastal regions from northern California to subalpine Alaska. It is often regarded as a separate species in the area and is described as a form of *V. ovalifolium* (Vander Kloet). Those who argue against this point to the more angled twigs and sparse hairs alongside the main veins of the underside of the leaves of *V. alaskaense,* as well as its darker, bloomless, less prolific and less sweet berries. Since populations of both intermingle, and since there is great variation between the plants of both, the problem is to all intents and purposes an academic one.

Where a clone with particularly favorable characteristics is found (for example, those with especially red young stems or more prolific fruit production), propagation by division is recommended. Additionally, cuttings of semiripe wood can be taken in late summer or early spring and rooted in a frost-free cold frame. Otherwise, propagation is from seed.

Vaccinium angustifolium Aiton. The species is the sweet lowbush blueberry of eastern North America and therefore very tolerant of cold winters, especially when a snow cover is available. It has not been appreciated for garden cultivation, but one or two clones are marketed for their superior appearance or heavier cropping potential as well as their usefulness as ground cover. The bright red or orange fall color is especially striking. It does best in full sun, and if about two-thirds of growth is cut back every third winter, the plant will actively produce young growth. (See chapter 3 for a full species description.)

'Brunswick'. A clone from Nova Scotia, it forms a dense mat about 6 to 8 in. (15 to 20 cm) high with glossy green leaves. It produces white flowers followed by sky-blue, pea-sized fruit in late summer that is quite tasty.

'Burgundy'. From Maine, this clone has very attractive gray-green foliage with deep purple-red young growth and light blue berries. It forms a compact plant about 3 ft. (90 cm) wide and 1 ft. (30 cm) high. Color in the fall is deep burgundy.

Variety *laevifolium* House. This form grows a little taller and spreads a little more than the species type. Its lanceolate, narrowly oval or oblong leaves are also larger.

Variety *nigrum* Wood. In Nova Scotia it is known as *V. brittonii*. It is a beautiful plant in the wild sand-dune habitats of Nova Scotia with very attractive glaucous foliage. Plants grow to approximately the same width as var. *laevifolium* but are not as tall. Its leaves are similar in dimensions to those of var. *laevifolium*. In cultivation (meaning it is grown in ordinary organic-based garden composts) it tends to have plain green leaves, but in the wild and in mineral soils, its fall color is plum red. Given poor sandy conditions, it makes a good, low-growing foliage plant. The berries are shiny and black.

The species is seldom propagated for garden use but when it is, it is usually done with seed. When a particular clone (such as one of those named above) is wanted, it should be requested by name. Propagation of these named clones is usually done by removing rhizomes bearing uprights from a parent plant. Cuttings from the current year's growth can also be taken and rooted in a cold frame.

Vaccinium arboreum Marshall. Known most commonly as farkleberry and sparkleberry, this is the only cultivated vaccinium with genuinely inedible berries. As its name implies, this is a shrub or small deciduous or semi-evergreen tree. It occasionally grows to about 30 ft. (9 m); the trunk can reach 15 in. (37.5 cm) in diameter at $3^{1}/_{2}$ ft. (1 m), but more often it forms a shrub 10 to 15 ft. (25 to 37.5 cm) tall. The bark on mature bushes is an attractive gray. Its leathery leaves are about 1 to 1.6 in. long (2.5 to 4 cm) long and $^{1}/_{2}$ to $^{3}/_{4}$ in. (1.25 to 2 cm) wide, shiny above and paler below, with an almost entire margin. They are shed over a long period in the fall and produce a rich range of fall color at any given time. The white, bell-shaped flowers are carried in racemes in summer. Black, shiny, inedible berries follow but tend to drop off without forming properly in cooler climates such as those in southern England.

Vaccinium arboreum grows wild from southern Virginia to central Florida and into Texas, Oklahoma and southeastern Missouri. It is found on dry, sandy or rocky sites in poor acidic soils. In cultivation this species has performed well in a variety of soils from dry to wet. It prefers some shade, especially in hot climates, and although it has been grown at Kew, London, it is not fully hardy in colder regions.

This species is propagated by seed as it is extremely difficult to propagate by cuttings. (Plate 38)

Vaccinium arctostaphylos **Linnaeus.** Native to Turkey and the Caucasus Mountains of southern Russia and its borders with Georgia, this species is also found in Bulgaria to the west of the Black Sea. It is hardy in temperatures down to 5°F (−15°C). The Circassian people of the Caucasus used a decoction of the leaves as a tea called "broussa tea," which looks like the more widespread and flavorsome black tea drunk throughout the world but lacks its flavor.

The Caucasian whortleberry is a slow-growing, densely branched deciduous shrub. It may grow to 10 ft. (3 m) high and 6 ft. (1.8 m) across in favorable situations, but it more often forms a much smaller bush, especially in poorer soils and colder climates. In poor, dry soils it will grow in quite exposed situations. The young, reddish brown shoots are followed by large, dark green lanceolate leaves up to 4 in. (10 cm) long and $^{3}/_{4}$ to $1^{1}/_{4}$ in. (2 to 3 cm) wide. They are finely toothed and prominently veined with a soft down on the veins of the upper surface, more so on the lower. The most attractive feature of this species is the fall color. The leaves turn brilliant purple and red quite early in the fall, with plants often exhibiting a kaleidoscope of these colors at the same time. They remain on the bush for several weeks.

217

Flowers are produced in midsummer, each in the axil of a bract, and are borne on racemes 1 to 2 in. (2.5 to 5 cm) long in midsummer on the previous year's wood. They are bell shaped, waxy and tinged white or pink-purple especially on the outer side of the blooms. Occasionally there is a second flush of flowers in the fall. Round, shiny, purple-black berries $^3/_8$ in. (1 cm) diameter from the first flowering may mingle with the colored leaves in early fall. The berries are edible but are not particularly pleasant.

It is propagated by seed or, if a particular clone is chosen, by cuttings. (Plate 39)

Vaccinium auriculifolium. This rather curious but aptly named vaccinium grows as a large shrub with woody gray stems. Its leaves are reminiscent of the auricula as they are large, pale green above and below and ovate or elliptic, some of the older, larger leaves being almost round. They are closely packed towards the tips of stems, forming an almost circular bowl shape within which the clusters of flower buds develop. The flowers are bell shaped, pink and waxy in appearance. Small black berries ripen over a long period in fall. The native habitat for this species is New Guinea where it is found in heavy shade in damp soil conditions in nothofagus forests.

It is not yet in general cultivation but should make an attractive plant in gardens in warm regions of the world or under glass in colder climates.

Propagation is by cuttings.

Vaccinium boreale **Hall and Aalders.** A dwarf, deciduous shrub that can be as small as $^3/_4$ in. (2 cm) and as tall as 6$^1/_2$ in (16.5 cm). It is often found associated with *V. angustifolium* and is regarded by some as a form of it. It makes dense clumps and spreads by surface rhizomes. Twigs are green, delicate, much branched and angular, and some hairs grow along its grooves.

Leaves are $^1/_2$ to $^3/_4$ in. (12 to 20 mm) long, $^1/_8$ to $^1/_4$ in. (3 to 5 mm) wide, bright green and smooth. The margins are sharply toothed. Flowers are cylindrical, about $^1/_8$ in. (3 mm) long and white to greenish white. The tiny blue berries are about $^1/_8$ in. (3 mm) in diameter, able to produce a good bloom, sweet and edible. It is a subarctic species that is native to Northern Quebec, Labrador, Newfoundland and along the coast of the United States as far north as New York State. Its habitat is in forest tundra and upland meadows on exposed, rocky sites. With its slow-growing, prostrate habit and beautiful red fall color, it is suitable as a garden plant in rock gardens or in pans in an alpine house, especially in cold climates.

Propagation is by seed or cuttings. It also propagates well by breaking off rhizomes.

Vaccinium bracteatum **Thunberg** (synonyms: *V. buergeri, V. idzuroei, V. taquetii*). This forms a large, well-branched evergreen shrub 3 to 9 ft. (9 to 30 m) in height, with slender gray-brown branches that are an attractive red-bronze when young. The light green, shiny, slightly serrate leaves are 2 in. (5 cm) long by ³/₄ in. (2 cm) wide, elliptic-ovate and pointed. They are also red-bronze when young. Flowers are borne in the axils of ¹/₈ to ³/₈ in. (3 to 10 mm) long, narrow, prominent bracts in racemes that are ¹/₂ to 2 in. (1.25 to 5 cm) long. Over ten flowers are contained in each raceme in late summer. These slightly elongated, goblet-shaped flowers are white, downy and small, ¹/₄ to ¹/₃ in. (5 to 8 mm) long with a ¹/₄ in. (5 mm) diameter. They have a slight scent. Berries are very small, about ¹/₄ in. (5 mm) in diameter, and often fail to ripen properly, failing to turn from red to purple-black in gardens in cooler climates. On the lower slopes of mountains in Japan, the fruit ripens in late summer.

Vaccinium bracteatum is worth growing because of its attractive general habit, young growth and profusion of flowers with the accompanying and persistent bracts. Native to Japan, Korea, China and Taiwan, it is not fully hardy in colder climates below −10°F (−23°C).

Propagation is by seed or cuttings.

Vaccinium '**Branklin**'. Very similar to *V. sikkimense*, it is slightly smaller in habit reaching 1¹/₂ to 2 ft. (50 to 60 cm). It is possibly a form of *V. sikkimense*. Tough, leathery, elliptic leaves are typically 1 in. (2.5 cm) long and ¹/₃ in. (8 mm) wide. They are a dark, glossy green above and paler below. Round red flower buds make an attractive feature during the winter. This cultivar is hardy to about 18°F (−8°C).

Propagation is by cuttings. (Plate 40)

Vaccinium caespitosum **Michaux**. Known as dwarf blueberry, bilberry, whortleberry and huckleberry, this is a dwarf, spreading, deciduous shrub from 1¹/₂ to 24 in. (3.8 to 60 cm) tall. It has rather angular, densely branched growth that forms a ground-hugging mat of yellow-green or reddish green stems. Young growth is reddish. The small leaves are variable in shape, dark blue-green above and paler and glandular below. These leaves are also finely toothed from their tip to at least their middle. The pinkish white flowers are pendent, round or cylindrical and are borne singly from the leaf axils in late spring and early summer. Round, blue-black berries are small (1/4 to 1/3 in. or 5 to 8 mm in diameter), sweet flavored and edible, with a good bloom to follow.

Vaccinium caespitosum grows over a very wide area of North America from Alaska to Newfoundland, New England and Maine. It was among the more important species used by the Native Americans in trade with the early settlers. It is also found in the coastal mountains of California and even as far south as the Colorado—New Mexico border. It was introduced into England in 1823 and makes an excellent plant for a large rock garden or as an understory among taller shrubs. It takes a while to become established but can become rampant once settled.

This species is very adaptable and is found in a wide variety of habitats from wet marshy sites to dry mountainous or woodland situations, and from high alpine sites to sea level. Its value is as a ground cover in acidic garden soils where it is difficult to grow other subjects and where there is plenty of room for it to spread.

Propagation is by removing runners with uprights and roots.

Vaccinium chaetothrix. An extremely compact, dwarf vaccinium that looks like a very dwarf form of *V. nummularia*. It forms mounds no more than 3 to 6 in. (7.5 to 15 cm) high. It is an evergreen, and young growth is an attractive red. Leaves are round, no more than 1/4 in. (5 mm) long and 1/4 in. (5 mm) wide and glossy green. It has tiny pink-white flowers and blue-black fruit.

Although native to New Guinea, this species comes from high altitudes and has been found to be hardy in upland gardens in southern England. An excellent subject for an alpine collection, it thrives in troughs or pots in a well-drained, acidic compost. A scattering of gravel over the soil around these plants improves the microclimate around them and reduces the risk of rotting.

Vaccinium chaetothrix is so slow growing that it is difficult to justify the removal of any shoots, but it roots quite easily from cuttings at almost any time of year. Propagation by seed is less invasive. (Plate 41)

Vaccinium consanguineum. A tall evergreen shrub to about 4 ft. (1.2 m), it is often compact and densely bushy with stiff, rigid, sometimes downy branches. Young stems may be red with purple growth when young. Leaves are lanceolate, up to two or three times as long (averaging $1^1/_2$ to 3 in. or 3.8 to 7.5 cm) as they are wide, shallowly toothed and pointed at both the tip and stem end. Each tooth may have a round, darkish tip.

Masses of highly ornamental, cylindrical flowers $^1/_4$ to $^1/_3$ in. (5 to 8 mm) long and $^1/_8$ in. (3 mm) in diameter interspersed with bracts are borne in late spring or early summer. They are creamy white with tinges of red or pink and are followed by a profusion of round, $^1/_4$ to $^1/_3$ in. (5 to 8 mm) fruit, which starts off sage green with attractive pink calyces. The berries turn dark red and then blackish purple at maturity. Although edible, the fruit tastes terrible. *Vaccinium consanguineum* originates from Costa Rica but has proved to be remarkably hardy in the British climate, where temperatures can drop below 18°F (−8°C). It makes a useful and interesting plant for a shrub border in most temperate climates.

Propagation is by seed or semimature or mature cuttings.

Vaccinium coriaceum. This plant forms an attractive, vigorous, markedly upright bush to about 6 ft. (1.8 m). Its main attraction is the foliage, which is small, glossy, and buxus-like. The green leaves mature from bright red young growth, which appears for most of the summer. Native to Borneo, this species is tender except in warm climates such as those of southern California. It makes an attractive plant for a conservatory.

Propagation is by cuttings. (Plate 42)

Vaccinium corymbosum. Known as the North American highbush blueberry, this species is native to eastern North America and occurs in a variety of habitats from open swamps and bogs in the sand on the edges of ponds, streams and lakes to drier situations in pine barrens, birch scrublands, sandy roadside verges and upland woods and meadows. Many forms, synonyms and varieties exist and have been named; Vander Kloet lists over 40. The northern highbush blueberry varieties I describe in chapter 4 are all derived from this species. (See a full species description in chapter 4.)

Propagation is by cuttings or seed. (See chapter 5 for a full discussion.)

Vaccinium constablaei Gray was identified in 1842 as a separate species. Nowadays, most botanists regard it as a form of *V. corymbosum.* It forms a compact plant about 3 ft. (90 cm) high and wide, with small to medium blue-bloomed, edible berries. It has very good, persistent fall color and is an excellent garden plant.

Propagation is as for *Vaccinium corymbosum.*

Vaccinium virgatum Aiton was given full species status but most botanists regard it as a synonym for a clone of *V. corymbosum*. Others regard it as a synonym for a clone of *V. tenellum*. It is worth disregarding the botanical complications since this is an attractive plant for gardens in cool climates. Less than 3 ft. (90 cm) tall and wide, with a delicate, twiggy upright growth habit, this species has arching branches and narrow, lanceolate leaves. The bright red fall color is superb and fairly persistent. Its flowers are slightly elongated and white or very pale pink.

Half highs and some of the more compact varieties of the northern highbush are particularly well suited to small gardens in cold areas, as are southern highbush varieties in warmer areas.

Propagation is as for *Vaccinium corymbosum*. Plants available for garden cultivation are greatly increasing as nursery owners select varieties that are particularly suitable for garden cultivation in different climates and in gardens of different sizes. I describe these varieties in detail in chapter 5.

Vaccinium crassifolium (synonym *V. sempervirens*). Known as creeping blueberry, this evergreen shrub creeps by rooting at the leaf nodes of horizontal branches, forming a dense mat. Upright, reddish stems reach 5 to 6 in. (12.5 to 15 cm), bear small, closely packed leaves and are covered with a fine down. The shiny, ovate leaves are only about $1/4$ in. (5 mm) apart on the stem, are tough, finely toothed and $1/3$ to $3/4$ in. (8 to 20 mm) long and $1/8$ to $3/8$ in. (3 to 10 mm) wide. They are dark green above and paler below. Small, urn-shaped, pendent flowers of white, pink or rose red are borne singly or in small clusters either as laterals or terminal racemes and become pendent. They are followed by shiny, purple-black edible berries about $1/2$ in. (1.25 cm) across. Its natural habitat is in dry situations that are often associated with pine trees, usually on verges or banks where there is little competition to provide too much shade.

Vaccinium crassifolium is native to the southeastern states of Georgia, Virginia and South Carolina. It was first appreciated in Britain after J. Fraser introduced it in 1794 and was quickly distributed to gardens throughout the country, often being used as a ground cover in acid soils. It is not fully hardy in colder areas.

'Wells Delight'. This has bright red-bronze young growth, which is particularly attractive set off against the bright, glossy, dark green leaves throughout the summer and into the fall. The small white flowers are followed by small dark purple fruit. 'Well's Delight' covers the ground a little more quickly than the type species and does better in a little shade. It should be planted about 2 ft. (60 cm) apart for good ground cover.

Propagation for both the species and 'Wells Delight' is by cuttings, which root very quickly.

Vaccinium cylindraceum. This forms a semi-evergreen, large, upright shrub that has proved to be a very hardy and attractive addition to the garden. What is more, it is remarkably drought tolerant and succeeds in neutral soils that are not too heavy. The attractive green-brown bark on older branches resembles the "snake bark" of some *Acer* species. The bright green, glossy leaves are 2 in. (5 cm) long, lanceolate and finely toothed, and many stay green until late winter when they turn yellow and fall, which is before new growth begins. Others turn bright red in the fall and are also persistent.

Flowers appear from midsummer onwards with some appearing up to early fall in certain gardens. They are borne in profusion in pendulous clusters all along the one-year-old stems. They start off from red buds and develop into $1/2$ in. (1.25 cm) long, narrow, cylindrical flowers that become yellow-green tinged red. Gray-green calyces add to the attraction. It is a most attractive flower especially when seen en masse on a mature bush in late summer. Most flowers form cylindrical blue-black, edible berries with an attractive bloom. Later flowers stay on the bush until the first winter frosts. If grown in full sun the leaves tend to develop dark spots as they age and drop in the fall. In shade they remain green until they fall in late winter. This species is native to the islands of the Azores. (Plates 43, 44)

'Tom Thumb' appears as a dwarf form about 12 in. (30 cm) high, with light pink flowers and thrives in full sun. It is useful for small gardens or containers. (Plate 45)

'Tinkerbell' is similar but even smaller than 'Tom Thumb'.

Propagation of the species as well as the forms I list is by cuttings using semimature stems in late summer.

Vaccinium darrowii. A species closely related to *V. myrsinites, V. darrowii* it is an evergreen shrub growing up to 3 ft. (90 cm) that spreads by rhizomes. It has pale green leaves $1/2$ in. (1.25 cm) long and $1/4$ in. (5 mm) wide. Round or slightly urn-shaped flowers are $1/4$ in. (5 mm) long, white or white tinged with pink or red. Attractive light blue, glaucous berries follow. Its native habitat is on scrublands among scrub oaks where it has adapted to hot dry conditions. It is useful as a border evergreen and a hedging plant, especially in climates similar to its native habitat in Florida and neighboring states. It is also extensively used by breeders, especially those working to produce southern highbush varieties. (See chapter 5) This species does not do well in gardens with cool climates.

Propagation is by seed or cuttings

Vaccinium delavayi Franchet. A compact, densely branched evergreen shrub that usually reaches between 1 to 3 ft. (30 to 90 cm) at maturity but may gradually reach 5 to 6 ft. (1.5 to 1.8 m) in warmer, more shady gardens where it sends out strong "leaders" or "water shoots" in late summer. These may be cut back if they offend. Young growth is angled, hairy and tinged red. Small leaves $\frac{1}{2}$ in. (1.25 cm) long and $\frac{1}{4}$ in. (5 mm) wide are borne on short stalks. They are dark green, glossy and leathery and are reminiscent of buxus with their smooth margins and notch at the tip. Tapered at the base, the leaves are closely packed on the shoots, up to 12 per inch.

Flowers are borne in $\frac{1}{2}$ to 1 in. (1.25 to 2.5 cm) racemes with a hairy stalk at the shoot tips. Pendent, urn-shaped blooms are greenish white flushed with rose or creamy white flushed with rose and very small at $\frac{1}{4}$ in. (5 mm). They are borne singly or in clusters of two to four from the leaf axils in early summer and are not a striking feature because they are often hidden by dense foliage. The edible fruit is round, about $\frac{1}{6}$ in. (4 mm) in diameter, and ranges from blue-purple to black.

Its natural habitat is growing as an epiphyte on trees or in cracks among rocks and on cliffs, which indicates a need for good drainage. Found by Abbe Delavay in Yunnan, China, described, it was named by Franchet in 1895 and introduced to Britain by George Forrest some time before 1923. *Vaccinium delavayi* is useful as an attractive evergreen, especially if planted in full or semishade. It has proved quite hardy in southern England where temperatures rarely fall below 18°F (−8°C).

Propagation is by seed or cuttings

Vaccinium deliciosum Piper. Known as cascade bilberry and blue huckleberry, this dwarf shrub is often confused with *V. caespitosum*, the dwarf bilberry. Closely resembling *V. caespitosum*, it forms tufted mats no more than 2 ft. (60 cm) high (more usually it is 4 to 12 in. or 10 to 30 cm high) and spreads by rhizomes into extensive colonies in the wild. The young twigs are gray-green and rounded. Leaves are $\frac{2}{3}$ to 1 $\frac{1}{3}$ in. (17 to 33 mm) long and $\frac{1}{4}$ to $\frac{1}{3}$ in. (5 to 8 mm) wide with serrations on the upper two-thirds of the leaf. In the fall it is said to set hillsides alight with its brilliant scarlet, flame and yellow colors.

Solitary flowers are creamy pink, globular and $1/4$ to $1/3$ in. (5 to 8 mm) wide. They are followed by edible, sweet, blue-black berries $1/4$ to $1/3$ in. (5 to 8 mm) in diameter. Its natural habitat is in alpine meadows or subalpine coniferous woods in the Pacific coastal mountain ranges of British Columbia into central Oregon. It is a hardy vaccinium and is ideal for a moist part of a rock garden.

Propagation is by seed or cuttings. (Plate 46)

Vaccinium densifolium J. J. Smith. A small, upright shrub up to 4 ft. (1.2 m) high, it has densely packed leaves that cover the branches. They are leathery, smooth and shiny above with the odd hair or bristle below, are just under $1/3$ in. (8 mm) long and just over half as much wide. The round flowers grow singly from the axils of the leaves, have a small opening to the corolla and are a bright, glossy red with a slightly velvety texture inside the corolla. They may be mistaken for berries at first glance, though the berries are blue-black. This species is native to New Guinea and is found in subalpine shrubberies and grasslands from about 10,300 to 12,600 ft. (3,100 to 3,800 m). As far as is known in gardening circles, it has not been tried in gardens outdoors but it should be hardy enough for sheltered gardens in temperate climates.

Propagation is by cuttings.

Vaccinium dunalianum Wight. This species, which is sometimes epiphytic, forms a large evergreen shrub that may reach 20 ft. (6 m) in the wild. There are no hairs on any part of the plant. Young stems are slightly angular. Leaves are an attractive and unusual feature of the plant as they are oval-lanceolate, 3 to 5 in. (7.5 to 12.5 cm) long and 1 to $1^3/4$ in. (2.5 to 4.4 cm) wide with long tapering points that may be about half the total length of the leaf. They turn under at the tips, have a broadly tapering base and are dark green and leathery with toothless, often incurving margins.

Flowers appear in early summer and are borne in racemes $1^1/2$ to 3 in. (3.8 to 7.5 cm) long from the axils of leaves. They are urn shaped, white or pinkish with green tones, $1/4$ in. (5 mm) long and have five triangular recurved tips to the lobes. The berries are round, black and about $1/4$ in. (5 mm) in diameter. *Vaccinium dunalianum* is native to the Himalayan region and is found mostly between 5,300 and 10,000 ft. (1,600 and 3,000 m). Although it occurs at high altitudes it does not thrive in the colder, more northern latitudes.

Propagation is by seed or cuttings.

Vaccinium erythrocarpum **Michaux.** Known as southern mountain cranberry and bearberry, this species is botanically interesting as it has been—and continues to be—particularly difficult to classify. Most botanists place it in the section *Oxycoccoides*, which acts as a link between two other botanical sections, *Oxycoccus* and *Myrtillus*. Broadly speaking, this classification makes it a blueberry-cranberry link. The only other species in this section is *V. japonicum*, to which it is very similar, the most obvious difference being that japonicum berries are always red while *V. erythrocarpum* fruit is a deeper shade of red through purple to black. *V. japonicum* is native to Japan while *V. erythrocarpum* is an American species. *Vaccinium erythrocarpum* forms an open shrub that averages 3 to 6 ft. (90 to 180 cm) high and that forms crowns at maturity. Its elliptic to ovate leaves are $1\frac{1}{2}$ to $2\frac{1}{2}$ in. (3.8 to 6.4 cm) long, $\frac{2}{3}$ to $\frac{3}{4}$ in. (1.7 to 2 cm) wide, mid-green on both sides and slightly downy below with small teeth.

The flowers are about $\frac{1}{2}$ in. (1.25 cm) long and narrow with four white, pink or red petals (the latter are very rare) that curve back sharply at the tip of the corolla. They are borne singly in leaf axils on long, $\frac{1}{4}$ in. (5 mm) pedicels. The red, deep purple or black berries are round, about $\frac{1}{3}$ to $\frac{1}{2}$ in. (8 to 12 mm) in diameter. They are almost tasteless.

Vaccinium erythrocarpum comes from high elevations from western Virginia to northern Georgia, where it is found as a woodland shrub from boggy areas to rocky slopes. It is often associated with unspoilt spruce forests. Although hardy (except in the coldest regions), it does not set freely except in climates similar to its native habitat.

Propagation is by seed or cuttings.

Vaccinium floribundum **H. B. and K.** Blessed—or cursed—in the mid-nineteenth century with seven synonyms, the most well known being *V. mortinia*, this is a very beautiful evergreen shrub that grows to between 3 to 6 ft. (90 to 180 cm) high and spreads to twice that distance. It can be a bit unruly as it produces long arching growths, especially in woodland gardens. These may be cut back to keep the bush tidier, which also encourages better flowering on the shorter stems. Ovate, dark green, shallowly toothed leaves are small, about $\frac{1}{2}$ in. (1.25 cm) long, and they crowd the stems. When young, the stems have an attractive, purple-red tinge. Masses of tiny, cylindrical, rose-pink flowers are ¼ to ½ in. (5 to 12 mm) long. They open from deep pink buds in the axils of the leaves almost all the way down the stems of the previous year's growth and are borne in tightly packed, 2 in. (5 cm) racemes in summer. They have a persistent blue-green calyx and are followed by edible round berries that turn from red to blue-black as they age.

Vaccinium floribundum is native to Ecuador and Peru, where the fruit is cooked to make, among other things, pies, jam and a beverage called "colada morada." It is also found in Colombia. Its habitat is quite diverse, ranging from mountainous dry or wet forests up to 1,450 ft. (4,350 m) to lower-level shrub and grass areas at 4,700 ft. (1,400 m). As with the North American lowbush blueberry species, *V. floribundum* thrives on being burned over, producing vigorous young shoots that rejuvenate the plants. Although a neotropical species, it is hardy in southern England, where it was introduced in about 1840.

Propagation is by seed or cuttings.

Vaccinium fragile **Franchet**. This beautiful species forms a compact evergreen plant that may grow to 1 to 3 ft. (30 to 90 cm), but it is often no more than 6 to 9 in. (15 to 23 cm). The young stems are an attractive red, and the young shoots are quite hairy. Glossy green, finely toothed leaves are ½ to 1 in. (1.25 to 2.5 cm) long, ¼ to ⅜ in. (5 to 10 mm) wide and slightly hairy below. It produces a mass of tiny, urn-shaped flowers in early to midsummer, which may be white with pink tips to the corolla and bright red calyces. Flowers are sometimes white with pink or purplish stripes, pale rose or salmon pink. They are borne on clusters of downy racemes, which arise from the terminal leaf axils, and are 1 to 2 in. (2.5 to 5 cm) long. Red bracts enhance the beauty of the racemes. The fruit is round and ripens from red to black, forming an attractive mixture of colors in the clusters in late summer. It likes a well-drained soil and makes a very attractive, flowering, evergreen plant in a shrub border or rockery. Collected in Yunnan, China, it is not fully hardy in colder climates below −10°F (−23°C).

Propagation is by seed or cuttings. (Plates 47, 48)

Vaccinium glauco-album **Hooker**. The most frequently found form, introduced from Nepal in the early 1970s, is an evergreen shrub that grows to 20 to 48 in. (50 to 120 cm) high and forms dense patches by suckering to 3 ft. (90 cm) or more. A more low-growing form that grows to no more than

12 to 15 in. (30 to 37.5 cm) is more suckering but less frequently available. The red stems set off the 2½ in. (6.4 cm) leaves, which are an attractive ovate or elliptic shape, gray-green above and bright, bluish white below. They may have small bristly teeth, but more commonly they are smooth margined. The cylindrical, pale pink flowers are borne in summer in pendent racemes 3 in. (7.5 cm) long. A distinguishing feature is the mass of silver white, pink-tinged bracts among the flowers. Round, black berries with a good, misty blue bloom are very persistent, and although edible, they have an unpleasant aftertaste.

Vaccinium glauco-album thrives in an ordinary garden situation with plenty of leaf mold. It prefers semishade and is hardy in the south of Britain but prone to damage in colder areas, especially if in an exposed, windy situation. This may seem odd given that the species comes from Nepal and Tibet in the Himalayas but is probably attributable to the wood not ripening in the more irregular British climate.

Propagation is by cuttings. (Plate 49)

Vaccinium griffithianum. A lovely, graceful shrub that grows to about 4 ft. (1.2 m) tall and a little wider than that. It has arching branches and young, slender stems that are a light, bright green if grown in shade and tinted red if grown in sun. It has long, lanceolate leaves that are 1 in. (2.5 cm) long and only about ¼ in. (5 mm) wide. It is semi-evergreen, with leaves turning a bright, light red in early fall and staying that way all winter, making a beautiful, colorful addition to the garden. The leaves fall only in early spring shortly before new growth starts. Young growth is an attractive pinkish red. Flowers open in midsummer and are small, pale pink-white. In early fall they are followed by small, inconspicuous and quite persistent blue-black, rather hard, berries. *Vaccinium griffithianum* originates in China and does well in semishade or full sun in the south of England but is probably not fully hardy. Frank Kingdon-Ward refers to it as "the most handsome of all vacciniums."

Propagation is by seed or cuttings of semimature shoots. (Plate 50)

Vaccinium hirtum Thunberg. At 3 to 4 ft. (90 to 120 cm) tall, this much-branched deciduous shrub is less wide than tall. The young stems are green, slender and may be slightly grooved.

Leaves are variable in size and shape, being narrowly to broadly ovate or broadly lanceolate, 1 to 2 in. (5 cm) long and ⅜ to 1 in. (1 to 2.5 cm) wide.

Bright green or with a reddish tint, they are rounded at the base, finely toothed and have a long, pointed tip. Bright fall color is an attractive feature. They are produced singly or in groups of up to three on shoots of the previous year's growth. Fruits are red, round or slightly oval and $1/3$ in. (8 mm) in diameter. This very variable species is native to and quite common on most of the islands of Japan and is found in the foothills of mountains and in clearings of pine forests in the hills. It makes a useful addition to a semishaded spot in a garden in temperate climates that has plenty of organic matter in the soil.

Variety *smallii* is similar to the type but has purple-black berries.

Propagation is by seed.

Vaccinium hirsutum **Buckley**. Known as hairy huckleberry, hairy-fruited blueberry and woolly berry, this small deciduous shrub has fine, green, twiggy branches up to 3 ft. (90 cm) long. It suckers freely and forms dense thickets. All aerial parts of the plant are covered in hairs. Deep green, oval to ovate, elliptical leaves are 1 to $2^{1}/_{2}$ in. (2.5 to 6.4 cm) long and hairy. They are borne on narrow, hairy stems, have pointed tips and no teeth. Cylindrical flowers are $1/4$ to $1/2$ in. (5 to 12 mm) long and white, sometimes tinged with pink. The black berries are particularly hairy, though edible and sweet. The plant has good fall color and grows naturally on dry, oak or pine ridges and in mountain meadows in very localized populations in mountainous areas of the southeastern United States. Although *V. hirsutum* is difficult to obtain for garden cultivation, it is worth seeking out for its curiosity value. It enjoys a moist, somewhat shady situation and is quite hardy in southern England.

Propagation is by removal of suckers or by seed or cuttings taken once the current year's growth has become firm in late summer.

Vaccinium japonicum **Miquel.** This beautiful vaccinium is best planted on a slope or on the edge of a wall above a path so that its slender, well-spaced branches can be seen from below as the flowers and fruit hang down from the undersides. It has a light, airy appearance and is especially beautiful when the sun shines through the foliage. It grows to 2 to 3 ft. (60 to 90 cm) high in the wild and its green branches are smooth in texture and sometimes slightly grooved. This species is usually deciduous but may be green in winter in warm climates. Pale green, slightly toothed leaves are ovate-lanceolate, 1 to $2^{1}/_{4}$ in. (2.5 to 5.4 cm) long and $1/2$ to $1^{1}/_{4}$ in. (1.25 to 3 cm) wide. They are often rounded at the base with pointed tips and small teeth along the margins. Bright green above, slightly paler below and light in texture, the leaves scorch in bright sunlight and develop unsightly brown blotches in exposed situations. They are often an attractive light red when young, with red stems.

In late spring or early summer, beautiful, dainty, ¼ to ½ in. (5 to 12 mm) flowers appear individually, hanging on quite long, slender stalks from the leaf axils of the previous year's lateral shoots. Borne on slender pedicels, the buds are long, narrow, pointed and reminiscent of cranberry buds, bright cerise for the most part, shading to pale pink or white at the base. This gives a most attractive bicolor effect. When the blooms open, the four petals reflex and curl back sharply at the tips, exposing a prominent boss of dull gold stamens. The anthers are more or less fused, fading to brown as the central pistil emerges.

Small, highly ornamental, glossy red berries about ¼ to ⅓ in. (5 to 8 mm) in diameter hang from the branches in early fall. *Vaccinium japonicum* thrives in the shade of a woodland garden. It also does well in a shrub border and is most attractive planted in the shelter of a larger shrub, particularly the purple-leafed *Cotinus* 'Grace' or *Acer palmatum* f. *atropurpureum*. This combination enhances the effect of its pale leaves. It is native to Japan and Korea, and a form is also found in China. The species is hardy in southern England.

Propagation is by seed or cuttings of semimature shoots taken in late summer. (Plate 51)

Vaccinium leucanthum. Young stems are an attractive red year round, bearing glossy, light green leaves that are paler below. They are serrate, averaging 1½ in. (3.8 cm) long and ¾ in. (2 cm) wide and with pointed tips. A very floriferous species, it has clusters of palest pink waxy flowers with bright red calyces. The berries are about ¼ in. (5 mm) in diameter and blue-black. It is hardy in the south of England.

Propagation is by seed.

Vaccinium macrocarpon Aiton. Called the American cranberry, this species is more associated with commercial growing but makes a good garden plant for those with acid soil who wish to grow their own cranberries. It also makes attractive ground cover with reddish foliage in winter, soon covering the bare soil, provided it is acidic and has organic matter such as peat or leaf mold. The nodding white or pale pink flowers that are produced in summer are an attractive feature, as are the persistent, glossy, red berries. There is something quite special about picking one's own cranberries to store in the refrigerator or freezer or to make straight away into sauces or compotes for Thanksgiving or Christmas. (See chapter 1 for a full species description as well as hardiness information.)

A layer of white sand covering the soil increases both water retention and weed control. It also creates an attractive background for the foliage and fruit of the plants. Many cultivars make good subjects for hanging baskets and window boxes, provided they are planted in an acidic compost and watered regularly. They prefer to have room to send roots down into soil from their stolons after a few years under such artificial conditions.

Propagation is by rooting uprights taken from plants and inserting them in prepared beds or in propagating beds, boxes or pots in early summer before growth starts. Alternatively, runners or rhizomes may be cut into pieces, each with a rooted node.

'Hamilton' is an attractive dwarf cranberry that is grown for its foliage and flowers, not its fruit. An ornamental form, this cranberry is much more compact compared with the species and is hardly recognizable as belonging to it. It looks equally good spreading over rocks and boulders in a rock garden or covering the ground in an ericaceous bed. It has tightly whorled, persistent leaves growing on densely packed branches, creating a whorl of deep green foliage that turns an attractive bronze in the winter. Two-inch uprights bear delicate pink flowers in spring, followed by small glossy red berries. An excellent hardy plant for a peat bed, rock garden or bog garden.

Propagation is by semihardwood cuttings taken in summer when the uprights have become firm. (Plate 52)

Vaccinium membranaceum **Douglas.** Common names for this species includes mountain bilberry, mountain huckleberry, twin-leafed huckleberry, blue huckleberry and black huckleberry. It is very similar to *V. myrtillus* and has similar ornamental value with exceptional fall color. *Vaccinium membranaceum* forms clumps of shrubby, twiggy growth 1 to 5 ft. (30 to 150 cm) high with yellow-green or red-green stems. Leaves are bright green and toothed until fall, when they turn red. Flowers are urn shaped, greenish white or pinkish white and are produced singly in the leaf axils. Purplish black, edible berries $1/4$ to $1/3$ in. (5 to 8 mm) in diameter follow. It is a hardy vaccinium that is native to the Rocky Mountains and north to Alaska, where it grows on alpine heaths or in coniferous woods, especially where trees have been cleared.

Propagation is by seed or by suckers that are cut off as they extend from the parent plant.

Vaccinium moupinense Franchet. A compact, dwarf evergreen that does not sucker but grows into a neat, rounded bush to 2 by 3 ft. (60 by 90 cm). Ovate or obovate, leathery leaves ³/₄ in. (2 cm) long and ¹/₄ in. (5 mm) wide crowd the branches; there are about 10 to 12 per inch. They are an attractive, very glossy green. Young growth remains red tipped all summer and well into the fall, and it is an attractive feature of the bush. Nine to fifteen nodding flowers are borne in racemes on reddish brown stalks in early to midsummer. They are urn shaped, waxy and a very deep, mahogany red. Some plants have rose-pink flowers. Attractively angular in appearance, they have five tiny, triangular lobes surrounding the open end of the corolla. Racemes grow mainly from the axils of terminal leaves. Round, purple-black berries are about ¹/₄ in. (5 mm) in diameter.

Originating in Sichuan, southwestern China, *Vaccinium moupinense* is very hardy and of great ornamental value, giving substance and body to a shrub border all year round. It is frequently epiphytic in its native forests, growing on old trees. Plenty of peat, leaf mold or rotting bark chippings are of benefit in the garden, where it makes a useful plant for the rock garden or shrub border, either as a feature plant or as part of the general display. It looks good in a tub.

Propagation is by seed or, more often, by cuttings taken in late summer or early spring before growth starts.

Vaccinium myrsinites Lamarck. With common names of Florida evergreen blueberry and ground blueberry, this colonizing species is often confused with *V. darrowii*. Characteristically, it is 18 to 36 in. (45 to 90 cm) tall, with green twigs that are very bright green when young. Leaves are persistent in warm climates, leathery and small, about ¹/₄ to ¹/₂ in. (5 to 12 mm) long and up to ¹/₄ in. (5 mm) wide. Round or urn-shaped flowers are ¹/₄ to ¹/₃ in. (5 to 8 mm) long and white tinged with pink or red. Round, shiny berries are black and just under ¹/₂ in. (1.25 cm) in diameter.

The native habitat of *Vaccinium myrsinites* is the coastal plain of South Carolina to southern Florida, where it grows in full sun or among scrub pines as an understory. It thrives there in dry, sandy soils, is popular as a habitat for birds and very important in the diet of black bears. It is surprisingly successful in the much cooler, damper climate of northern Europe and first began to be cultivated in England from about 1880. Useful as an evergreen in warm climates, it can be grown as a hedge or as a single plant, especially in dry exposed gardens.

Propagation is by cuttings in late summer or early spring.

Vaccinium myrtilloides **Michaux**. Known as sour-top blueberry and velvet-leafed blueberry or huckleberry, this blueberry is often found as part of the "wild" lowbush blueberry population of commercially harvested blueberry barrens. It is much like *V. angustifolium* and just as hardy but can be distinguished by its entire or irregularly serrate hairy leaves. (See chapter 3 for a full species description.)

Propagation is by seed or by removing runners from the parent plant.

Vaccinium myrtillus **Linnaeus**. This species has many common names: bilberry, whortleberry, blaeberry, blueberry, brylocks, hartberry, hurtleberry, hurts, whortleberry, whorts and wimberry. There are also thousands of different forms of this species. Its ornamental value is in the red, orange and yellow fall color, which is evident on plants in full sun. Some leaves on plants in sheltered gardens under shade will remain all winter. The plant makes good ground cover among rhododendrons and other taller ericaceous shrubs. However, the main reasons for planting *V. myrtillus* is as a source of fruit, which has an exceptionally high antioxidant value and an intense flavor that many have a particular fondness for. Plenty of room and soil with sufficient acid content are needed to grow enough plants to get a quantity of fruit that makes it worthwhile. (Of course owners will need to keep the backache balm handy!) *Vaccinium myrtillus* that is planted in wildlife gardens along with heather for the bees also provides food for birds, mice—and bears.

Forms that have particularly bright or deep red leaf color in the fall are favored for ornamental garden cultivation. There is also a form in Iceland that produces larger than usual amber-colored flowers that are produced in sufficient quantities to make quite an impact in the garden. Another form produced albino berries but it appears to have been lost to cultivation.

Nurseries propagating any quantity of *Vaccinium myrtillus* usually do so from seed, producing clumps of plants with slightly different characteristics. If a particular form or clone is required, it should be propagated vegetatively.

Division of clumps produces independent plants quickly, but if material is scarce, pieces of rhizome carrying an upright can be removed, although this method does take longer to get a reasonable sized plant.

Vaccinium nummularia **Hooker**. A most attractive evergreen dwarf vaccinium, this plant spreads to 3 ft. (90 cm) and reaches no more than about 2 ft. (60 cm) tall. The arching stems are brown and hairy. Glossy, dark green leaves are ovate or elliptic, small (⅝ in. or 16 mm long by ¼ in. or 5 mm wide) and very finely toothed. They grow in alternating, double rows, are tough and tend to have downward, curving margins. The new, spring growth is deep red, and in full sun the leaves take on a purplish tinge, especially in the fall when the next year's pink flower buds cover the stems.

Flower buds open in early summer to form small cylindrical flowers in dense pendent racemes that are carried from leaf axils near the tips of last year's shoots. Depending on the form of the species, the flowers may be of bright rose-red or paler with red tips. The round black berries are ¼ in. (5 mm) in diameter and edible, but they are seldom picked as they are so small. Although this species is said to be slightly tender, it is worth growing in most urban gardens or in mild areas not subject to frosts of 14°F (−10°C) or more. Native to Sikkim and Bhutan, it trails over rocks in the Himalayan wilds. In theory it should make good ground cover, but in practice it tends to make a neat bush about 2 ft. (60 cm) tall and 2 ft. (60 cm) wide in gardens. Dwarf forms can be found in cultivation.

Propagation is by cuttings of semimature or mature wood taken from the current year's growth between summer and early spring and rooted in a cold frame. (Plates 53, 54)

Vaccinium oldhamii **Miquel**. A compact, upright, deciduous shrub growing up to 3 to 9 ft. (90 to 300 cm) with slender, dark brown older branches. Oblong, oval or elliptic leaves are slightly pointed at the tips and base and are 1¼ to 3 in. (3 to 7.5 cm) long and 3/4 to 1½ in. (2 to 3.8 cm) wide. They are paler green on the undersurfaces, and sometimes coarse hairs are scattered on the upper surface. Flowers are ⅙ to ¼ in. (3 to 5 mm) long with downy flower stalks bearing leaflike bracts at the base. These flowers are borne in considerable numbers on racemes 1½ to 2½ in. (3.8 to 6.4 cm) long on the ends of young shoots. They appear in midsummer and are bell shaped and pale yellowish brown or reddish. The berries are round, ⅓ in. (8 mm) in diameter, black with a good bloom and have persistent calyx teeth remaining from the flowers. The plant's main feature is its bright red fall color and red winter stems. Although it is native to Japan and Korea, where it grows in thickets and woods near the foot of mountains, it is also found in China. It is quite hardy.

Propagation is by seed or by cuttings taken in summer when the young growth has become firm. Cuttings should be rooted in 100 percent humidity under plastic in a cold frame with some shade to prevent scorching and wilting.

Vaccinium ovalifolium Smith. This species is known as the oval-leafed blueberry and, in Newfoundland, as the highbush blueberry. Closely related to *V. myrtillus*, it is very hardy and deciduous. It grows to $3^{1}/_{3}$ ft. (1 m) in the wild, forming small bushy clumps and rarely spreading by suckering except when injured by cutting or other damage. In cultivation in favorable situations it may reach 12 ft. (3.7 m). It is fairly narrow and upright in habit. Young stems, which are angular and often grooved, are an attractive feature, and they are also often a handsome reddish or yellow-green color. Ovate leaves have smooth margins and rounded tips, are a pale green (the lower surfaces are even paler) and are 1 to $2^{1}/_{2}$ in. (2.5 to 6.4 cm) long and $^{5}/_{8}$ to $1^{1}/_{4}$ in. (1.6 to 3 cm) wide.

Flowers usually appear in late spring to early summer before the leaves, emerging from a characteristic pale green calyx that has no lobes. Flowers are $^{3}/_{8}$ in. (1 cm) long and $^{1}/_{4}$ in. (5 mm) wide and vary in color from greenish white to deep pink. The berries are blue, dull purple or black, often with a blue bloom, up to $^{1}/_{3}$ in. (8mm) in diameter and edible. However, they are not very palatable because they have a gritty texture. They also rot quickly on the bushes.

Vaccinium ovalifolium is native to the western coastal areas of Canada and the United States, from Alaska to south-central Oregon to sea level in the more northern areas and to subalpine elevations in Oregon. Some isolated populations occur further inland in Idaho and South Dakota, in Newfoundland and in one or two areas to the west of that province. *Vaccinium ovalifolium* enjoys moist conditions and can provide a useful plant for a bog or marsh garden. Forms or varieties are found elsewhere, such as variety *coriaceum*, which grows in Japan. This species is found in moist boggy situations in the coastal mountains, where it is often associated with coniferous woodlands and scrub, especially where it gets partial shade such as on the verges of roads and clearings. Inland, it may be found in drier, more open habitats. It can produce good fall color if growing in more light. (Plate 55)

Propagation is by seed.

Vaccinium ovatum **Pursh**. With common names such as box blueberry, evergreen huckleberry and blackwinter huckleberry, this species is among the most widely grown and versatile for ornamental purposes in gardens. David Douglas introduced it into cultivation in 1826. Many features are attractive; for example, over about 12 years it forms a large, bushy, evergreen shrub that can reach 12 ft. (3.7 m) and spread to 10 ft. (3 m), by which time it tends to sprawl a little. It responds well to being cut to ground level, which rejuvenates it and creates a bushier plant. The current year's stems remain bright red throughout the winter, and the glossy, green, upper leaf surfaces contrast well with the paler undersides. The leathery, ovate leaves are reddish bronze when young, finely serrate, 1$\frac{1}{4}$ in. (3 cm) long and $\frac{1}{4}$ to $\frac{3}{4}$ in. (5 to 20 mm) wide, depending on habitat. Flowers are globular, urn shaped, white with a pink flush and $\frac{1}{4}$ in. (5 mm) long. They are borne in 1 in. racemes in early summer.

The edible berries, which are $\frac{1}{4}$ in. (5 mm) in diameter, start off as red but turn purple and glaucous when ripening. They are very persistent, becoming glossy and black by midwinter. They have a sweet, slightly musky taste, and it is said that the flavor improves after the first frosts and after the berries have persisted for a month or more on the bushes once ripe. They ripen so late, which means that some may fail to reach maturity before being destroyed by the more severe frosts in colder areas. They do not appear to be high on the culinary list for birds.

Vaccinium ovatum is native to the coniferous forests of the coastal regions of the Pacific Northwest, from central British Columbia to central California. Although often found with *V. parvifolium*, it prefers more light so is more often seen in clearings or by roadsides. It prefers a moist environment and plenty of organic matter, and is sometimes seen on rotting logs or above head level colonizing the remains of toppled trees. It even grows close to the sea, where it is unaffected by salt spray.

Generations of Indians have made use of this berry, and it was particularly valuable because it ripened after all other berries had been harvested. It is harvested today and sold in tourist and gift shops as huckleberry jam. It has been called "blackwinter huckleberry," "shot huckleberry" and "evergreen huckleberry." In addition to its use as an ornamental garden shrub with year-round attraction, branches of *Vaccinium ovatum* are also useful as foliage in floral arrangements. It grows well in the garden in full sun or partial shade.

'St. Andrews' had been growing rather anonymously in the university botanic garden at St. Andrews in Scotland for several years when Starling realized that it was a particularly good form. He was given a cutting, eventually naming the dwarf form in 1987. It grows to about 9 in. (23 cm) and spreads, forming mats up to about $3^1/_3$ ft. (1 m) in diameter, which makes it a good ground-cover plant. Apart from its dwarf habit it has similar features to the species and is very hardy. A particularly attractive feature is the young, bright orange-red growth that emerges as very short uprights from the dense mats and contrasts so well with the dark green of the main plants. This bright coloring is an enduring feature, lasting all summer and well into winter. It is useful for gardens in cold areas and is particularly attractive in a rock garden. (Plate 56)

'Clyde Robin' is a similar clone that is being offered in nursery catalogs.

'Thundercloud' is a patented clone from British Columbia with, as Oregon's Fall Creek Nursery puts it, "outstanding intense red-bronze spring foliage, profusion of pink flowers and good tasting berries." It is fully hardy.

Propagation is by cuttings taken when the wood of the current year's growth has become firm. Cuttings can either be rooted in pots or trays in a cold frame in the spring or in a frost-free propagator in late summer or early fall.

Vaccinium oxycoccus **Linnaeus**. Called the small cranberry, this species is widely distributed in boggy situations, usually among sphagnum moss, throughout the cooler regions of Europe, Britain, and in those states of the United States north of about latitude 40°N. The species is so similar to the much bigger *V. macrocarpon* or large cranberry that it is not normally cultivated except in areas where winters are too severe for the flower buds of *V. macrocarpon* to survive. It is very hardy indeed. (See chapter 1 for a full species description.)

Propagation is by cuttings or by severing sectors of rooted runners.

Vaccinium padifolium **Smith**. Known as Madeira whortleberry, this species forms a small tree on its native island where it is found in the mountains between 1,000 and 3,000 ft. (300 to 900 m). In cultivation in Britain it thrives best in the south of England, where it forms a shrub about 6 ft. high and wide. It has been confused with *V. arctostaphylos* as the flowers are similar, but *V. padifolium* has smaller, more persistent leaves and is taller but more compact in habit.

Lanceolate leaves are 1³/₄ in. (4.4 cm) long and ¹/₂ in. (1.25 cm) wide. They are distinctly persistent and still purple-red in midwinter. Flowers are produced in racemes, typically in early summer, but can appear in early spring in warm climates. They are bell shaped, greenish cream tinged with pink or purple. The berries are round, blue and ¹/₃ to ¹/₂ in. (8 to 1.25 cm) in diameter. Although hardy, it thrives in temperate or subtropical gardens.

Propagation is by cuttings taken in summer when growth of the current year has become firm.

Vaccinium pallidum **Aiton**. This species, called the hillside blueberry, is sometimes associated with and may be confused with *V. angustifolium* and is just as variable. A deciduous plant, it forms colonies of shrubby plants from about 4 to 28 in. (10 to 70 cm) high depending on its situation. Its stems are twiggy and angular, green or yellow. Leaves are ovate to broadly elliptic, 1 to 1¹/₂ in. (2.5 to 3.8 cm) long and ¹/₂ to ³/₄ in. (1.25 to 2 cm) wide, sometimes but not always serrate. They are usually pale green but may be a dark blue color in some colonies.

Flowers are slightly cylindrical and have very attractive pink stripes on their greenish white corollas. The edible berries are usually blue, occasionally black. Regarded as a drought-tolerant species, it thrives in full sun or partial shade, and because it is native in a wide range of climates from as far north as southern Ontario and as far south as Georgia, it is useful in many gardens.

Propagation is by seed or by cuttings taken in summer when growth has firmed.

Vaccinium parvifolium **Smith**. Known as red huckleberry, red bilberry and red whortleberry, this very attractive shrub is popular not only with gardeners but also with florists, particularly in Germany. Light green, rather fine leaves are ¹/₂ to 1 in. (1.25 to 2.5 cm) long and ¹/₄ to 1¹/₄ in. (5 to 30 mm) wide, and as they are borne on fine, twiggy, angular young stems, they give an almost lacy look to the plant. Young growth is a pleasing bronze. The plant needs some shade as too much exposure to sun causes unsightly blotching on older leaves. It grows into a large shrub if left to its own devices, reaching 8 ft. (2.4 m) in the wild. Although described as deciduous, the plant tends to be evergreen or semi-evergreen in cultivation in milder areas. In cooler areas it loses its leaves quite quickly in fall, leaving its green winter stems bare. The stems are reminiscent of *Jasminum nudiflorum*, and the bright red of the buds that will form the next year's flower buds make an attractive winter feature. Also surprisingly attractive is the bright red of some older leaves scattered among the younger ones before they fall.

The globose or urn-shaped flowers are not particularly significant (only about ⅛ to ¼ in. or 3 to 5 mm in diameter), a waxy cream or pale pink and borne singly or in pairs from the leaf axils in early summer. Round berries with a ½ in. (1.25 cm) diameter are prominent, however, being bright red and glossy. They persist on the bushes for at least two months, well into winter, until a hard frost spoils them. They are edible and continue to be harvested, especially by Native Americans, and eaten fresh or used for making preserves. They were also dried, either singly or mashed together, and made into cakes, which are then also dried. Sometimes the juice was extracted and used as a mouthwash or to stimulate the appetite. The sharp flavor is not unlike that of cranberries. They have also been used as "salmon egg" bait to attract fresh-water fish.

The native habitat of *Vaccinium parvifolium* is in the coastal regions of western Canada and the United States from Alaska to northern California. It is concentrated in British Columbia, Washington and Oregon, where it grows on the fringes of coniferous woods, often in quite dark conditions and on rotting tree trunks and stumps. More berries are produced in light, dappled shade, but the delicate tracery of the light green leaves is better appreciated in more heavy shade, especially if viewed from below. It is tolerant of relatively dry conditions.

Plants available for purchase tend to be very variable in habit as they are usually propagated from seed. Some are more markedly compact with smaller leaves and upright, while others are rather spreading. It responds well to pruning.

Propagation is by seed. If an especially good clone is found, however, it is better to propagate this species by cuttings taken when the wood is firm enough, which is usually in July.

Vaccinium praestans **Lambert**. This attractive little vaccinium forms a dwarf, creeping, deciduous shrub with upright shoots 1¼ to 4 in. (3 to 10 cm). It spreads by rhizomes to 12 in. (30 cm). Ovate leaves are slightly toothed, 1 to 2 in. (2.5 to 5 cm) long and curiously rounded towards the apex but pointed at the tip. Pale green in summer, they are tapered at the base and have a short stalk. In the fall the leaves turn yellow then flushed red and eventually bright red.

Bell-shaped flowers are white flushed with pink and borne either singly or in 2 in. (5 cm) racemes in early summer. Surprisingly large (up to ¹/₂ in. or 1.25 cm in diameter), bright red, round berries are juicy and edible, and they grow near the shoot tips nestling among the leaves. They have a sweet flavor and a pleasant fragrance.

This species prefers a cool, moist spot in the garden since its natural habitat is often among sphagnum moss in boggy situations among or on the edges of pine forests in northern Japan. In fact, *praestans* means "of meadows." It comes from the cold climate of northern Japan and the Russian islands even farther north so it is extremely hardy.

Propagation is by seed or by removing suckering side shoots that have rooted into the soil surrounding the plant.

Vaccinium retusum. A delightful small evergreen reaching between 18 in. to 3¹/₃ ft. (45 to 100 cm), this plant has quite hairy stems. Tough, bright green, oval leaves are small, about ³/₄ in. (2 cm) long and ¹/₃ in. (8 mm) wide. They are characteristically terminated by a recession at the rounded tip and are red when young. In winter, bright red buds are attractive features among the leaves.

Flowers appear in early summer and are borne in terminal racemes. They are urn shaped and pink, with a mass of contrasting white bracts among them. Found wild in the eastern Himalayas, this is a good plant to grow in well-drained soil and especially among rocks, although it is not fully hardy in colder, more exposed gardens. In shade it tends to be more vigorous and sprawling.

Propagation is by cuttings taken in summer or in early spring before growth starts. (Plate 57)

Vaccinium sieboldii (synonyms: *V. ciliatum* var. *sieboldii, V. longeracemosum, V. nagurae* [Japan]). This large evergreen shrub is very slightly hairy when young and has gray-brown branches. Ovate to broadly lanceolate leaves up to 2¹/₂ in. (6.4 cm) long and 1¹/₂ in. (3.8 cm) wide are pointed at the tip and slightly pointed at the base. Flowers are borne in long, 2 to 4 in. (5 to 10 cm) racemes at the tips of the previous year's shoots. Each flower is borne on the end of a flower stalk ¹/₈ to ¹/₃ in. (3 to 8 mm) long. Lanceolate bracts ¹/₄ to ¹/₃ in. (5 to 8 mm) long are a prominent feature. The flowers are bell shaped and white or cream. Round berries are $^1/_4$ in. (5 mm) in diameter and blue-black with a bloom. *Vaccinium sieboldii* is native to Japan's Honshu and Kyushu islands. It is not fully hardy.

Propagation is by seed or by cuttings taken in summer when growth has firmed.

Vaccinium sikkimense. A small evergreen that grows to 2 ft. (60 cm) tall and 3 ft. (90 cm) across, this is an attractive plant for the shrub border. Its dark green, glossy, ovoid leaves have a very slight serration and are $1^1/_2$ in. (3.8 cm) long and 1 in. (2.5 cm) wide. Dense clusters of white flowers appear in midsummer and are flushed pink; they look good against the background of dark leaves. The berries turn blue-black in the fall. It is quite hardy in southern England.

Propagation is by cuttings taken in summer or in spring before growth starts. (Plate 58)

Vaccinium sprengelii Sleumer (synonyms: *V. donianum, V. leucanthum* [?]). A beautiful deciduous shrub up to 9 ft. (3 m) high with attractive, flame-colored young growth.

Ovate-lanceolate leaves are $1^1/_2$ to $3^1/_2$ in. (3.8 to 9 cm) long and $^1/_2$ to $1^1/_2$ in. (1.25 to 3.8 cm) wide with long narrow points. Flowers are borne in late spring on the underside of long racemes that may be up to 3 in. (7.5 cm) long. Cylindrical blooms are white or tinted pink, only about $^1/_4$ in. (5 mm) long and with a narrow mouth. They are smooth on the outside and downy within. Small, black-purple berries are freely produced in warm climates. *Vaccinium sprengelii* is native to China's Hupei and Sichuan provinces and the Khasia Mountains and state of Assam in India and is not regarded as fully hardy in cold climates. It is found in woodlands and thickets and is very variable in the wild.

Propagation is by seed or cuttings.

Vaccinium uliginosum Linnaeus. Called bog blueberry and whortleberry, this small deciduous shrub with an open rather sprawling habit forms loose mats with branches 1 to 2 ft. (30 to 60 cm) tall. Young branches are yellowish green, slightly hairy and rounded rather than angled. Older branches are usually gray with a hint of red. Leaves are $^1/_3$ to $^1/_2$ in. (8 to 12 mm) long, $^1/_8$ to $^1/_3$ in. (3 to 8 mm) wide and of quite a robust texture except on plants grown in heavy shade. The leaves turn bright red in fall. Pale pink flowers emerge in early to midsummer and are produced singly or in small clusters in the leaf axils. The ¼ to ½ in. (5 to 12 mm) round berries are tasty, sweet and blue-black, often with a good blue bloom.

Vaccinium uliginosum is a widely distributed, very hardy, Northern Hemisphere species with a range that extends into the Arctic. It occurs in both the United States and Canada as well as in Europe, Scotland and northern England. Many different forms exist, and one particularly good one with very glaucous leaves comes from Poland. In North America it is a favorite food of caribou, and in northern Europe it is eaten by red deer that browse the leaves all year round. This species is found in moist, moorland situations, often with sphagnum moss. Its potential garden use is in a moist or bog garden, especially where birds and small mammals are welcomed, and in cold climates where its hardiness is appreciated.

All parts of this plant have been used by native peoples for medicinal purposes, and the fruit is used in jams, jellies and pies. One rather unusual use is as an indicator during the prospecting of minerals, particularly uranium, copper and lead, because the mineral concentrations in the soil below are reflected in the leaves when they are analyzed.

Propagation is by seed or portions of rooted suckers that have been removed. (Plate 59)

Vaccinium vitis-idaea **Linnaeus.** Known as cowberry, lingonberry, mountain cranberry, rock cranberry and many other common names, this *Vaccinium* species is probably among the most valuable in the garden. The forms available provide a low-growing, spreading and relatively dense evergreen plant with delightful flowers of varying shades of pink and white that last for a long period beginning in late spring or early summer. They frequently continue to provide interest among the red berries well into the fall. The stems are greenish brown, often with reddish overtones, and new growth may be covered with fine hairs. Older stems are dark brown and hairless, and the bark may peel. (See chapter 2 for a full species description and hardiness information.) (Plates 60, 61)

Many wild forms or clones of the type species are available because the species has great variability in the wild and is widely dispersed. The minor differences between them involve slight differences in growth habit and fruiting. The original selections, now propagated and named, are all from the wild, with the most widely available described below. (See chapter 2 for information on hardiness and propagation methods.)

'Aalshorst', 'Autumn Beauty', 'Autumn Red', 'Erntedank', 'Erntekrone' and 'Erntesegen' are all forms available in Europe, as is 'Dolinda', which has variegated leaves. 'Sussi' and 'Sanna' from Sweden are also available in the United States.

'Gillian Dennis' is probably the most stable of the forms with variegated leaves. Found in 1973 on moorland in Yorkshire, it is quite vigorous and spreads rapidly. Plain green shoots appear every now and then and need to be removed to retain the variegation. It is tolerant of both dry and wet conditions.

'Koralle' is a very compact, low-growing plant that crops very heavily. It seldom reaches more than 12 in. (30 cm) and spreads quite slowly because of its heavy cropping. It does have "off" years, especially following extra heavy cropping ones when the plants do not grow enough vegetatively to produce enough growth to support a crop the next year. It has relatively pale green leaves. Deep pink flowers appear all summer and can often be found among the fruit in fall. The berries are large, about $^3/_8$ in. (1 cm) in diameter. 'Koralle' is a favorite with those growing lingonberries commercially for fruit production. (See chapter 2 for a fuller discussion of its commercial use.) In 1976 it was awarded an RHS Award of Merit for garden use as an ornamental.

'Leucocarpum' is a cream-white, fruited form that may still be found in catalogs. It does not reliably produce white fruit.

'Red Pearl' is an excellent and popular form for gardeners with its upright growth and brilliant, glossy, dark green leaves. With a good balance between growth, flower and fruit production, it is more reliable than 'Koralle'. It grows to about 16 in. (40 cm) and spreads rapidly in a suitable site. Beautiful, clear pink flowers are more or less continuously produced throughout the summer until late fall when they mingle with the bright red berries from earlier flowering. The first crop of berries ripens in late summer, the latest blooms getting caught by the frost. In some years there is the added bonus of late, red-colored young growth, but it too is unlikely to survive the winter.

'Variegata' is a variegated clone that has been around since at least the mid-1950s. It is less stable than 'Gillian Dennis'.

Subspecies *minus* ('Minus') is one of the botanical nightmares that beset the genus. Vander Kloet (1988) lists three different classifications for this plant: *Vaccinium vitis-idaea* var. *minus*, *V. vitis-idaea* subsp. *minus* and *V. vitis-idaea* f. *minus*. It is also widely available in the nursery trade under

V. vitis-idaea 'Nana'. Both W. J. Bean and the Royal Horticultural Society Encyclopedia give it subspecies status. Whatever its correct botanical classification, it is a dwarf version of *V. vitis-idaea*.

Subspecies *minus* is very widely distributed throughout the more northern regions of all of the Northern Hemisphere. It is found in North America, Europe, Japan and the coastal islands of Russia just north of Japan. In Korea, it is similar to the type species but of smaller habit, leaves, flowers and fruit. It has a mound of branches covered by tiny, glossy leaves on a very compact plant, which is ideally suited to the ornamental rock or peat garden. Its natural habitats are on alpine slopes among rocks or on the margins of coniferous forests. (Plates 62, 63, 64)

There are innumerable clones of subspecies *minus*. Some are more free flowering than others, so it is worth seeking out the floriferous clones. One that makes mats only 1¼ in. (3 cm) high with very small leaves was awarded an RHS Award of Merit. Two forms from Nova Scotia, 'Red Dome' and 'Betty Sinclair', are also good.

Propagation is by cuttings taken when young growth is firm.

Hybrids

A number of interspecific hybrids are being produced, combining the best features of some of the species.

Vaccinium **'June Ashburner'** (*Vaccinium floribundum* × *V. ovatum*) is a highly ornamental shrub that has deep red, young stems that grow long and arching. Serrate, evergreen leaves are densely packed, shiny and leathery. They are ovate, ½ in. (1.25 cm) long and ⅓ in. (8 mm) wide, dark green above and light green below. The young leaves growing on the top 6 in. (15 cm) or so of the plant are reddish purple. The flowers are borne all along arching branches and are bunched at the tips. They are white with pink at the base of the corolla, ⅛ to ¼ in. (3 to 5 mm) long and ⅛ in. (3 mm) wide. Round, black, shiny berries are ⅛ to ¼ in. (3 to 5 mm) in diameter. Kenneth Ashburner introduced this hardy hybrid in the early 1970s.

Vaccinium **'Cinderella'** (*Vaccinium ovatum* × *V. floribundum*) is an F_2 hybrid from 'June Ashburner' introduced by Starling in 1996. A small, highly ornamental and hardy shrub with arching growth, it forms a bush 3 ft.

(90 cm) tall by 3 ft. (90 cm) wide. Young growth is a beautiful coral-red all summer into late fall, and older growth is a glowing red all winter on deep red stems. Leaves are densely packed along the upper side of the stems, $^3/_4$ in. (2 cm) long and $^1/_2$ in. (1.25 cm) wide. Bell-shaped flowers are pink and white, about $^1/_4$ in. (5 mm) long, pendent from the undersides of branches and bunched towards the tips. Berries are black, ovoid, $^1/_3$ in. (8 mm) long and $^1/_4$ in. (5 mm) wide.

Vaccinium '**Prince Charming**' (*Vaccinium arctostaphylos* × *V. cylindraceum*) is a bushy shrub with branches to ground level that was introduced by Starling in 1996. It is semi-evergreen with ovate leaves that are $1^3/_4$ to $2^3/_4$ in. (4.4 to 7 cm) long by $^1/_3$ to $1^1/_4$ in. (8 to 30 mm) wide. In summer the leaves are light to mid-green, and in the fall the older leaves turn gold and red. Younger leaves remain on the bushes through the winter and fall just before growth starts in spring. The current year's growth has red stems.

It flowers very prolifically with large clusters of pendulous, bell-shaped flowers on long pedicels. They are $^1/_3$ in. long (8 mm), $^1/_4$ in. (5 mm) wide, reddish amber in sunny situations and pale orange tinged green in shade. 'Prince Charming' produces a heavy crop of black berries that are $^1/_2$ in. (1.25 cm) long and $^1/_3$ in. (8 mm) in diameter with a good bloom. (Plate 65)

Appendix I: Chart of Scientific and Common Names

Scientific Name	Common Name
Empetrum nigrum	black-berried heath, blackberry heath, black crowberry, crakeberry, crauberry, crowberry, crow pea, curlew berry, hog cranberry, monox, monox heather, pigeon berry, wire ling
Gaylussacia baccata	black huckleberry
Gaylussacia frondosa	blue tangle, dangleberry
Vaccinium angustifolium	lowbush blueberry, low sweet blueberry, narrow-leaved whortleberry, sweet lowbush blueberry, sweet-hurts
Vaccinium arboreum	farkleberry, sparkleberry, tree whortleberry
Vaccinium arctostaphylos	broussa tea, caucasian whortleberry, oriental whortleberry
Vaccinium ashei	rabbiteye blueberry
Vaccinium caespitosum	bilberry, dwarf bilberry, dwarf blueberry, dwarf huckleberry, tufted whortleberry,whortleberry
Vaccinium corymbosum	highbush blueberry, North American highbush blueberry, northern highbush, swamp blueberry, tall blueberry
Vaccinium crassifolium	creeping blueberry
Vaccinium erythrocarpum	bearberry, southern mountain cranberry
Vaccinium hirsutum	hairy-fruited blueberry, hairy huckleberry, woolly berry
Vaccinium macrocarpon	American cranberry, large cranberry, cranberry
Vaccinium membranaceum	big huckleberry, black huckleberry, blue huckleberry, mountain bilberry, mountain huckleberry, thick-leaved bilberry
Vaccinium myrtilloides	sour-top blueberry, , velvet-leafed blueberry, velvet-leafed huckleberry

Scientific Name	Common Name
Vaccinium myrtillus	bilberry, blackheart, blaeberry, blueberry, brylocks, bullberry, fragham, frocken, hartberry, horts, huckleberry, hurtleberry, hurts, whinberry, whortleberry, whortle bilberry, whorts, wimberry
Vaccinium ovalifolium	mathers, oval-leaved bilberry, tall bilberry
Vaccinium ovatum	blackwinter huckleberry, box blueberry, Californian (or California) huckleberry, evergreen huckleberry, shot huckleberry
Vaccinium oxycoccus	bog berry, cranberry, cornberry, crauberry, crone berry, European cranberry, fen berry, fen grape, marshberry, monox heather, moorberry, mossberry, small cranberry
Vaccinium padifolium	Madeiran (or Madeira) whortleberry
Vaccinium parvifolium	red bilberry, red huckleberry, red whortleberry
Vaccinium praestans	kamchatka bilberry
Vaccinium uliginosum	bog bilberry, bog blueberry, bog whortleberry, moorberry, whortleberry
Vaccinium virgatum	rabbiteye blueberry, southern black blueberry, twiggy whortleberry
Vaccinium vitis-idaea	brawlins, cowberry, flowering box, foxberry, hurtleberry, hurts, linbenberry, lingberry, lingen, lingonberry, mountain cranberry, munshock, partridgeberry, red whortleberry, rock cranberry, upland cranberry, whinberry
Viburnum edule	highbush cranberry, mooseberry, squashberry
Viburnum trilobum	American cranberry bush, cranberry bush, cranberry viburnum, highbush cranberry

Metric Conversion Chart

inches	centimeters		inches	centimeters		Fahrenheit	Celsius
1/8	0.3		30	75.0		-50°F	-46°C
1/4	0.6		36	90.0		-40°F	-40°C
1/3	0.8		40	100		-30°F	-34°C
3/8	1.0		48	120		-20°F	-29°C
1/2	1.25		60	152		-10°F	-23°C
5/8	1.6		65	165		0°F	-18°C
2/3	1.7					10°F	-12°C
3/4	2.0					15°F	-9°C
1	2.5		**feet**	**meters**		20°F	-7°C
1 1/4	3.0		1/4	0.08		25°F	-4°C
1 1/3	3.3		1/3	0.1		30°F	-1°C
1 1/2	3.8		1/2	0.15		35°F	2°C
1 3/4	4.4		1	0.3		40°F	4°C
2	5.0		1 1/2	0.5		45°F	7°C
2 1/4	5.4		2	0.6		50°F	10°C
2 1/2	6.4		2 1/2	0.8		55°F	13°C
2 3/4	7.0		3	0.9		60°F	16°C
3	7.5		4	1.2		70°F	21°C
3 1/4	8.0		5	1.5		80°F	27°C
3 1/2	9.0		6	1.8		100°F	38°C
4	10.0		7	2.1			
5	12.5		8	2.4			
6	15.0		9	2.7			
7	18.0		10	3.0			
8	20.0		15	4.5			
9	23.0		20	6.0			
10	25.0		25	7.5			
12	30.0		30	9.0			
15	37.5		35	10.5			
18	45.0		40	12.0			
20	50.0		45	13.5			
24	60.0		50	15.0			

Bibliography

Austin, Max. E. 1994. *Rabbiteye Blueberries: Development, Production, and Marketing.* Auburndale, Florida: Agscience.

Bean, W. J. 1951. *Trees and Shrubs Hardy in the British Isles.* Ed. D. L. Clarke. 8th ed. London: John Murray. 1980–89

Beckett, V. A. 1989. *Vaccinium vitis-idaea* 'Gillian Dennis'. *Alpine Garden Society* 57 (238): 345.

Caruso, F., and D. Ramsdell, eds. 1995. *Compendium of Blueberry and Cranberry Diseases.* St. Paul, Minnesota: The American Phytopathological Society.

Cousins, Pierre Jean. 2001. *Food Is Medicine.* London: Duncan Baird

Coville, Frederick. 1910. Experiments in blueberry culture. U. S. Department of Agriculture Burl. Plant Indus. Bulletin 193.

Eck, Paul. 1990. *The American Cranberry.* New Brunswick, New Jersey: Rutgers University Press.

Fall Creek Nursery. 2002–2003. *Nurseryman's Blueberry Source Book.* Lowell, Oregon: Fall Creek Nursery.

Gough, Robert E., and Ronald F. Korcak, eds. 1995. *Blueberries: A Century of Research.* New York: The Hawarth Press.

Hall, Tony. 1986. *Vaccinium vitis-idaea* Loddiger subsp. *minus. Alpine Garden Society* 54 (226): 350–355.

Hillier Nurseries. 1994. *The Hillier Manual of Trees and Shrubs.* Newton Abbot, England: David and Charles.

Ingold, C. T. 1975. *The Biology of Fungi.* London: Hutchinson.

International Society for Horticultural Science. 1999–2000. *Acta Horticulturae.* Third, Fourth, Fifth and Sixth International Symposia on *Vaccinium* culture. Papers.

Kingdon-Ward, Frank. 1954. *Berried Treasure: Shrubs for Autumn and Winter Colour in Your Garden.* London: Ward, Lock.

Luteyn, James. 2002. Neotropical blueberries: The plant family Ericaceae. Retrieved 2002. http://www.nybg.org/bsci/res/lut2/

Moerman, Daniel E. 1998. *Native American Ethnobotany.* Portland, Oregon: Timber Press.

Musgrave, Toby, Chris Gardner, and Will Musgrave. 1998. *The Plant Hunters.* London: Ward Lock

Pritts, M. P., and J. F. Hancock, eds. 1992. *Highbush Blueberry Production Guide.* New York: Northeast Regional Agricultural Engineering Service.

Pojar, Jim, and Andy MacKinnon. 1994. *Plants of the Pacific Northwest Coast.* Vancouver, Canada: Lone Pine Publishing.

Shoemaker, James Sheldon. 1955. *Small Fruit Culture: A Text for Instruction and Reference Work and a Guide for Field Practice.* 3d ed. Columbus, Ohio: McGraw-Hill.

Starling, Barry. 1977. *Vaccinium vitis-idaea* 'Koralle'. *Alpine Garden Society* (December) 45: (190) 322–323.

Stickney, Peter. No date. *Field Guide to the Vaccinium of Western Montana.* Missoula, Montana: U.S. Forest Service Intermountain Forest and Range Experimental Station.

St-Pierre, R. G. 1997. *The Brooks and Olmo Register of Fruit and Nut Varieties.* 3d ed. Alexandria, Virginia: ASHS Press.

Stearn, William T. 1995. *Botanical Latin.* Newton Abbot, England: David and Charles.

Trehane, Piers, ed. 1995. *International Code of Nomenclature for Cultivated Plants.* Wimborne, England: Quarterjack Publishing.

Vander Kloet, S. P. 1988. The genus *Vaccinium* in North America. Publication 1828, Research Branch, Agriculture Canada, Ottawa.

Van Royen, P., and P. Kores. 1982. *The Ericaceae of the High Mountains of New Guinea.* Vaduz, Germany: J. Cramer. Reprint from Van Royen, P., The alpine flora of New Guinea 3:1485-1911.

Other Helpful Information

Nursery catalogs

Dierking, Wilhelm
   Beerenobst, Deutsche Markenbaumschule, Kotnerende 11, 29690 Gilten-Nienhagen, Germany.
   E-mail: info@dierking.de

Dorset Blueberry Company
   Hampreston, Wimborne, Dorset BH217LX United Kingdom.
   E-mail: info@dorset-blueberry.co.uk

Web sites

Too many Web sites dealing with vacciniums exist to list here, but one of the most helpful on blueberry culture is the site by the Northwest Berry and Grape Information Network at http://berrygrape.orst.edu/fruitgrowing/berrycrops/blueberry

For neotropical vacciniums, the Organization for Flora Neotropica (OFN) can be accessed at http://www.nybg.org./bsci/ofn/

Index